Bobby Chinn

Wild, Wild East

Recipes & Stories from Vietnam

Bobby Chinn
Wild, Wild East
Recipes & Stories from Vietnam

Foreword by Anthony Bourdain
Photography by Jason Lowe

CONRAN OCTOPUS

Dedication

This book is dedicated to my grandmothers,
Essie Chinn & Zinat Metwally

Published in 2007 by Conran Octopus Limited,
a part of Octopus Publishing Group,
a Hachette Livre UK Company,
2–4 Heron Quays, London E14 4JP
www.conran-octopus.co.uk

British Library Cataloguing-in-Publication
Data. A catalogue record for this book is
available from the British Library.

Publisher: Lorraine Dickey
Editors: Lewis Esson, Jenni Muir
Art Direction and Design: Jonathan Christie
Photography: Jason Lowe
Production Manager: Katherine Hockley

ISBN: 978 1 84091 445 0

Foreword
by Anthony Bourdain

Bobby Chinn, chef, long time resident of South East Asia, television personality, hustler, International Man of Mystery and now author, is the first guy you want to know in Hanoi if you want to find where to get the good stuff to eat, how to make it and why it's made that way. His pioneering Restaurant Bobby Chinn is a long-time international crossroad and what Bobby doesn't know about Southeast Asian food is not worth knowing. _Wild, Wild East_ is an important contribution to Western knowledge of some of the oldest, most nuanced and sophisticated cuisines in the world, explained in easy-to-follow fashion.

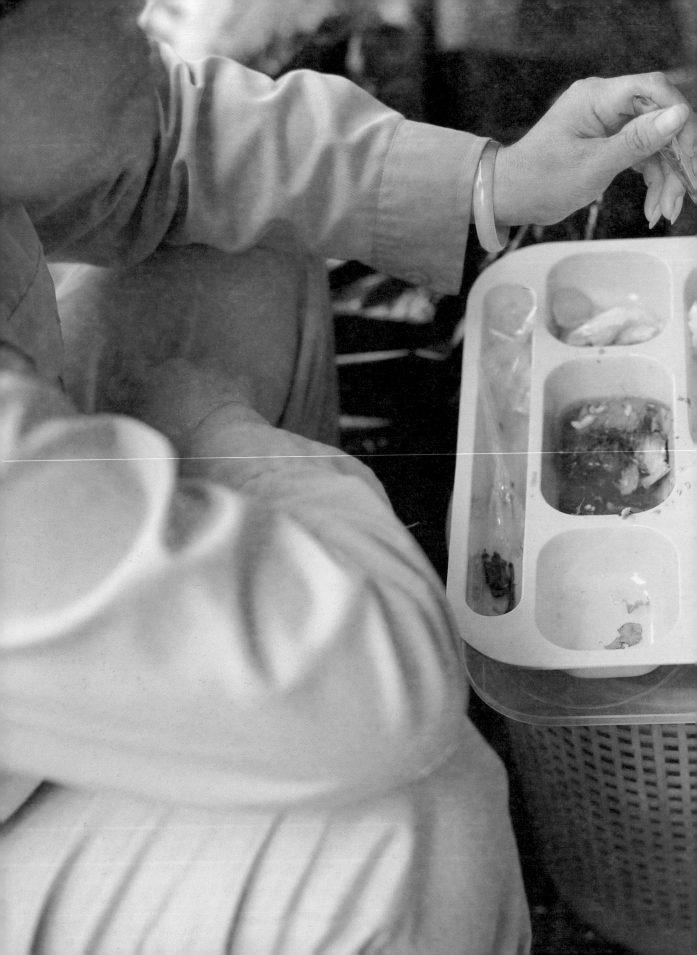

Bobby's Story

It took me a while to figure out that I was an ethnic mutt. Half Egyptian, half Chinese, born in Auckland, New Zealand, educated primarily in England, with the sense San Francisco was home.

I am the son of two very unusual parents: my mother, an Egyptian aristocrat, and my father, an American Chinese, born in Shanghai who after World War II moved to America and was raised in San Francisco. My father was self-educated, from the encyclopaedias he peddled to the British colonies during the '60s. His goal was to see the world, so he moved from country to country, hiring people in direct sales to sell his books.

I was privileged to be brought up with two grandmothers who were both really great cooks. My Chinese grandmother from Shanghai made Chinese food that I had never tasted in any restaurant anywhere. She was cooking a 'fusion' type of Chinese food back in the '50s, substituting for ingredients not readily available in the USA at that time. Somehow she made light sauces, greaseless noodles and entirely unique tastes.

My Egyptian grandmother cooked all manner of North African food – a wicked couscous, bisteeya and highly addictive. Quite frankly, I do not remember ever having a bad meal until boarding school in England.

'I have lived my life like an algebra equation. You find out the answer through the source of illumination, finding out what you do not like versus doing what you think you will like. I tried planning it all out, but it never really worked out that well when I did, so I stopped planning and started to feel my way through it all.'

My educational background is a trans-global mosaic including intermittent years of elementary school in San Francisco, a year at an all-boys' school in Egypt, as well as a stint at the Cairo American College in Maadi, until my Egyptian grandfather was appointed Ambassador of Egypt to the Court of St. James, which meant moving to England. There I was sent to several boarding schools, began playing rugby and was awarded a sports scholarship to Millfield School in Somerset.

When it came time to enrol in college, I returned to the USA and enrolled at College of Marin, then the University of Nevada in Las Vegas (UNLV), and St. Mary's in Moraga, California.

Uncertain of what sort of career I wanted to follow, I returned to London and began a business degree. I graduated from Richmond College in London with a BA in Finance and Economics, and worked in many positions in the securities industries, eventually moving to New York City to begin working on the floor of the New York Stock Exchange at 11 Wall Street. It did not take me long to realize that I really did not care for that sort of life at all, much to the displeasure of my parents who had paid a fortune for my English public school education.

I left, pursuing an interest in anything outside of wearing a suit and tie. I sold seafood to the mob and was reintroduced to the restaurant industry. I studied improvisational comedy at The Groundling and ended up doing a little bit of stand-up in both Los Angeles and San Francisco.

'In my life, I have been through many schools on three continents and had many jobs. My first was as a shoe shine boy at the age of 12 in the financial district in San Francisco. I worked the mail room when Charles Schwab was called 'Chuck', flew a kite on Fisherman's Wharf for $20 a day, and sold t-shirts on the Wharf. I was an elevator operator in the Fairmont Hotel, until I refused to send the owner up a couple of storeys.'

To support myself I worked as a runner, busboy and server in various restaurants. While waiting tables, I began hanging out in the kitchen of Elka, a cutting-edge Franco-Japanese restaurant in San Francisco. It was about this time that I discovered my love and talent for cooking.

'Elka was so cutting edge that you really needed to have a food lover's guide to explain the menu. I needed to learn and I volunteered my time in the kitchen to observe so I could understand food, the preparation and the operation. I learned how to make a chicken stock, and then a lemon grass chicken consommé. I was thrilled with myself. I was working with my senses and I started really getting into food. The chefs were like doctors to me and I liked the look of the white jacket.'

One day my father came to lunch at Elka. He started selling me on the idea of taking a trip to have a look at Vietnam. I was then working as a waiter and he started to go over my work experience. 'Your resumé is looking very sketchy. Research analyst in Boca Raton, trader for a hedge fund in San Francisco, floor of the New York Stock Exchange, stand-up comic, waiter...'I think you lost focus,' he said. Then the sell came in.'

'Vietnam is the next Baby Tiger,' he said. 'Or more like the Tail of the Dragon, with China being the head. Eighty million people with a per capita income less than 5% of the US minimum wage. A country the size of California, rich in natural resources, that has been economically isolated for the last 25 years. It is now at peace for the first time in a thousand years. I have seen this all before. The opportunity is now. Come and take a look.'

A couple of other people at the table started to encourage me to come out with them. We would be a group and I would be an added member. I looked into the food, but only found two cookbooks on the subject. I turned to Elka and asked what she knew about Vietnamese food, and she knew close to nothing, just like most chefs that I talked to. Vietnam in our vocabulary was not a country, but a war, and most people knew nothing about it. I started seriously to think about it and it all made sense.

When I arrived there in 1995, there were no foreigners to speak of really. We were a strange breed, and people would just stare at you. More than 60% of the population were born after 1975, when the war ended, so you felt old in a country of teenagers. English-speaking people were hard to find. The office we used as a base was in Ho Chi Minh City, where most of the manufacturing output comes from. It was like a poor man's New York. The multinationals had just arrived and obviously they knew what they were doing.

My father had set up a consultancy business and was advising the State Bank of Vietnam on investments and the establishment of a stock exchange. I realized I could not work for him, as I am not an obedient Chinese son. The western restaurants were bad at best, and the Vietnamese food was either scary or not that good. The country reminded me of an Asian version of Egypt back in the 1970s. I said 'Let's open up a restaurant. We will be the only place in town, and we will meet the who's who of Vietnam.'

When I got back to the States to develop the idea, I was met with a pretty dismal response. All the chefs thought I was crazy. I realized then that none of them had the vision. What would possess anybody to go learn a cuisine in a country that they had no roots in, especially when these days you could learn from the ethnic restaurant around the block? When you are doing haute cuisine, you want to work for a name, so that when you open your restaurant they will say 'He was Thomas Keller's sous chef,' or 'He worked with Nobu,' or whoever.

Nobody ate Japanese food in the states 25 years ago. You couldn't find a Thai restaurant in

San Francisco 15 years ago. When there is business, though, there is travel, and those emerging market cuisines crossed over to the American palate at about the same time. Vietnamese food was about to get discovered. I figured that Vietnamese food would be the next cuisine and I would be on the crest of the wave when it did hit in San Francisco.

So I begged Hubert Keller from the Fleur De Lys restaurant in San Francisco for a job. He did hire me, but rather reluctantly, as I had no real skills, although I really developed them there. Later I worked with Jeff Inahara at opening the Coconut Grove (Jeff had worked at Elka). I was working with friends, so I got to tailor my jobs to accelerate my learning curve, since I was pretty much starting in my 30s.

Unfortunately, while working as a saucier, I had a bad accident resulting in a back injury that derailed my career as a chef for a full year, during which time I laid in bed, read cookbooks, watched Great Chefs, Great Cities, watched PBS, and learned a lot without actually cooking.

After a brief sortie cooking in France, I returned to the US and had surgery for my back. After this I was diagnosed 'stationary and disabled', which meant that I could no longer work as a chef in the US. It was clear then that my cooking days there were over and Vietnam now made a hell of a lot more sense.

> *'I like to live on the edge, and sometimes you see more that way. No one gets out of here alive, and you are not going to take anything with you when you die, except the experiences that you had. I like to stay in swank hotels, but eat street food. I like to visit markets, museums as it is an express lane into a culture. I like to eat cheap food next to the locals because there is an added sense of acceptance as well as better sense of the people and the culture. I am also more generous in poorer countries, as I fee it is good karma."*

So I moved to Ho Chi Minh City and began by working at a beautiful restaurant called Camargue, but it did not really work out. After four months I left, and then started my own place, Saigon Joe's, with my girlfriend, Laura Flourens, who ran the front of the house. That lasted three months, until a dispute with our partner ended the whole thing.

We then moved back up to Hanoi and started a restaurant called Miró, which lasted three months until we were kicked out. Then Laura got a job in a hotel and I was later hired to open the restaurant in The Hanoi Towers, an apartment block built over the old 'Hanoi Hilton' – the notorious prison camp where captured GIs were held during the war.

We called this the Red Onion, and that is where I started to get attention from the international press. Basically a lot of foreign correspondents knew what I went through and liked my cooking, so they supported me for not giving up where most people would have quit.

I raised investment capital from the US to take ownership of The Red Onion, but the deal there fell through. As fate would have it, however, One Ba Trieu Street in the fashionable Hoan Kiem Lake district in Hanoi's Old Quarter became available soon thereafter. In 1997 Restaurant Bobby Chinn was built there, which I was able to design exactly to my requirements.

When I built this restaurant I wanted to do something that no one had ever dreamed of here. I named the restaurant after myself to protect myself. I had been kicked out of every restaurant that I had ever worked in over here and if it happened again they would have to rename it. If it was good, then I would have developed a reputation.

I had a feng shui guy come in and make the sacrificial chicken, whisky, cigarettes, etc. for the ancestors and kitchen gods at the alter in the kitchen. The guy wanted me to add a pond in the middle of the restaurant, but the last place had a pond and it went bankrupt, so I doubted the pond was going to help.

> *'Vietnam is a sweet, affectionate country full of love, with kind-hearted people. I want to send my love via dishes, pieces of music and books.'*

Bobby Chinn, October 2007

The Food of Vietnam

Vietnamese food is, has been and will continue to be one of the hippest cuisines of our time. Pick up any cookbook on Vietnamese cuisine and it immediately takes you through its history like no other cuisine. When I read a French cookbook, it never goes into the influences of the Roman Empire, or how duck à l'orange was really a Middle Eastern dish. Vietnamese cuisine is different. The dishes have a history that is as diverse as the country, yet it is quite distinct from all the other Asian cuisines. To understand and appreciate this, one should look at the history as well as the region.

What is now Vietnam was once divided into countless regions and occupied by many other nations such as the Chinese. In fact, from the 2nd Century BC, the Chinese ruled over Vietnam for over 1,000 years, leaving behind cultural traditions that echo in many Vietnamese traditions still observed today. Conspicuous culinary influences can be found in Vietnamese stir-fried foods and the widespread use of chopsticks.

Before the Chinese aggressively expanded their boundaries to envelop their contending neighbours, the Indianized Cambodian Kingdom of Funan ruled the southern portion of modern-day Vietnam from the 1st through to the 6th Century BC. Following that occupation were the Champa around Da Nang during the 2nd Century AD. While these cultures were present, they imported spicier foods, which were also made heavier with the addition of coconut milk.

Although Vietnamese cuisine was probably already robust on its own, it massively benefited from 16th century European trade, along with cultural traditions imported along with those goods, especially the traditions brought in by French colonials. Over time, these international influences helped Vietnamese cuisine evolve into the delicate, diverse and highly finessed cuisine that it is today.

Revisiting the influence of other cultures, the French in their near century of colonial rule in Indochina brought much of their refinement in cooking methodology, as well as their panoply of pantry ingredients into Vietnam's modern personal store. While bringing along kitchen techniques, the French had also imported their produce, agricultural technologies, Burgundy wines, chocolate, pastries and even truffle harvests.

French chefs have always been considered the masters of technique and have perfected it like no other country. It has evolved from heavy rich cream dishes to 1970s' nouvelle cuisine and cuisine minceur, which is actually a style borrowed from classic Japanese cuisine. With minceur's simplicity in ingredients, light food and many different tiny courses, the French sold

this latest cuisine to foodies and critics alike, inspiring extolling articles and the expenditure of hundred of dollars to eat well-crafted food in very small portions. Today, the French are extracting inspiration from their students in California, Australia, and still Japan.

However, what has taken the French hundreds of years of culinary evolution, the Vietnamese have already been perfecting it over the last thousand. How they missed Vietnamese cuisine as a turning point when they were there is its own travesty.

Vietnam has had the key ingredients and techniques at its fingertips for centuries. Its food is light, healthy, and generally easy to make. It can be subtle, yet bold, and is about quality ingredients, colour, contrast, texture and execution. Spanning from oil-less marinades for charcoal grilling and the caramel cooking in clay pots, to the pungent dipping sauces and the finishing of dishes with raw herbs, to the pungency of nuoc mam, their fermented fish sauce, the diversity is astounding.

Their broths and stock-making processes alone deserve enormous acknowledgement. While in the West stocks are influenced heavily with herbs, in Vietnam, spices take on a subtler role. Most people take this process for granted, but what is so unique about the Vietnamese stocks is that they are cooked for a long time, so the spices that are used fade in intensity with the long process. This delivers broths that are uniquely subtle, punctuated with herbs that highlight the broth and the accompanying meat.

I am dumbfounded as to why the food critics of the world have not really caught on to the cuisine. It is world-class global cuisine that has been perfected like no other. One of the problems is some of the meats they eat here. I'm talking about dog, bear and wild snakes.

Sucking on a snake's beating heart and dousing my insides with alcohol (very close in character to rubbing alcohol) mixed in with blood from the snake and its bile gland to get some form of manliness movement does not impress a food critic. I would much prefer to down Viagra with Veuve Clicquot when given

the choice and see who gets a rise first. Don't be biased about an entire cuisine just because there are some dishes that are not to your liking.

Travel throughout the region, and you will discover that Vietnamese cuisine is not like any of its South East Asian neighbours. Firstly they use chopsticks and yet bread can be found with your meal here. The other countries use spoons and forks. It is easier to define and explain Thai, Cambodian, Malay and Indonesian cuisine, which I like to refer to as spice-driven food. Vietnamese cuisine is much harder to explain.

Is it noodle-based, or is the basis the sophisticated subtle broths? Is it the oil-less marinades for the grill? Fresh spring rolls? The use of fish sauce as a dipping sauce, or as a vinaigrette, or to mix with anything from chicken stock to sugar to make a wide variety of sauces? To simplify Vietnamese cuisine as Chinese- and French-influenced cuisine would not do it justice. Perhaps in technique yes, but although both countries played an important role, spice traders, ethnic minorities and the creativity of cooks, as well as the natural culinary evolution through time have created a cuisine that is more complex then most people that eat it ever really appreciate. It would be like eating Chinese food and saying, 'Dude its Chinese food.'

Chinese food? That is too simplistic today for foodies. Chinese food varies as much as the region. Sichuan food is very spicy and somewhat oily, similar to that of its neighbours Pakistan and India. Beijing was the imperial city, so the cuisine there is more sophisticated and delicate. Shanghai food is the most European-influenced cuisine of China that also influenced Taiwan's cuisine, with dishes like chilled meat terrines and sophisticated stocks. Then you have the very popular Cantonese foods, which were the first to introduce their cuisine to the West, as they were the first major link to the West. Imagine taking all those cuisines and having each region messing around with the others' food for a couple of thousand of years and then what do you get? Chinese food. Same, same, but different.

As foreigners pop in to discover Vietnamese food, their preferences tend to gravitate towards the foods of the South. The reason for this is that the seasoning and style of cuisine down South are more familiar to them, as most Vietnamese chefs who introduced Vietnamese Cuisine to the West came from the South, similar to the reason for the popularity of Cantonese Cuisine. Yet, when celebrated Vietnamese chefs from the West pop by for a visit and ask me to take them to my favourite spots, I watch them with stunned eyes and flabbergasted palate. I joke: 'Not same, same as down South. Different!'

The Dishes

On a recent trip, the most celebrated Vietnamese chef in the USA, Charles Pham from the Slanted Door paid me a visit. I took him to eat banh cuon at my favourite street place. The lady there (see page 61) has perfected the whole package, all she really needs are chairs for grown-ups.

Her rice-based noodle is so thin, it is almost transparent. As she pulled the sticky thin rice crêpe from the steamer, and rolled the minced chicken mushroom mixture up like a Cuban cigar, with all the expertise of a great sushi chef, he just laughed. 'She didn't even garnish the damn thing!'

He didn't even try the ca cuon (the pheromone gland of a Beatle that if I saw it in the same vicinity as me I would run!), but I could see the admiration in his eyes. She has perfected her craft, and very well I might add. He walked away blown away, admitting 'I have never been able to get my rice crêpe that thin.' No one else has that I know of.

Then more questions. I'm a foreigner trying to figure it all out, and I've got a famous Vietnamese chef asking me as if I know the answers. The more I learn, the stupider I get. The dish in question is very Chinese, but the way it is eaten is totally different. In China it is sauced, in Vietnam, herbs and a dipping sauce used, which in my mind makes the dish more dramatic.

Take a dish like bahn xeo, often described as a crispy crêpe, like the French had something to do with it! But the roots of the ingredients come from other influences, namely India, through the Thais and Cambodians, indicated by the use of a spice like curry or turmeric, and coconut milk for the batter. If I was French and someone served me banh xeo calling it a crêpe, I would ask them 'How many times do I have to tell you, I like it soft! Not overcooked and crispy! It is suppose to be soft... spongy, like a real bad American pancake! Why do you make it crispy and throw in pork fat and shrimps and then tell me to rip it up and eat it with herbs and salad?' The correct response could be:

'Because it is not a crêpe, mallet head. It's a crispy thin Indian bread! Like a pappadum. We just decided to add our cooked prawns in fish sauce, mung beans, beansprouts and a little pork fat, to scare the Muslims away, but don't tell them that. And you know how we love herbs, and salads…. It's same, same, but different.'

Tale clay pot cooking with caramel sauce, The Chinese are a huge fan of the clay pot, but the use of fish sauce in the caramel, with chilli peppers, ginger, garlic and prawns, and chicken or fish is quite unique. This dish varies from region to region. In the North it is not as sweet and is little more subtle than a lot of the versions I have tried down South.

Geography

Vietnam can usefully be split into three geographical regions, with each region producing a unique recognizable culinary style. Over the years, there have been different interpretations of the original dish where it is harder to distinguish the origins. How did it start? Where did it come from? Where is it going?

The North

In the North, The weather gets a little cold, and the food reflects the season more than down South. The Chinese and Mongolians, influenced by the cooler mountainous terrain indigenous to them, contributed their seasonal menu together with appropriate cooking utensils and style. Due to the limitation of produce available, pickling is more prevalent and dried goods (seafood, mushrooms) play a more integral role in recipes. There are lots of soups for the chilly mornings and nights, where beef is more heavily prized.

Then, you may ask, why do they eat it in the South, where it is warm and hot? Because it is just that good! Stir-frying, learned from its Chinese neighbours, is deep rooted in Vietnamese culinary heritage and found all over the place.

Central Vietnam

This is where the old capital of Hue is situated. Due to the lack of diversity in cultivation and produce, chefs and cooks alike were pretty much short on ideas. Even the Emperor got tired of the same old food. In fact, King Hung Vuong VI had a competition to pass down the throne to one of his 22 sons who could produce a dish he had never had before. The one that produced the best and most unusual dish would get the kingdom.

That is how the Rice Cake for New Year was created. If that does not give you an idea of how hungry they were for new dishes, I don't know would. What I can tell you is that all those bite-sized dishes from Hue were created to please a kingdom tired of mung beans, noodles and rice.

The chefs went out of their way to reintroduce dishes with the same ingredients but camouflaged and disguised beyond recognition. You don't want rice any more?! You can't tell the king! Take a good look around you! All we seem to have is a muddy river and rice fields! No. What you do is say: 'You're going to love the rice pancake with crispy shallots and mushroom dipping sauce! MMMMmmmm. Rice dumpling? Sticky rice dumpling! I'll steam it, I'll fry it, and I'll wrap it in banana leaves. I'll stuff it, and give you dipping sauces that will complement each uniquely prepared dish. That is the 'Court Cuisine' Delicate, intricate, and highly imaginative out of necessity!

In the mountainous region, a place I have not spent much time to speak of, they eat a lot of game, and the fish sauce they use there is generally more salty. I think they are also skinnier than the majority of the Vietnamese.

South

In the south, where the climate and soils yields produce all year round, one finds the food more heavily spiced then the North. Foods are sweeter

and spicier. The Indian influence seems more prevalent in the cuisine down there than up in Hanoi. Put it all together and you have a cuisine that is bordering on Nirvana.

Cooking Techniques

The Vietnamese have a couple of techniques that are unique to their cuisine.

Grilling

Before grilling, oil-less marinades are usually used. Now that seems pretty easy. It is, but some of the styles borrowed are heavily influenced by the Indonesians. Take satay, with peanut and coconut dipping sauces and you can appreciate the origins.

Then you have grilled chicken marinated in chopped lemon grass and finished with a fermented chilli purée and hoisin sauce, and you see both Vietnamese and Chinese influence.

With ground pork patties, buon cha, you mix in a little caramel and you have a unique caramelizing technique that gives slightly crisped pork patties. Where the delicate pork patties sweat their fat into the hot coals, creating subtle smokiness, and the hot coals caramelized the meat only to be served with chilled rice noodles, herbs and dipping sauce is a true culinary masterpiece. Hot and cold, and contrasting textures are all achieved in a dish that sells for a measly buck!

China has been the biggest influence from the East, with its wealth of culinary techniques and styles. In the 14th century they had over 43 different techniques for cooking. Today it is estimated that there are over 80,000 dishes from which to choose. Their contribution to world cuisine is easily recognized, with the wok, chopsticks, soy sauce and the array of condiment sauces up the Ying Yang.

Vietnamese cuisine will evolve further with the introduction of new ingredients, and once local chefs look at themselves as culinary artists, as in other countries, where they are respected by the society as 'chefs' and not just cooks, then the new breed will be more inclined to create new dishes that we will all get to savour eventually.

Vietnamese Ingredients

This is a brief guide to many of the ingredients commonly used in Vietnamese cuisine, but which tend not to be widely sold in grocery stores. Many of them can, however, be found at speciality or gourmet food stores. Shopping online is usually the quickest way to track down rare ingredients. It may not always be the most cost-effective solution, but is certainly a great way to source things when you don't have a friend from Vietnam to deliver something personally for you.

Rice

Rice paddy fields are a familiar sight in many parts of Asia. Behind corn and wheat, rice is the world's third largest crop, feeding about two-thirds of the planet's population, and Vietnam is the second largest exporter of rice, after Thailand.

As in many other parts of the world, in Vietnam white rice is used as an anchor for daily meals, either as a satisfying, starchy filler or to balance potent meat and vegetable dishes. Traditionally in poorer regions of Vietnam, rice is eaten in sizeable amounts with very salty side dishes in order to compensate for the lack of food. However, it is also used for special dishes such as fried rice, and the fermented rice dish on page 180. Rather than boil or steam it in water, some households cook rice in chicken stock to add flavour. Adding more stock or water produces congee, a rice porridge, which is served for breakfast.

While rice can be eaten at virtually any meal in Vietnam, when it is eaten differs by region. In the North, rice is eaten last, usually as a palate cleaner. Sometimes it is followed by a simple, clear soup, which also tends to indicate prosperity, as diners do not have to stuff themselves with bland filler. In the South, rice is eaten right along with the meal.

There are a number of rice varieties used in Vietnam and in this cookbook.

Black sticky rice

I first encountered this rice and some of its uses in Bali. In its rare table appearances, black sticky rice is typically used for sweet puddings, but I use it as an ingredient in a savoury duck dish (see page 145). The techniques that we use in the kitchen are influenced by how I was taught in Bali. While the rice has its own unique flavour, I also incorporate charred ginger, pandan leaves, raisins, sultanas and lotus root while the rice is cooking. This turns this Asian ingredient into a very Middle Eastern style of dish. When you steam black sticky rice covered in pandan leaves, the leaves perfume the rice with a very dense, organic aroma.

Fermented rice

Red and white fermented rices are sold, and the one I use in this book is the white variety. It is easily made by adding some yeast to plain, cooked white rice and leaving it to ferment for three or four days. Fermented rice has a pronounced scent of yeast and a very delicate, sweet taste. It is used for making wine and desserts, but can also be a notable addition to savoury dishes.

Glutinous rice (also called sticky white rice)

This grain is typically short and rounded. In Vietnam, it is usually found in the form of xôi, which is a dish of steamed rice that may be served

savoury or sweet. As a savoury dish, it might be accompanied by steamed pork pâté (gio heo), topped with ground mung beans and soy sauce, or dried shredded pork. Sticky rice is also bound in a savoury cake, banh chung, eaten during the Lunar New Year. In its sweet form, it can be dyed red and sweetened for weddings and engagement parties.

Young rice

Called com in Vietnamese, young rice is eaten by itself steamed in a colander or banana leaves, or added to savoury and sweet dishes, such as fried pork patties (cha com) or the traditional soup dessert, che. Down the street from my restaurant is an infamous ice-cream shop, which has kem com, a creamy iced lolly of young rice that is popular even during the coldest of winters. The grains of this rice are very light in weight, almost like flakes, and a delicate celadon colour.

Fresh herbs and flavourings

Betel leaves

You are not likely to find these at your typical greengrocer unless they really do the legwork to import unusual fresh ingredients. Often used in the mouthwatering dish bo la lot, this dense and slightly sour herb can be easily replaced with grape leaves.

Galangal

There are two types of galangal: greater galangal and lesser galangal. The lesser version is not generally used as a spice, but as a Chinese medicinal herb. Greater galangal is a peppery spice best used in soups and curries. An off-white rhizome that's the doppelganger of ginger, it is generally sliced thinly or cut into chunks and worked into a paste using a mortar and pestle. Galangal freezes well.

Lemon grass

Long and light green, lemon grass conveniently grows in Southeast Asia where lemons do not grow easily. It shares the same essential oil, citral, as lemons, giving this herb a sour lemon taste and

scent. Popular with any grilled meat, it is also used in some stir-fried dishes and as a fragrant garnish. For storage, place the stalks in a plastic bag and refrigerate or freeze them. To prepare lemon grass, pull off the hard outer layers and thinly slice the interior.

Pandan leaves (also called screwpine and pandanus)

Often used to wrap, colour and perfume rice as it steams, pandan leaves have a uniquely vegetal, nutty taste that works in both savoury and sweet dishes. They are readily available fresh in Oriental supermarkets, and can also be found frozen in packets.

When they do not have pandan leaves, some cooks make rather weak substitutions, such as adding green food colouring to their rice, and vanilla to their sweet dishes. Pandanus juice, made from simmering the leaves in water and sweetening the result, is sold as a tonic drink and may be available when you can't get the leaves.

Shiso (also called perilla and beefsteak plant)

Best known as rau tia to in Vietnam, this herb is commonly used fresh in salads, or cooked with aubergines or omelettes. Its dramatic green and purple leaf makes an interesting salad topping, while its spicy aroma and taste of cinnamon, lemon, cumin and star anise make it the perfect herb to use when you want to give a haunting bite to a light dish.

Sugar cane

Some small streets in Vietnam showcase heavy metal grinders that are devoted to crushing sugar cane in order to extract the juice. Served on its own or with a little bit of lime, the juice is a refreshing drink but also a great ingredient to add a light, sweet flavour to beverages and food dishes. Sugar canes are also used as thick skewers for grilling (page 164), and after eating, one can chew on the sugar cane to cleanse the palate.

Tamarind

There are two types of tamarind: sweet and sour. Although the sweet version is still noticeably tart, sour tamarind is tangy and acidic. I first learned about tamarind as a child in Egypt and had it as a drink. In the West, it is used as a base ingredient for Worcestershire and HP sauces, while in Asia tamarind's numerous, highly palatable uses include chutneys, candies, sauces, glazes and juices.

At my restaurant, we serve it with crab (see page 160), because the flavours are highly complementary. The concentrated pulp of the fruit is sold in many forms, usually as a brick-like block that has to be cooked in water, strained then reduced to thick paste. If your tamarind turns out to be ultra-sour, you can adjust this with brown or palm sugar.

Turmeric
Apart from its exceptional reputation as a scar remover (dab it daily on a freshly dried abrasions to avoid scarring), turmeric is also antiseptic and has been linked with all manner of medicinal properties from healing liver disorders to easing the symptoms of Alzheimer's Disease.

A rhizome of the ginger family, turmeric is a bright persimmon colour when freshly cut. The dry golden powder is more widely available in the West, and is a key component of curry powder. The colour of this root is quite resilient, so if you accidentally get it on your favourite shirt, you can remove the stain by rubbing plain yogurt into it. Allow it to set and dry and then wash it with warm water.

Chillies
Vietnamese cuisine is not in general as spicy as that of its the neighbours India and Thailand, however dipping sauces and chilli oils allow you to take up the hotness a few notches if you so wish.

Looking at the Scoville Scale (which measures the pungency of a chilli based on its level of capsaicin, the chemical that stimulates our heat-sensitive nerve endings), you will find that the chillies used in Vietnamese dishes score no higher than the upper mid-range, with the Thai bird's-eye chilli being the hottest. Although they are not flaming-hot, like South American habaneros, these chillies are still hot enough to make your eyes water.

Normally, the smaller the chilli, the fierier it will be. To give a milder taste, use a small spoon to carefully remove and discard the seeds and pith. If you prefer to use your fingers take particular care to avoid touching your eyes, nose and mouth, as the pungent oils easily linger. Wash your hands thoroughly afterwards.

In Vietnamese cuisine chillies are typically used fresh, unless they have been pickled. It is not advisable to use dried chillies or chilli flakes as a substitute, unless you are experimenting and desire a different taste and/or texture.

Serrano chilli
This very meaty green chilli turns a scarlet red and perhaps even yellow as it ripens. Often used in Thai and Mexican cuisine, it adds the perfect complementary bite to many Southern Vietnamese dishes, as well as the very simple, yet essential, dipping sauce. Best to buy it fresh as needed rather than try to store it.

Thai bird's-eye chilli
Affectionately known as 'mouse shit chilli', this little variety is incredibly potent and has a stinging bite. It can usually be found quite easily in greengrocers and supermarkets. If necessary you could substitute a Serrano chilli.

Sauces
Vietnamese cuisine could not be what it is without its sauces. They round out the flavour and complete a dish. (Sometimes, it is difficult to identify the individual flavours in a Vietnamese dish, because the main flavour it imparts is so unique.) The sauces listed below are usually bought ready-made and easily found in supermarkets and specialist shops. You may have more difficulty finding the shrimp sauce, but online shopping should prove successful for those who want to get the recipe to taste just-so.

Chilli sauce
The Vietnamese make a great chilli sauce used in bun bo and pho. This condiment can be home made, but to save some time, it can also be bought bottled at the grocers. It pairs very well with

oyster sauce, and when mixed together, you can never tell that the resulting sauce is made of either ingredient. While walking the food stalls of Hanoi, I learned this trick for the grilled chicken on a skewer on Ly Thuong Kiet Street.

Oyster sauce

What is oyster sauce and what is in it? This mystery condiment is quite simply oysters, brine and a bit of that ubiquitous Asian seasoning monosodium glutamate. A less expensive version (and what is usually sold in Western grocers) is thickened with starch, coloured with caramel and contains preservatives. Imparting a very sweet aroma and an addictive umami flavour, oyster sauce is useful for steamed vegetable and stir-fried dishes. Combined with a few different flavourings for variety, it is probably the most indispensable Asian ingredient in my kitchen.

Shrimp sauce

This very, very pungent sauce requires a highly adventurous palate. Vietnamese shrimp sauce is a thick, purple and slightly mealy looking substance that is made of fermented, crushed shrimp. When made in its very elemental form, it is shrimp fermented in salt, crushed and – depending on one's taste – later mixed with a small amount of caramel sauce. In North Vietnam, dog meat served with this bubbling fermented sauce is considered a rare delicacy.

Soy sauce

Inherited from the Chinese, soy sauce is more commonly used in the north of Vietnam than the south for authentic cuisine. However you are also bound to find soy sauce and its various forms – low sodium, light soy sauce (which is saltier and thinner in consistency), soy sauce with chilli, wasabi, etc – at dim sum or vegetarian restaurants further south. In Vietnam, typically speaking, soy sauce is an understudy for fish sauce, used when there is a desire to change the taste, or when you want another dipping sauce on the table.

Soy sauce is made from soy beans and some form of roasted grain like wheat, barley or rice. The tradition of soy sauce use dates back to the Chinese Zhou period, and its numerous forms vary from light brown to viscous dark brown. Mushroom soy sauce is a mixture of straw mushrooms and thick soy sauce.

Spices

Charred chillies

Charred spices are quite popular in this cuisine, as there is also charred ginger, onions and shallots. Charring imparts a nice, smoky taste without any work on the grill. As you will see in some of my recipes I often do it by placing the spice, say a chunk of fresh ginger, in the flames while I am cooking something on the hob, then I scrape off the blackened skin and give it a whack with a cleaver to encourage the lovely smoky juices to come out.

Curry powder

Depending on the household that is cooking the curry, this powder can include a very diverse assortment of spices. Generally speaking, this powder is quite similar to that of Indian cuisine. It can include cumin, turmeric, mustard seeds, cloves, ginger, garlic, cinnamon, nutmeg and black pepper. Adding a little water and yogurt turns this mixture into a light paste that can be coupled well with chicken.

Five-spice powder

This is yet another adaptation from Chinese cuisine, which entails balancing the five basic flavours of Chinese cuisine: bitter, pungent, salty, sweet and sour. This potent combo entails a fragrant mixture of star anise, cloves, cinnamon, cloves and fennel. There are other combinations with include licorice in lieu of star anise, cassia, cloves and nutmeg, but you can experiment to your liking. A savvy grocer would carry a seven-spice powder, which would include additional spices like peppercorns.

Mustard seed

The mustard seed is not actually an essential ingredient in Vietnamese cuisine, but it does come in handy for a sharp, pungent flavour that

can be used with fish or pickles. Mustard seeds and sauce are generally added to egg noodle dishes like won ton noodles or other Chinese adapted dishes.

Oils, Vinegars etc

Peanut or groundnut oil

Peanut oil, also known as groundnut oil, is very pragmatic and resilient, so it is widely used for deep-frying. However, be careful of your guests' dietary needs and allergies, as many food lovers are allergic to peanuts.

Rice wine

Made from steamed fermented glutinous rice, rice wine has a very low alcohol content and makes for a light beverage or sweet additive to desserts. Sake is a well-known type of rice wine, which is crafted by Japanese rice wine makers. Sake is readily acquired in cosmopolitan parts of Vietnam, but can easily be made at home over the course of a week.

Rice vinegar

This variety of vinegar is made from fermented rice under a controlled process, where fermented rice is introduced to bacteria to ferment further. Rice vinegar is commonly used in creating clear dipping sauces, salad dressings and pickling.

Sesame oil

Pressed from toasted sesame seeds, this potent oil is used very sparingly as a flavouring. Used to separate egg noodles, stir-fry vegetables, and in salads, this oil is yet another adoption from Chinese cuisine.

Dry Goods

Cassava flour

Contemporary use of cassava flour is in tapioca balls, like those in boba tea drinks. This flour is made from the cassava root, which is also used in Vietnamese cuisine, and eaten like a steamed potato.

Coconut milk

Extracted from the flesh of mature coconuts, coconut is generally used to sweeten glutinous rice and other desserts like sweet soup desserts. In more savoury dishes, like curry, coconut milk adds to the thick consistency of the sauce and gives the sauce a smooth and creamy consistency. Coconut milk can be made, but is easily bought in a can at the grocer's. Be careful with immediate refrigeration, as coconut milk spoils easily in room temperature.

Dried yellow mung beans (also called mung dai beans)

This pale yellow bean is a skinned version of a light green mung bean. Typically used skinned or unskinned in a sweet soup, che dau sanh, yellow mung beans are also used in sticky rice, xoi, as well as savoury or sweet cakes for special occasions (e.g. banh chung, banh com, etc). Yellow mung beans are also made into a paste to top certain sweet soup desserts. This bean can also be found in vegetarian versions of banh beo and used as a filling substitute for meat.

Dried small red beans

This bean is found as filling for sweet cakes and the main ingredient for certain sweet soups. Generally a softer bean than the yellow mung bean, this type is found in more sweet dishes than savoury. When prepping red or yellow beans, it is best to soak them for a few hours, but careful not to soak them for too long, as they tend to affect people who are susceptible to flatulence.

Dried shrimp

These are terrifically salty and chewy like jerky, and are great for topping or garnishing salads. Dried shrimp can also be used in powdered form as the topping for banh beo or whole in rice porridge or soups. Dried shrimp is typically sold in an Asian or specialty grocery store.

Palm sugar

Made from the sap of the date palm, palm sugar has a very rich taste, similar to molasses. Also used in desserts, this sugar is often used to counterbalance salty dishes.

Rock sugar
This pretty amber-coloured sugar is used in sweetening teas or glazing meats. Store dry in a cool cupboard.

Sesame powder
This is the ingredient you can use to make a wonderful tea. We use this for our sauce in the rice pudding. Black sesame is puréed into a paste. Afterwards, I add a coconut cream, which creates a sweet, nutty sauce.

Tapioca pearls
These are tiny balls of tapioca that are rarely used outside of adding to the sweet Vietnamese soups. Often sold dry to be boiled soft, these balls are made from sago flour.

Tapioca flour (also called tapioca starch)
When water is added, this flour becomes a very sticky and effective thickening agent for savoury soups, sweet soups and stir-fries. Tapioca flour is also a critical ingredient for banh beo and other foods from Central Vietnam.

Vanilla powder (also called vanilla sugar)
At the restaurant, we make it ourselves. Take some vanilla pods and stuff sugar into them. The pods will absorb the fragrance, so do not throw them away.

Mushrooms

Dried wood ear mushrooms (also called dried tree ear mushrooms or dried black fungus)
Typically used finely julienned in soups, spring rolls and banh cuon, this ingredient does not impart much flavour. However, it is often used to add a soft but crunchy texture.

Oyster mushrooms
The cap of this mushroom is quite large, and comes in thick and thin varieties. This type is also commonly used in stir-fries and rice dishes.

Shiitake mushrooms (also called Chinese black mushrooms or black forest mushrooms)
Thick and juicy when fresh and having a very earthy and perhaps even salty taste, these mushrooms make a fantastic substitute for beef. I like to sear them to get them crispy on the outside and moist in the middle. When dried, I soak them and reserve the water to make soup.

Straw mushrooms
Soups and stir-fries generally feature this type. If not dried, this mushroom is sold canned. It has a light, organic taste, and has a soft crunchy texture.

Noodles & Wrappers

These ingredients are slightly more difficult to find in a regular grocery store, but if your town or city has a specialty food store, they are liable to carry at least the noodles and rice paper listed below. Italian pasta makes a poor substitute, so it is best to find these ingredients as they are key to their dishes.

Cellophane noodles
Called mian in Vietnamese, these tough stringy noodles are eaten after being boiled to a soft, glutinous or an al dente consistency. This noodle type is commonly found in very comforting chicken soups and light salads that are mixed with vegetables and/or meat. Cellophane noodles can also be used as a binding agent in spring rolls like rice vermicelli.

Fresh flat rice noodle sheets
These are sold in Vietnamese food stores, and are best when bought fresh early in the morning. These are brought in from a village near Truc Bach in Hanoi. This inspired the dish pho cuon. These noodles are very light, fresh and sticky and sold by the kilo. You can cut them up into thin strips as noodles or you can use them as wraps. The thin noodles are generally eaten like a pho in broth or with Vietnamese pork sausage as a quick snack.

Rice paper

This handy wrapper is used to wrap spring and summer rolls. It is also a fun alternative for filo dough. I used to make bisteeya with the filo. When there was a time the filo was bad, I made a substitution, and it worked out great. The thing you need to look out for is overly dry rice paper.

Rice vermicelli (also called Vietnamese rice vermicelli)

This type of noodle is common in dry noodle dishes, but can also be served wet with broth. If you serve them with a chicken broth, it is best to eat the soup immediately, as the noodles easily become mushy after a few minutes, especially if they are overcooked. I use this as a binding agent, like in spring rolls.

Miscellaneous

Rice crackers (also shrimp crackers)

These are dry rounds of thin hard dough that you would deep-fry and serve as a light table snack or with certain Vietnamese salads .

Tofu

As in other Asian countries, tofu comes in both firm and soft forms. Made of pressed bean curd and sealed with wheat gluten, tofu has a very moist consistency. Firm tofus can be eaten fried with a fish dipping sauce or in stir-fries, while soft tofu is often served in a light sugar and ginger sauce for dessert. Tofu is best covered and refrigerated, and covered when not being eaten, and will last at least 4 days.

Vietnamese pork sausage (also called pork paste)

Pork sausage is made of blended pork meat with fish sauce, rolled and steamed in banana leaves. Eaten with a baguette, steamed sticky rice or regular white rice, this form of meat is a light way to eat pork. Pork sausage can last quite a while if well wrapped in plastic and refrigerated. It should last for at least a week in your refrigerator.

Fruit

Asian pear (also called Nashpati, Nashi pear, Sand pear, Korean pear, and Apple pear)

Watery and delicately sweet, this pear can easily make a great thirst quencher, with its very juicy flesh. I use this grilled and served with a foie gras terrine. When served hot, the pear is quite lovely with a light glaze.

Green mangos

These mangos are your typical unripe mangoes that are very fibrous and have a very tart taste. Often used julienned in salads and eaten with small dried shrimp, green mangoes are also cut into large matchsticks and served with salt and chilli powder as a snack.

Jackfruit

This is a fruit that is incredibly sweet and fragrant, which did not appeal to me. However, in its raw form, it is a wonderful dish to sauté. There are some tricks, however. When cutting through the thick, green skin, the fruit excretes a white sticky substance, which resembles Elmer's Glue.

In order to cut the young jackfruit, your knife should be well oiled, as should your hands. Otherwise, it would be impossible for you to extract the fruit. The jackfruit has seeds that can be blanched and roasted. These almost taste like almonds. The flesh of the young jackfruit is cooked in boiling water for about 30–40 minutes with garlic. Once removed, it is shredded by hand and sautéed with garlic, shrimp paste, a little Vietnamese herb and garnished with sesame seeds. This is a traditional Hue dish.

Young jackfruit can also be found cooked and canned if you wish to avoid the headache of preparing it.

Lychee (also called litchi)

Native to Southern China, Vietnam and regions as far southward as the Philippines, this fragrant fruit has a very light and sweet taste. The white flesh is quite tender, and is generally eaten alone or in a sweet compote or dessert soup.

Mangosteens

Called 'Queen of Fruits' in different parts of Asia, one would never guess that such a delicate fruit can emerge from its very tough and thick purple shell. Although mangosteens are illegal to import in places like the USA, because of their potential to carry the Asian fruit fly, some individuals would still risk hand carrying this fruit for its light refreshing juice.

Segmented like an orange, but with the consistency similar to a dense, fibrous lychee, mangosteens are a refreshing fruit that can be used in salads and puréed to make sorbet. The juice can also be used as a substitute for sugar and can be well paired with poultry.

Pomelo

I was never a fan of the grapefruit. A fruit that you have to sprinkle sugar on to make palatable never appealed to me. The pomelo is more subtle in flavour. Its large, thick segments make it easy for preparation, removing seeds and separating the small juice capsules. Pomelo has a natural affinity in salads.

Rambutans

In the same family as the lychee, this dynamic fruit has a wild soft shell, which looks similar to a sea urchin. Fleshier than its cousin, rambutans make an addictive snack, and can be thrown into a salad or garnish for a white meat dish.

Star fruit (also called Carambola)

Light and tart and with the dry aftertaste of a light tea, this star-shaped fruit is often found in - or as a garnish for – salads, as well as a fresh fruit juice in Vietnamese cafes.

Vegetables

Aubergine (also called Eggplant)

In the tradition of Central and Southern Vietnamese cuisine, the aubergine is often served grilled, topped with shredded crabmeat and a light fish sauce mixed with garlic and chilli. Aubergine is also great in stir-fries.

Banana Blossom

This is commonly used as a noodle. My huge revelation came when I hired Tuan, a chef from Hue, who would cook them in acidulated water until the banana blossoms inner leaves were tender. When deep-fried in a batter, the flavours have a subtle flavour of tender artichoke. By simply shredding the meat, throwing in salt, pepper and seasoning with sugar, it has the texture of shredded cooked chicken.

Chayote

This wrinkled, pear-shaped gourd has a very bland taste and is generally boiled in a soup, pickled or stir-fried.

Chinese mustard greens

Available year round, these leaves can come with flat, crumpled, scalloped or toothed edges, and are generally stir-fried or pickled.

Daikon

My appreciation of daikon comes from the Japanese. In its healthiest form of preparation, it acts as a backdrop for sushi. The Japanese also braise it in dashi and soy sauce. In Vietnam, we braise it in fish sauce and sugar. I also like to use it as a wrapper, cutting it very thinly into sheets, and throwing mixed herbs and vegetables into it as a wrap.

Lotus root

This tough, fibrous root is from the lotus water lily, which is often used in soups (e.g. crab soup) or in salads.

Luffa squash (also called Chinese okra and silk squash)

When cooking this spongy squash, make sure you skin it to remove its bitter outer layer. Often served in soups or stir-fries, this vegetable makes for a highly refreshing and lightly sweet dish.

Taro stems (also called cocoyam, dasheen, edo and elephant's ear)

Both the leaves and tuber root of this plant can be eaten. Taro leaf stems are quite tasty in stir-fries and are quite nutritious. High in vitamins and minerals, these leaves are a great source of iron, phosphorous, riboflavin and thiamine.

Water spinach

Water spinach can be found in abundance in many Asian markets. This is one of the vegetable of choices among my staff. Generally, it is boiled and served chilled, accompanied with a bowl of fish or dipping sauce. The water from this is used as a soup – a palate cleanser of sorts. The efforts made to sauté it also yield very pleasing results with fermented bean curd.

Equipment

Banh Beo moulds

If you cannot find these moulds in a store, you can easily use small porcelain or metal saucers as replacements. Make sure that they are resilient enough to be steamed many times.

Clay pots

These are generally used to slow cook its contents, as the evaporation process is slow, allowing the contents to cook in its juices for a prolonged duration of time. I often use this for my Caramel Fish (see page 171) or even a fancy macaroni and cheese dish.

Cleaver and kitchen shears

I have a growing appreciation for these two. It is more a sense of re-education in technique. When I bone a chicken with a paring knife, I think of the Vietnamese chefs, and how they bone more efficiently with shears. Just as there are many types of knives designed for specific tasks, two cleavers and some kitchen shears would suffice in a Vietnamese kitchen. A vegetable cleaver, which is light and has a thin blade, can be used for anything from boning a fish to shovelling up small items. The large, thick cleaver is the perfect instrument for chopping meats with bones.

Colander

This is a perfect instrument for steaming, draining and smoking.

Mandolins

In Vietnamese food, there are a lot of very thinly sliced ingredients. The mandolin grater is perfect for achieving that for making noodles and slicing.

Mortar and Pestle

Although it may appear labour-intensive, using a mortar and pestle is ideal for pulverizing ingredients into pastes. This could be pushed aside for the food processor, but for one's ability to control the consistency of whatever is being pulverized.

Rice cooker

This is one of the greatest inventions in cooking. Its application does not have to be limited to making rice. At the restaurant, we use the rice cooker to hold pre-cooked items, from paella to savoury custards. You can actually use this to cook paella with very satisfying results.

Skewers

Always use wooden ones and soak them for a couple of hours to make sure they do not burn nor stick to what you are skewering. These come in handy for quick barbecuing.

Spider

This is a special sieve that picks up items in oil when you are deep-fat frying. It is indispensable.

Wok

These come in different sizes and grades of thicknesses. The point of the wok is designed for multi-purpose cooking. It has a very low bottom base, which transforms heat quickly, and rounded sides that allow easy sautéing. The small bottom base is small and somewhat narrow. When it comes to deep-fat frying, you don't need much oil to fill it up. When using it, it imparts a smoky flavour to whatever you're cooking. The key is to have ample BTU to get it to a high temperature.

In Asian cooking, cooking quickly at a very high temperature is prevalent. The wok is designed for just this kind of cooking.

Building Blocks

Most of the recipes in this section are simple to make and store very well, so you can make more than you need for one dish and keep them ready to use on another occasion. The crispy shallots are a good example. They're used in a lot of Vietnamese dishes to add an extra dimension of taste and texture – and, if you're making them, you might as well make the shallot oil. Caramel sauce can be made in large quantities and stored – it's not going to go off because it is just sugar and water. I make large pots of beef stock then reduce them to a demi-glace and freeze them in ice cube trays. That way I can take just one or two cubes per person out of the freezer and, bam..., there's you're sauce. Here you will also find recipes for Vietnamese pickles, which punctuate dishes by bringing a contrast of taste, texture and colour. The first time people try them they tend to be delightfully shocked.

Crispy-fried Shallots and Shallot Oil

HÀNH PHI VA DAU HANH

The advantage of making crispy fried shallots is that you also get to reuse the oil in which you have fried them. Used in modest amounts, this oil makes a wonderful enhancement to other dishes and lends a subtle toasty undertone of flavours that is hard to identify, transforming a simple dish into something a little more complex.

The oil is a wonderful dark golden colour and is used in many dishes like Banh Cuon (see page 61), and the crispy fried shallots add colour, texture and flavour to some of my favourite Vietnamese dishes, like Bun Bo (see page 73), Banh Cuon again, stir-fried rice, Grilled Aubergine (see page 110), Congee (see page 81) and various salads (see the Salads chapter). Do not use the oil if it has had something overcooked in it, as the burned food will spoil the flavour.

Frying the shallots is not as simple as it seems. There are a couple of little tricks to making the fried shallots deliciously crispy. Firstly, it is ideal to have the shallots cut to the same uniform thickness, as this allows them to cook in the same time. The best tool for achieving this is a food processor with the slicing attachment. A mandolin grater is not very useful as it is too hazardous and a little too time-consuming. In the event that you do not have a

food processor with the right attachment, then a very sharp knife is pretty much your best bet.

The second trick is to dry the shallot slices overnight on a baking sheet pan. We leave them overnight in the oven at a very low temperature – actually, with just the pilot light on.

The third tip is probably the most important. You need to ensure that the oil is not too hot. If it is too hot, the shallots will rise too quickly to the surface, where the sugars burn and you end up with non-crispy burnt shallots. The temperature of the oil needs to be consistent. When we make the shallots for the restaurant, we cook them in batches to ensure that we do not reduce the oil temperature too much when we add each batch.

MAKES ABOUT 40G

250ml vegetable oil

200g thinly sliced shallots

Heat the oil in a wide frying or sauté pan to 130°C or when a pair of chopsticks create small bubbles when they are submerged.

Add one-quarter of the shallots and move them back and forth occasionally to ensure they are not touching each other and cook equally.

Once they turn golden brown, remove the shallots with a perforated spoon or a fine-mesh strainer. (Make sure not to overcook them as you will ruin the oil as well as the shallots.) Place on a

baking sheet lined with kitchen paper. Place in a warm oven with the door slightly open so they don't lose their crispness to keep them warm.

Strain the leftover oil through a coffee filter and reserve for other dishes.

Note: The cooked shallots will keep for up to a month in a tightly covered jar. They can also be frozen for up to 3 months. Whenever I use them, I first put briefly in a preheated oven so they come out hot and crispy, especially when serving them with cold dishes. This makes a huge difference, although many people do not bother to do this simple pre-preparation. I also use paper towels to remove as much oil from them as possible.

Roasted Peanuts ĐẬU PHỘNG RANG
Although peanuts were not a staple in Vietnamese cuisine until the French imported them in the mid-to-late 19th century, they are now - particularly the roasted type - very popular. Whether sweetened, salted, boiled, cooked, steamed or roasted, peanuts have become an invaluable ingredient in local dishes.

Apart from being a tasty snack on their own, roasted peanuts are used as a garnish and as a main ingredient for food such as Bun Bo (see page 73) and Peanut Sauce (see page 46). They also are great for adding texture to salads. Wherever you see roasted peanuts, you generally find the Crispy-fried Shallots (see page 38).

This recipe is so simple I even wonder if it will actually make it into the book. The reason I have added it is that it is so absurdly easy and the simple addition of warm chopped peanuts to so many dishes gives incredible pleasure to anyone.

SERVES 5
500g raw shelled peanuts

Preheat the oven to 180°C/Gas 4. Place the peanuts on a baking sheet and cook in the preheated oven for about 10 minutes.

Alternatively, you can cook them in pan over moderate heat, making sure you stir them constantly until the nuts turn golden-brown, about 5 minutes. Allow to cool.

If you have chosen nuts with the skin on,

place them on a baking sheet and cover with a damp towel while the peanuts are hot. After about 20 minutes, rub the skin with the wet towel so that the skins come off.

Marinated Chillies ỚT NGÂM GIẤM
Although Vietnamese food is not particularly spicy, there are often condiments set on the table that are, allowing diners to pep up their dishes. Sometimes it is a vinegar, perhaps a chilli vinegar, or a chilli sauce, or even just lime juice. The pickled chillies here can be puréed and used as a chilli sauce. If you do this, it would be wise to remove some of the seeds to make sure that the resulting sauce is not too excruciatingly hot.

Popular chillies used in Vietnam are the well-known ones from Cau Nhi village in the Quang Tri Province, which have been written about as far back as 1553, by Doctorate Minister Duong Van An. In an official report about the province, the official also wrote about the chillies in the province, which had fiery effects, burning the mouth and stomach.

MAKES ABOUT 40 (600ML)
350ml seasoned rice wine vinegar
115g sugar
1 tbsp sea salt
10 small garlic cloves
30g each red, yellow and green chillies (making sure they are roughly the same size so they cook in the same time)

In a pot over a gentle heat, combine the vinegar, sugar, and salt. Once the sugar and salt have dissolved, pour into a clean glass jar.

In another small pot, bring some salted water to the boil. Reduce the heat and blanch the garlic for about 30 seconds, then remove and refresh in iced water to stop further cooking - the idea is just to soften them a bit. Remove from the ice water when cool to the touch and dry off in a kitchen towel, then drop into the vinegar mix.

Repeat the blanching and refreshing process for the chillies, cooking each colour separately. Once all of the garlic and chillies have been placed inside a jar, there will be a tendency for them to float to the top. Place a kitchen towel over the mixture to ensure that all of the ingredients are submerged.

These keep for some time in the refrigerator and work well as a garnish for many dishes.

Crisp Carrot and Daikon Pickles

GỎI DƯA CHUỘT

This dish is not only simple to make, it is very colourful and tasty. If you wanted to make them spicy that would also be easy as well. They make great bar food, and a wonderful snack. Their light crunchy consistency also lends them well to complementing many dishes.

SERVES 4

1 small carrot, peeled and cut into julienne strips
175g daikon radish, peeled and cut into julienne strips
Dressing
100g caster sugar
2 tsp salt
150ml seasoned rice wine vinegar

Make the dressing: combine the ingredients and stir until the sugar is completely dissolved.

Add the carrot and radish to the dressing and mix thoroughly to make sure you coat all the vegetables. Leave to marinate for half an hour, stirring the contents twice.

You can serve immediately or store for up to 24 hours. Serve with the dressing or drain first. Notes: If you do not mind a little more work for a more aesthetically appealing product, use a large carrot instead, cutting rounds from the bottom half of the carrot. Cut small triangles into the circumference of each piece to create flat carrot flowers, making sure you leave space in between each triangle. The same can be done with the daikon. Do not forget the salt, as it removes the bitterness from the daikon.

Dried Shredded Pork RƯƠC HEO

Dried shredded pork is a great snack all by itself, but it is usually served with white glutinous rice with steamed chicken or on top of fresh French baguette. This light - almost cotton-candy-like - dish can also be made out of chicken or fish. This is one of those recipes that really makes you wonder who the first person to figure this out was. It makes great bar food and is very simple to prepare.

Pork loin is the best cut to use, as there is hardly any fat and the grain of the meat is very easy to distinguish. This recipe make a lot, but it stores very well and you might as well make more than usual, as it goes very quickly.

MAKES ABOUT 800G

2 kg lean pork loin
115 ml fish sauce (preferably nuoc mam)

Chop the pork into 7.5-cm cubes and marinate in the fish sauce for 2 hours, turning it from time to time to ensure that all sides are coated with the marinade.

In a large pan, simmer the meat in the marinade, covered, for about 45 minutes on a very gentle simmer, until all the liquid has evaporated. The meat has a tendency to stick to the pan, so be careful when removing it from the pan as it may stick. Place the meat on a rack and allow to cool to room temperature.

Once cool enough to handle, shred the pork by tearing away at the meat, following down the length of the grain. This process is a little time consuming, but if you like sewing, this is an activity that can be done in front of the TV or with a group of friends. Shred the pork into very thin strips, making the strips thinner and thinner.

Once all the pork is shredded, return it to the pan and stir until completely dried. Alternatively, place it in an oven preheated to 107°C/Gas ¼ and simply let the pork dry out completely, about 20 minutes, but make sure to move it around to prevent unnecessary browning.

This golden fluffy pork will store quite well in a glass container for several months without refrigeration.

Toasted rice powder THÌNH

I first stumbled on toasted rice powder in Thailand. Its wonderful toasty flavour is rather like that of ground sesame seeds. During the craze for garnishing with carrot or beet powder, I found this powder much more appealing as its flavour was not mellowed by the process of getting it to powder form – so much the case with the other powders. On the contrary, the flavour enhanced my Thai beef salad, by dulling the spice and adding a toasty taste.

I never really explored using the powder much further than that, until on a hot sunny day I ate on Food Street with my sous chef Hung. He went to a side store and ordered a brown drink served in a plastic bag with a couple of ice cubes in it and then told me that it would cool me down. One sip and I laughed. It reminded me of the horchata (also known as rice milk), a Latin drink that I used to consume in the Mission district of San Francisco.

This toasty sweet, nutty drink was so pleasing that I immediately became incredibly sad not to have discovered it years before. Till this late date, I am often surprised by the many expats who have lived in Hanoi for many years and have still to discover this drink. So far in my eleven-year search, I have only found one place that sells it. So not only is this a wonderful dish enhancer, it can be made into a surprisingly delectable toasted rice drink (see below).

MAKES 1 CUP
1 cup of uncooked white rice

Place the rice in a dry pan over a medium heat and toss the rice constantly to ensure that it browns evenly. This will take a little bit of time, about 30 minutes, to reach a golden brown.

Process the toasted rice in a blender or a spice grinder to a fine powder. Sift through a fine-mesh strainer and remove any large bits. Store in an airtight jar and refrigerate.

Simply use the toasted rice flour as a coating for fish, or as a dust garnish for plates.

Toasted Rice Drink

NUOC THÌNH

SERVES 2
1 cup Toasted Rice Powder (see above)
115g sugar
1.2 litres warm water

Place the rice powder, sugar and half the warm water in a large bowl or pan and soak overnight.

Next day, strain through a fine-mesh strainer. Add the remaining water and stir.

The exact sweetness of this drink is up to you: simply add more sugar if you would prefer it sweeter. You may also add cinnamon to this drink for an additional flavour dimension.

Fish Sauce Dip NƯỚC CHẤM

This is an absolute must on any Vietnamese table. It not only brings out the different flavours of a Vietnamese dish, the sauce also rounds it out or completes it. I suggest making four times the amount recommended in this recipe, because it is quite addictive. Once made, it can be stored at room temperature, but I suggest refrigeration for a longer shelf-life and containment of the lingering garlic scent. For a little variety, it can also be used as a light salad dressing.

MAKES ABOUT 120 ML
1 tsp rice vinegar
3 tsp sugar
1 finger-length Thai bird's-eye chilli, finely chopped (deseed if you prefer a milder sauce)
2 garlic cloves, crushed
1 tbsp freshly squeezed lime juice
2 tbsp fish sauce

In a saucepan, mix the vinegar, sugar and 60 ml water. Bring to the boil and set aside to cool.

When cool, combine with the chilli, garlic and lime juice. Mix well and stir in the fish sauce. For a variation, add some grated carrot or Carrot and daikon radish pickles (see page 42) to the dip.

Caramel Sauce THANG NƯỚC DUONG

Desserts like crème caramel may have been popular French imports in Vietnam since the late 19th century, but in Vietnamese cuisine caramel is usually far from sweet.

Generally in a burnt liquid form, this distinctive additive makes for a unique flavouring and colouring agent. In dishes like the savoury Bun Cha (see page 77), caramel sauce is the one additive that can never be omitted, because of its key role.

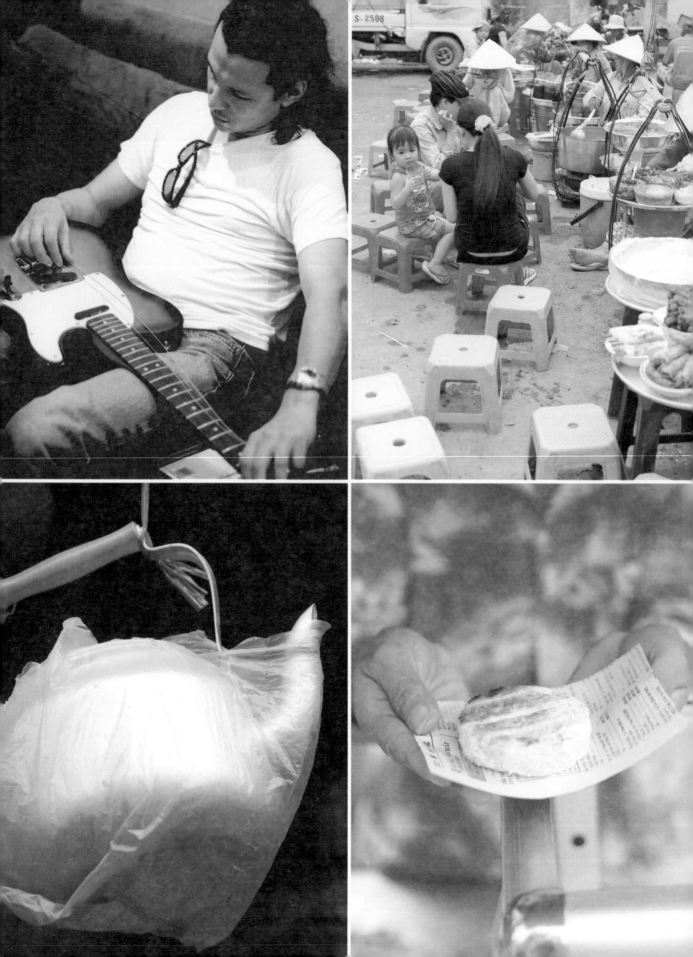

Generally most people make caramel using refined white sugar. You can use that if you can't find palm sugar. Using palm sugar or brown sugar, however, means that it takes less time and imparts a more complex flavour. We make this in bulk at the restaurant, as it stores well.

MAKES ABOUT 150ML
200g palm sugar
180ml hot water

Place the sugar in a saucepan and, over very low heat, melt it. Once the sugar is totally melted, increase the heat to high, swirling the pan constantly until it browns and begins to caramelize, taking on a darker colour. When it starts to smoke, immediately remove it from the heat and pour in the water. Serious caution should be taken here, though, as it will spit, and sugar burns are evil! If there is some crystallization, return the mixture to a low heat and cook a little more until the crystals dissolve. Notes: When using this sauce, make sure that, whenever you add foods to it, it should be warm to prevent it from crystallizing.

Burnt caramel water for grilling

NƯỚC HÀNG

Ok, in the event that you made some cardinal mistakes with making the caramel that we all know and love, this recipe is to be your saviour.

Actually, you should really try making the regular caramel sauce with white caster sugar and taking the caramelization as close to the burning point as possible before you throw in the water or cream. In the event you overcook it, so it burns and takes on a bitter flavour, keep cooking it for a couple of seconds more until it gets almost black – then add the water. This will give you a better understanding of the timing of caramel, as it takes very little time to ruin it at the end.

I remember showing staff how to make caramel. I decided to make it in bulk, making more than we needed. Unfortunately (for my ego, that is), I cooked it a few seconds too long. I could immediately smell that I had burnt it.

Aware of my mistake, a young prep-cook jumped up to my side and suggested that he keep it for the staff meal. I thought, 'Am I that much of a prick to serve my staff burnt food? My God what do they take me for?' I told them not to be silly, and then a bunch of staff protested, telling me that it really wasn't a problem. I was floored.

They took the pot with the bitter caramel and proceeded to bring the heat level back up, cooking it a little more until it was literally black, then poured hot water over it, and boiled it further to ensure that there was no crystallization. They cooled it down and poured it into empty bottles. It looked like soy sauce. It turns out you can buy this stuff in the markets of Hanoi; it's called keo dang or bitter candy.

I had no idea what they were going to use it for, and I honestly thought that they pulled off this whole little act so I would not be upset. It was not until Michael DiGregorio, program officer for arts and culture at the Ford Foundation, took me to a scholar working on a dissertation on street food that I actually learned about this recipe. Nguyen Thi Bay, lecturer at Hanoi Culture University, gave me answers to all my questions.

I wanted to know the secrets of the ubiquitous grilled pork dish bun cha (see page 77). How do they get it moist and crispy at the same time? Bay explained to me – it's the water, called nuoc hang, literally 'water for goods', a burnt sugar water that adds colour, as well as caramelizing on the fire.

When I asked the street vendor, she told me that it is just the way it is done, passed down from generation to generation. In a lot of recipes no one bothers to explain to you that if you add regular sugar, it will not generate the darker colour for the inside of the patty, and the outside of the patty will also burn just a wee bit more then by using burnt caramel water.

One needs to be very light-handed with this and it can make a huge difference. I only use it for the bun cha, as pork meat needs to be cooked well done, whereas for the salmon cha, we do not use either. Either way, if you do burn your caramel, trust me – save the burnt water and use it for the bun cha. It is bitter, but just a little will add a lot more complexity to a grilled dish.

225g caster or palm sugar
225ml hot water

Place the sugar in a saucepan and melt the sugar over a very low heat. Once the sugar is totally melted, increase the heat to high, swirling the pan constantly until it browns and begins to caramelize, taking on a darker colour. When it starts to smoke, at this point other cookbooks tell you to remove the pan from the heat immediately and pour in the water? Don't! Keep on cooking for a couple of seconds more, while it smokes and turns black at the sides, THEN pour in the water (with serious caution, as burnt sugar burns are even more evil then the other sugar burns!)

If there is some crystallization, return the mixture to a low heat and cook it a little more until the crystals dissolve. The liquid should be black, with the colour and texture of soy sauce! Notes: When using this sauce, use just a little, as it is very subtle in flavour. You should hardly taste it. It is used more for colour, as well as aiding the grilling of meats, than for taste. It could also be useful in small amount for marinades.

Peanut sauce SOT LAC

An essential dipping sauce accompaniment to Fresh Spring Rolls (see page 58), this robust peanut sauce is also phenomenal with chicken and fish. There are so many variations of this sauce that I really do not know which one could be claimed to be authentic.

For example, there are peanut sauces that have hoisin sauce added to them and in some places I could swear they add fermented shrimp paste, which is a little overpowering. For me, I have had my fair share of great peanut sauces, and my favourites are the ones that have the coconut milk added to them.

This is what we use at the restaurant. It is a mixture of Balinese, Singaporean and Vietnamese. We serve it with our seafood satay on lemon grass sticks and have even paired it with squid salad with pleasing results.

90g peanuts
3 tbsp vegetable oil
1 tbsp shrimp paste
1 small onion, finely chopped
3 garlic cloves, finely chopped
2.5cm piece of root ginger, finely chopped
5.5cm piece of galangal, finely chopped
2 pieces of lemon grass
3 tbsp chopped deseeded hot red chilli
3 tbsp water
1 tbsp brown sugar
4 tbsp coconut milk/cream (optional)

Roast the peanuts in the oven preheated to 120°C /Gas ½ for about 20 minutes until lightly browned. Grind one-third and set all the peanuts aside.

Heat the oil in a small pan. When hot, add the shrimp paste and cook until it releases its odour and smells up the entire house. Add the onion and garlic, and sauté until soft. Throw in the ginger, galangal, lemon grass and chilli. Allow these spices to release their wonderful aromas for a couple of minutes.

Add the water and brown sugar, as well as the roasted peanuts, ground and whole. Bring to the boil and simmer for 15 minutes.

Transfer to a blender and pulse to get a chunky sauce, or purée for a smooth sauce.

Finish with a little coconut milk and more sugar to taste. Serve at room temperature or hot. Notes: This sauce freezes well, so you may wish to make it in bulk as it is very popular. If you do, don't add the coconut milk. Make the mixture and freeze. When you want to use it, defrost some, throw in a little of the coconut milk and reheat.

Chilli-lime Dipping Sauce

NƯỚC MẮM CHANH

Commonly used as a dipping sauce for chicken or fish, you can add this to almost anything. For the more adventurous, you can hazard more garlic and add a little more water to dilute its expected pungency. Add fish sauce to taste.

I love this very simple recipe with steamed chicken or Ga Tan, the medicinal soup (see page 139). Either way, this is a very powerful sauce that will awaken any palate. It is one of my favourite dipping sauces as it can give many of the bland boiled vegetables dishes served up for staff meals a kick of spice, saltiness and sourness, which convert it into a bold flavourful dish that needs to be diluted with mouthfuls of rice.

MAKES ABOUT 100ML

4 tbsp lime juice (juice of 6 small limes)

50g sugar

8 garlic cloves, finely chopped

10 red chillies, freshly chopped (choose the variety according to your preference and taste)

4 tbsp fish sauce

Take the limes and roll them across a work surface until they are soft. This will make it much easier for you to squeeze out a lot of the juice. Remove the seeds, but keep the pulp, as these little segments of sour juice are all part of the pleasures of the dipping sauce.

Using a mortar and pestle, mix in the sugar. The sugar will act as an abrasive, making it easier to pound your garlic. Throw in the chopped chillies and continue to grind the mixture into a rough paste. (An alternative is to dilute the sugar with the liquid ingredients and garnish it with minced garlic and chilli.) Either way, the results are very pleasing. Clean the mortar and pestle by drizzling the lime juice over them. Pour their content into a jar then pour in the fish sauce. Cover and keep refrigerated.

This sauce develops its flavour over time and will keep in the fridge for about a week, but make sure it is covered, otherwise the odours of garlic and fish sauce permeate the refrigerator!

Sweet-and-Sour Sauce SỐT CHUA NGỌT
There are so many ways to make this great Chinese sauce that is used in fish, beef, and chicken dishes. A sweet-and-sour sauce is a very simple thing to make, but there are many variations of it that I think I should explain here. A sweet-and-sour sauce in French culinary terminology is a gastrique – equal parts sugar to vinegar or other acid.

Every time I think I've seen it all, someone else comes along and shocks me. In France I was cooking for a famous caterer by the name of Yaffa Edry, who had hired a Vietnamese chef from Nice to cook for a bar mitzvah. The chef made a sweet-and-sour dipping sauce using raspberry jam, strawberry vinegar, sugar and tomato paste. At first I thought it was too odd, yet strangely enough, a fruity sweet-and-sour dipping sauce was a liberating breakthrough for me.

A chef I hired from Ho Chi Minh City made a wicked sweet-and-sour, using ketchup, leftover tomato scraps, cinnamon sticks, brown sugar and rice wine vinegar with very pleasing results.

When I cook this for my mother, who does not like to see me cooking in the kitchen for a long time as she prefers to spend quality time with me (if you can imagine that), I take canned pineapples, cut them into quarters, drain the juice into a pot, add ketchup and vinegar, and season with sugar. Quick, simple and easy. If you want to throw in a flavoured vinegar, or add cinnamon as a little twist, go ahead… live a little!

MAKES ABOUT 550ML

1 tbsp vegetable oil

2 onions, sliced

100g diced yellow sweet peppers

100g diced green sweet pepper

475g can of pineapples in juice (cut the pineapples pieces into quarters and reserve the juice)

240ml tomato ketchup

1 tbsp tomato paste

4 tbsp rice wine vinegar

¼ teaspoon ground white pepper

1 tbsp cornflour mixed with 1 tsp water

2 tbsp sugar

Heat the oil in a frying pan over medium heat and stir-fry the onions for a couple of minutes, stirring constantly. Add the peppers, and cook until fragrant, about 1–2 minutes. Throw in the pineapple and put this mixture aside for later use

In a separate pot, mix the ketchup, tomato paste, pineapple juice, vinegar, white pepper and cook, stirring constantly. Throw in the cornflour mixture and allow to thicken. Reduce the heat to low, simmer and season with sugar.

Tamarind Sauce

MAKES ABOUT 1.4 LITRES
725ml tamarind purée
475ml palm sugar syrup (450g palm sugar
    dissolved in 125 ml water over a low heat)
240ml apple juice
2 tbsp ground cumin

Mix everything together and that is it.

Hot Chilli Oil DAU OT

This is a very popular condiment out here in
Asia. Let's face it, it is packaged in plastic
pouches in many freeze-dried noodle mixtures.
It is generally used in modest amounts,
particularly in the northern regions of Vietnam,
probably due to the heavy Chinese influence
there. Vietnamese cuisine is generally not spicy,
but as you travel further south, the food tends
to get sweeter and spicier, as well as bolder than
that in the North, due to the Thai and
Cambodian influences.

MAKES ABOUT 750ML
20g dried hot red chillies , stems removed and
    broken up
500–950ml vegetable (groundnut or rapeseed) oil

To reduce the intensity of the chilli oil, first
remove the seeds that are at the top of the chilli.
Make sure to oil your fingers or wear gloves to
prevent unnecessary burning sensations (you also
do not want to be touching your eyes, etc.). The
easiest way to do this is to cut the chilli in half,
and then roll your fingers back and forth from
the stem or tip down to the opening. Reserve the
seeds for another use. Place the dried chillies in a
non-oiled pan and stir over a low heat for about
5 minutes or until very dry and toasty.

Add the oil and cook over a low heat until
the chillies develop bubbles by their side. Cook a
little longer until the oil takes on a darker colour.
Set aside and let the oil cool down.

You can strain the chillies from the oil or keep
them in it. The oil keeps well for several months
in a glass jar or a squeezy bottle in the refrigerator.

Lemon Oil DAU CHANH

Lemon oil has a very refreshing essence and
everything I love in a good lemon. Its flavour is
clean, bright and fresh, but without the acidity of
lemon juice.

Using lemon oil is also rather like killing two
birds with one stone – I love its refreshing taste in
salads and emulsified into sauces, and the zest,
after being strained out, I throw into breads,
custards or mashed potatoes.

The zest can also an essential ingredient in
marinades for birds or whatever else you wish.
Dishes in which you can try this oil include the
Seared Alaskan Day Boat Scallops (see page 176).

MAKES ABOUT 220ML
3 medium-sized lemons
240ml vegetable oil

Pare the zest off the lemons and make sure there
is no bitter white pith left on it as this will add an
unpleasant bitter flavour. The best instrument
would be a micro-plane. If you don't have one of
those, use a zester, and if you want to be a
traditionalist, there is nothing wrong with using
a sharp knife. Once you have enough zest, chop it
as finely as you can.

Place the zest in a pan, cover with oil and
gently heat until small bubbles form. Remove
from heat and let the flavours infuse.

Once the oil is cool, strain it through a
coffee filter or a fine-mesh strainer. Reserve
the zest and use for marinating chicken or
other dishes.

Vinaigrette

MAKES 425 ML
120ml balsamic vinegar
120ml olive oil
120ml vegetable oil
4 tbsp sugar
¼ tsp salt
½ tbsp mustard

Blend all the ingredients well by whisking or
shaking in a jar.

Beef Stock NƯỚC IÉO BÒ

It was not until I came to Hanoi that I learned how to make Vietnamese beef stock. In the West, time was money and money was time, and the process was totally different. I was taught to soak the bones for making stock and later bring them to the boil and then reduce the heat to a simmer, constantly skimming the scum rising to the top.

For a brown stock, the bones would be browned in the oven to add flavour and colour. To sweeten the stock and round off the flavours we would add a mirepoix, a mixture of chopped onions, carrots and celery, with a sachet of herbs, garlic, peppercorns, bay leaves, etc.

I took real pride in my stock-making abilities, as a great stock was the basis of an even better sauce. Since a lot of the sauces were reductions of the stocks, it was imperative to have a well-balanced stock, otherwise any flaws would be concentrated, something that a critical palate could detect. The Vietnamese technique, in my opinion, is better in achieving a much cleaner broth without losing any of the essential flavours brought on by the slow cooking at low heat.

The Vietnamese soak the bones overnight in water and then drain them the following morning. They then cover the bones with cold water and bring to the boil, drain off the water and repeat this process three times, or until most of the impurities are removed, leaving a cleaner stock with a better flavour. By cooking it gently for a long time, you also extract the gelatine.

It did not take much convincing for me to give up my old technique. I actually decided to take it a step further, by soaking the bones overnight with a little lime juice and limes, so their acid would help in the extraction of the blood and impurities.

MAKES ABOUT 3.5 LITRES

3kg beef bones
½ onion
5cm fresh ginger root, peeled and sliced
5 whole shallots

15g cinnamon stick
4 large bay leaves (fresh or dried)
3 star anise pods
⅓ teaspoon salt, or to taste
⅓ teaspoon black peppercorns

Start three days ahead. Soak the bones in water to cover overnight.

Next morning, drain, cover with fresh cold water and bring to the boil. Drain and repeat the process three times or until the impurities that rise during each boiling are much reduced.

Under the pot, while you are bringing the bones up to the boil in 7 litres of water, char the onion, ginger and shallots until they are charred on all sides. Rub and wash off the loose ashy peel. Pound them with a good whack from a cleaver. This will help release the complex flavours when added to the simmering stock together with the rest of the ingredients.

Once the stock has simmered for a couple of hours, skim off as much of the scummy impurities as you can.

Once cleaned, add all other ingredients and simmer for 3 hours, skimming off the foam and fat that float to the surface and tasting all the time. The flavours of the spice will dull over time, leaving a wonderful subtle stock of which you can be justifiably proud.

Remove from the heat, strain the stock and set aside to cool. For fat-free stock; refrigerate overnight, and all the fat will solidify on the top. Remove the fat with a spoon, and reheat.

Chicken Stock NƯỚC DÙNG GÀ

This light stock can be used as a substantial base for Pho Ga and other soups and sauces.

Here I use the traditional Western way of cooking chicken stock with a mirepoix of vegetables and herbs. This gives my stock and sauces more depth. I later season the stocks with the traditional Vietnamese spices to give it the necessary accents, depending on the dish. For example if I wanted to turn it into a Pho Ga stock, I simply add the cinnamon, star anise and black cardamom, and season with fish sauce.

5 kg chicken bones

25g parsley

10 garlic cloves

1 tablespoon black peppercorns

3 bay leaves

Mirepoix

2 large onions, chopped into quarters

2 large carrots, chopped into slices 2.5 cm thick

5 celery sticks cut into pieces 5 cm thick

1 leek, chopped into slices 2.5 cm thick

Clean the chicken bones. Chop them into 2–3cm pieces and soak in water for about 2 hours.

Drain well, then cover with 6 litres of fresh water and bring to the boil. Reduce the heat to a low simmer and cook for about 30 minutes, skimming off the impurities that rise to the top.

Add the mirepoix and bring back to the boil. Reduce the heat and simmer for 5 hours.

Add the parsley, garlic, peppercorns and bay leaf, and simmer for another 1 hour.

For a fat-free version, let the stock cool, then place in the refrigerator overnight. Spoon off the hard solidified fats on the top.

The stock can be frozen for a month or kept chilled for 3 days.

Fish Stock NƯỚC DÙNG CÀ

This is one of my favourite stocks to make as, in my opinion, it is the most delicate of the stocks. Fresh bones have to be used and again I like to soak them a couple of times to remove as much impurities as possible.

One of the tricks in making this stock is to ensure that you extract as much gelatine as possible. In order to do this, I like to cut the bones so that the gelatine is exposed in between the vertebrae. Salmon bones are the easiest in this respect, as the vertebrae are small and easy to cut, otherwise get your fishmonger to cut them for you.

The key thing to remember is that there is no salt added to the stock, so it should be a little bland. Also, unlike other stocks, fish stock should not be cooked for a long time. It is a quick stock and should cook for no more then 30 minutes or until the gelatine has dissolved.

This is a great base for any seafood soup or lobster stock, or liquid for steaming clams. Instead of using water, try using fish stock instead and you will get an idea of how it transforms a simple, good dish into a fantastic, great one.

2 kg fish bones

½ celery stalk, chopped

2 leeks, cut into 5cm lengths

½ onion, chopped

7 parsley sprigs

2 garlic cloves, lightly smashed

pinch of black pepper

3 bay leaves

4 tablespoons dry white wine or to taste

Clean the fish bones. Chop them into small pieces about 1 cm in length. Soak in water for about to 2 hours, then drain.

Cover with 6 litres of fresh water and bring to the boil. Reduce the heat to a simmer and cook for about 10 minutes, skimming off the impurities that rise to the top.

Add the celery, leek and onion, and simmer for another 10 minutes.

Add the parsley, garlic, peppercorns and bay leaf, and simmer for another 30 hour minutes.

Finish with the white wine, remove from the heat and let cool.

This stock should be used fresh and not frozen, as it does not freeze well.

Cooking with gas

People love the way we serve our gazpacho soup at the table. It's a simple combination of cucumber and tomato with a blanched onion and splash of Tabasco sauce. For me, the key to a good gazpacho is to make it tasty and serve it very cold. To ensure this we keep the bowls in the freezer and, in front of the customer, shake the gazpacho over ice in a cocktail shaker. It's creative, yes, but something I am not so proud of as it was inspired by the events below.

Business was okay. Dinners were picking up, but our lunch had deteriorated with the introduction of a new decree that prevented people parking their bikes at the restaurant during the day. We were averaging five to ten lunches a day and, even with our central location, I basically wrote off the idea of ever building a decent lunch business. I had arranged a marketing meeting in the middle of what I thought would be another fairly dead lunch service when all of a sudden Michael Frisby from the Commercial Services Department arrived.

Michael was entertaining a group of visiting Americans from the treasury. They looked a little out of place, as many people visiting Vietnam do. Suits and ties on a hot summer's day was not the norm for expats doing business here. Generally a shirt and trousers would suffice.

In a jolly voice, Michael showed his guests that he had a close rapport with me. 'Bobby – how are you? Let me introduce you to Bobby Chinn of Bobby Chinn's. He is the young American who owns this fine establishment and has been in Vietnam for eight years, a symbol of what can be done in Vietnam.'

They stood there scanning the place, tilting their heads down the strings of roses and admiring the art. It was a quiet and cool retreat from the ruckus and heat outside.

'We would like to have a little privacy, so can we sit in the back?'

'With pleasure,' I replied, picking up the menu from the hostess station and escorting them to the table. Mike was calling all the shots to make their lunch quick and easy. 'Bobby does a great gazpacho. How is the gazpacho today?'

I was not supervising the day-to-day operation of the kitchen at the time as my old sous chef, Fucker, had returned. Although Fucker and Hai did not get along, the competition between them was healthy as they both worked to gain the respect of the junior staff. Come to think of it – I had not even stuck my head in the kitchen that day. I couldn't lie to Mike, so I went with the most honest answer I could muster: 'I hope it's good!'

'Also a great burger. Great burger!'

Burgers? Burgers to me are not so easy. Cooking them to perfection is hard. Most people order a burger well done, but nine times out of ten a kitchen will cook it to the point that it smells bad because it is way overcooked.

In any case, I was in the middle of a marketing meeting and was not about to supervise the kitchen over four simple lunches. Gazpachos were a go, a couple of burgers well done, and a sandwich. I quickly placed the order with the kitchen, instructed them that it was a VIP and went back to my marketing meeting at the front of the restaurant.

As the first course was served, my name was shouted out across the restaurant. The last time I

heard that tone was when I was being called for a beating or a serious bollocking from my parents. Whatever the problem was, I would fix it.

'Bobby!'

'Yes?'

'Bobby, can you tell me why the gazpacho tastes like gasoline?'

'What?'

My brain raced across the possibility of it being a joke. Gasoline? How could that happen?

'The gazpacho tastes like gasoline!'

'What?'

I could not comprehend what he was saying, but moving closer to the table, the smell of gasoline became stronger and stronger. I grabbed the bowls from the table, my hands trembling with anger.

'How does that happen?'

'I have no idea, but I can tell you that there will be death and destruction.'

I took two bowls of the soup, placed them on the pick-up line and slammed my hand down to get everyone's attention. I dipped a spoon into the soup and proceeded to walk to the cold station from where the dish had came.

Miss Thuy, was working with us, having been sacked from the last restaurant for selling burnt food to guests.

'Thuy – Eat it!' My arm stretched out to her face.

'No!'

'No? You will eat it! You made it. It is good enough for my customers, it's good enough for you!'

Her face bright red, she refused again. 'NO!'

Fucker quickly came to her rescue, running

'Bobby!'

'Yes?'

'Bobby, can you tell me why the gazpacho tastes like gasoline?'

'What?'

My brain raced across the possibility of it being a joke. Gasoline? How could that happen?

across the kitchen yelling, 'What the hell is your problem!'

'What the hell is my problem? No, what the hell is your problem? You're the kitchen supervisor! Why don't you tell me what the hell my problem is, you fuckwit?!'

My arm quickly rotated in Fucker's direction. 'Eat!'

He quickly slurped the soup to find the taste of gasoline filling his mouth. It looked like he was planning to swallowing the concoction when the spoon entered his mouth, but all of a sudden he sprayed it all out, mostly over me, as he proceeded to cough, choking on the gasoline, falling to his knees, streams of saliva dangling from the side of his mouth.

I stood over him like a fighter looking down at a challenger with one knee to the ground, taking his time to gather the strength and composure to stand back up.

'Come on, tell me Fucker! What the fuck is my problem? Come on, tell me! Tell me! I've got a kitchen sending out gazpacho. How the fuck does this happen?'

None of the staff had any idea why I was screaming this time, but their fearless leader was on the floor coughing from one spoon of gazpacho. One of the staff ran for water. Fucker was so shaken that he spat out the first sip, gargling before he could even talk. He stood there in silence. He was too quick to defend a person that should not have been defended. Then the words came out quietly and humbly.

'You got to fire her right now! Women that fall in love, stop thinking. This is why she is so stupid now!'

'You tell me what I should do now! Sorry, I am not trained to tell guests "yes, that was high octane gasoline in your gazpacho!" What the fuck am I supposed to do now? Tell me Fucker! I want your advice!'

'Fuck you! I just told you what to do. Fire her now!'

'Thanks – that is great! She's fired! What do I tell the guests? How the hell does this happen? FIRE THE SECOND COURSE RIGHT NOW!'

As I walked back to the table, Michael looked a little uncomfortable, belching gasoline with his VIP guests. 'Are they trying to kill me back there?' he asked.

Was he joking? Were they trying to kill me and the business? I could not respond, the anger was too deep.

'How does this happen?'

'Michael, I fired the person that made it, and I will fix it.' But somehow it seemed nothing was going to be fixed. The burgers were taking forever and Fucker was a very long time producing the other main courses.

Michael said: 'We've got to get back to the embassy. How long is this going to take Bobby?'

By the time I got back to the kitchen, their order was being plated and waiting to be picked up. I ran the food out to find that all the burgers were rare.

'We do not have any more time. We have to go. This was a really disappointing lunch.' And right there they all got up at the same time and made their way to the door.

I was destroyed. After they walked out I closed the restaurant to any other diners. Fucker walked by me like I was invisible.

'Fucker? Where the fuck are you going? I need to talk to you.' With one arm up, he raised his hand, flicked me the finger and walked out the door. Quickly following him was Thuy, bright faced and humiliated.

Back in the kitchen, Hai gave me the rundown.

To ensure the gazpacho was served cold, we used one-litre La Vie Water bottles to store it. They were placed in the freezer, then during service they would sit in an ice bath – a Kitchen-Aid bowl filled with iced water.

The problem was that Thuy decided to use a smaller La Vie bottle. She found one that had been filled with gasoline, and poured the gazpacho into it without checking.

You might be wondering why there was bottle of La Vie with gasoline inside. Well, the night before, our waitress Ha had ran out of gasoline, and in Vietnam gasoline is still sold on the side of the roads in La Vie bottles.

So, that's why we now serve our gazpacho from a cocktail shaker and the bowls are stored in the freezer to ensure that the soup is served perfectly chilled.

Staples, Snacks & Street Food

The recipes in this chapter range from light appetizers to one-dish meals that can satisfy at breakfast, lunch or dinner. (You only need one, but I sometimes have two, because they're so good.) Pho is a breakfast dish but everyone who stays out late in Vietnam has it before bed. It combines intensely flavoured stock with noodles and I can tell you from many years' experience of staying up late and drinking a lot that having all that liquid going into your system prevents hangovers. Dishes such as Bun Bo are very handy to know as they are made largely from storecupboard ingredients: you just slice the beef, throw the noodles on top and enjoy the contrast of hot and cold. I like using rice paper rather than Chinese wonton wrappers for making deep-fried spring rolls – the result seems so much lighter and crisp in a way that I find comforting. Also here are recipes for fresh spring rolls, which are wonderfully light and clean to eat and can easily be made suitable for vegetarians.

Fresh Spring Rolls GỎI CUỐN

These are great for functions, as an appetizer or hors d'oeuvre. They are best served with the Vietnamese Peanut Sauce on page 46 or, for a lighter taste, the Nuoc Cham on page 43.

You can also turn them into a vegetarian snack with cucumber slices, sliced cherry tomatoes and jícama. Grilled portobello mushrooms also make a great addition for a more substantial and meaty taste. Any vegetable lover can make these with an array of vegetables without the shrimp.

Try reclassifying spring rolls as a salad, using rocket or watercress, or you could use fruit like apples. Pork is often thrown into the spring roll, but I have omitted it for the sake of my Muslim and Jewish brothers.

When buying rice papers look for ones with no crumbs! Crumbs indicate they are a bit dry and these are difficult to work with, they crack when you are trying to fold them.

MAKES 8 (SERVES 4 AS AN APPETIZER OR 8 AS AN HORS D'OEUVRE

8 rice papers
4 large lettuce leaves
225g thin Vietnamese rice vermicelli
handful coriander leaves
handful mint leaves
8 cooked peeled prawns, halved lengthwise

24 chive stalks
Peanut Sauce (see page 46) or Nuoc Cham (see page 43), to serve

Lightly moisten the rice papers, spreading some water over the surface by hand and then store under a damp towel.

Place a rice paper on a damp towel and put a lettuce leaf on top, centred and covering about a third of the bottom of the rice paper. On top of the lettuce, add one-eighth of the noodles, coriander and mint leaves.

Roll the rice paper halfway into a cylinder, pressing down while you are folding in order to make it tight. Fold 3.5cm of the two ends of the paper over the filling. Lay 2 shrimp halves along the crease, with the cut side downwards. Place 2 chive sprigs on top of the shrimp at one end. Leave about 10cm of chives extending from the roll. Continue rolling until you complete the cylinder and seal by putting a bit of water on your finger and wetting the leading edge of the paper.

Repeat with the remaining ingredients to make 7 more rolls in the same way.

You can cut the rolls in half and stand the halves end up, with the chives sticking out of it for a traditional presentation.

Serve with peanut sauce or Nuoc Cham. These are best eaten fresh, but will hold for an hour or so in the fridge.

Steamed Rolled Ravioli

BÁNH CUỐN NONG

This heavenly delicacy is a Thang Thi District original. Like most popular foods just outside of Hanoi, they always find their way into the city centre in a niche of a busy street. Down on Hang Bo Street there is a very small stall where about twenty short plastic chairs – always filled – crowd around small worn wooden tables. The owner, Ms. An, is the resident Banh Cuon master, who takes only minutes to complete a full dish. With queues always winding from the door, she has to!

The place was a rundown meat market from early morning until afternoon, and after that it converts itself into a Banh Cuon stall. Ms An is the third generation in her family making this dish. She learned it from her mother and her mother learned it from her mother, and she has been making this dish for the last 25 years.

I took just one bite and I was immediately converted – like the many food critics and chefs I have since taken to her establishment. Her rice noodles are so tender; they almost melt in your mouth as the perfectly seasoned stuffing tumbles on to the tastebuds. I became instantly addicted. Even her sauce was perfect. For years I ate there, asking her to teach me, and for years she just smiled and laughed at me. After about 8 years, she finally broke down and told my staff that if I wanted to learn, she would teach me.

I visited her house, which was about 20 metres from her stall, in the back alley on the second floor. There I watched her preparing all the mise en place for the dish. There was no wasted motion, everything she did had a purpose and she seemed incredibly at ease.

Oil is poured into a wok and she tips about three-quarters of the sliced shallots into the oil, where they sink to the bottom. With a spider, she constantly moves the shallots from side to side until the temperature of the oil rises, sending the shallots up to the surface, where they sizzle away, then she reduces the heat.

Once the shallots are golden brown, she drains them, then places them into a bamboo basket and positions a fan over it to accelerate the drying and cooling to make them crisp.

The oil was reserved and used as shallot oil as well as to cook the rest of the ingredients. Drained presoaked dried Chinese mushrooms, stripped of their stems, sat in a food processor.

The food processor was old, tinged yellow from age and years of use. The machine lacked the usual speed control buttons in the front and in their place was a hollow dark space. Ms An reached inside the dark hole and pulled out two wires with exposed copper tips. She placed one wire to her left and the other to her right. She turned to me to see if I was paying attention and then holding the two wires, brought them together to 'hot wire' the food processor, tapping the wires together, sending small electric sparks, pulsing as the mushrooms in the topless bowl are sliced smaller and smaller. I started to laugh, and it became contagious.

The process is repeated for the wood ear mushrooms. The bowl is thoroughly cleaned, and the process continues with very small dried shrimps which she pulverizes to a powder.

Ms An reserves a generous amount of shallot oil in the wok and cooks the remaining shallots until they are soft and translucent. She adds the finely chopped mushrooms and wood ears, and cooks them. She removes chicken from a pot, pulls the meat from the bones and chops it up finely. She folds this back into the mushroom shallot mixture and it is pretty much done. It is seasoned lightly with salt and pepper, but to me it is not as exciting as I once thought.

So often in Vietnamese cuisine, if the actual dish is not a showstopper, then the dipping sauce is. A duet of a dish tied together with a sauce that brings it additional complexity. I realize that it is the dipping sauce that ties it all together.

Her dipping sauce is bolder, darker, richer and more complex than those I have tried elsewhere. It is made with chicken stock from the braised chicken, with caramel and brown sugar adding colour, and fish sauce and vinegar seasoning the sauce and rounding off the flavours. To me the sauce in this dish is more intense, while the meat stuffing is subtler, but when combined the flavours and textures come together in a harmony that exemplifies the wonders of Vietnamese street food.

Her secret… I share with her, as it is her livelihood, and it is all in her batter. You can watch this dish being made out in the wide-open. I had asked all the pertinent questions but somehow my batter did not come out correctly after much trial and error. I did not mention my failures to her, but I returned to her six months later to get her to teach me again.

On my second visit she informed me that there was a secret that she did not share with me the first time. Her reason being that she did not want to divulge her secrets to my translator, knowing full well that he was one of my chefs.

On this second attempt, she showed me the rice that she used. Bought fresh daily, she uses two types of rice, and it is their ratio that yields the results. If that was not enough, the ratio was also quite unconventional, and could only make sense to a person who has been perfecting the dish for 35 years with two generations already having passed the recipe down. Then there is soaking time as well as slight fermentation. It was so technical, that I never bothered to try and make the batter again. I think one can get very pleasing results from packaged rice flour, something that most of the restaurants use.

Critic after critic, foodie after foodie is clear of her natural skill. I think it is an established consensus that one of the greatest culinary masters sits in her pyjamas on a busy street in the old quarters of Hanoi, making a dish that will eventually be extinct, or at least no longer made to the standard that she now makes it.

The preparation is rather labour-intensive, but it is worth the effort just truly to appreciate a master at work. The actual process of assembly and final cooking is rather difficult as well. For me, watching her is part of the Banh Cuon experience. She ladles the rice flour mixture quickly and evenly over a fine-mesh – somewhat elastic – sieve, moistened by the steam beneath. Placing a lid on top, she waits for it to cook for about a minute or so. With the flick of her wrist she runs a flat wooden stick across one edge, pushing the down sticky soft mixture and in the process creating a thicker end to the rice sheet.

She places her stick flat and perpendicular to the thick edge of the rice sheet, presses the flat wooden stick to slip underneath the crepe, then flicks her wrist, peeling the rice crêpe with one smooth action as she removes it and slaps it on to a shallot oiled surface to prevent it from sticking. With mechanical precision, she adds the filling and rolls them up while piping hot and then tosses them on to a dish, topping them with crispy shallots and dried shrimp powder. The version below does not require as much technical skill and I have simplified it to make it easier to assemble.

MAKES 12

125g rice flour
4 tbsp tapioca
¼ tsp salt
Filling
4 tbsp vegetable oil
4 shallots, finely chopped
10 dried Chinese mushrooms, reconstituted in water, stems removed and the mushrooms finely chopped
6 dried wood ear mushrooms, reconstituted in water, stems removed and the mushrooms finely chopped
225g cooked chicken (I use poached thigh)
¼ tsp sugar
1 tbsp fish sauce
freshly ground black pepper to taste
Accompaniments
handfuls of basil, dill, shiso, mint and coriander (all of these or whatever you have)
Garnish
240ml Nuoc Cham (see page 46)
40g Crispy-fried Shallots (see page 38)
8 tbsp dried shrimp, pulverized to a powder in a food processor

In a mixing bowl, mix the flour, tapioca and salt together well. Slowly pour in 300ml water in a steady stream until it is well incorporated into a paste, making sure that there are no lumps. Pour in another 300ml water and set aside.
To make the filling: place a pan over medium heat, add some of the oil and, when that is hot,

sweat the shallots until soft and tender. Add both the Chinese and wood ear mushrooms and sauté until cooked and well coated with the shallots and shallot oil, about 10 minutes. Add the finely chopped chicken and season with the sugar, fish sauce and pepper. Let cool, but cover with cling film to prevent the mixture from drying out (make sure the film touches the mixture). To make the rice noodle crêpes, mix in the late-added water to the flour paste to produce a smooth batter. Place a non-stick pan that has been lightly oiled over medium heat. Pour the batter into the pan, swirling the pan to ensure that the batter is equally distributed over the surface of the pan. Cook for about 2 minutes, and then flip the thin crêpe on to a well-oiled surface to prevent it from sticking to the surface. Make two more crêpes in the same way. Sprinkle a generous amount of the filling a couple of inches from the bottom edge horizontally across each crêpe. Fold the crêpe over the mixture and roll up into a cylinder, like rolling a cigar or other smokable object. Repeat the process until you have three such cylinders. Place on a plate and, using kitchen shears, cut the cylinders in half, then cut each half cylinder in half again. Garnish with fried shallots and sprinkle with the dried shrimp powder. Serve with Nuoc Cham as a dipping sauce, adding the herbs to it.

Rice Noodle Wraps with Grapes and Duck Gizzard Confit

PHỞ CUỐN MÈ VỊT VÀ NHO

I've never been fond of duck gizzards as I always find them chewy and tough. I was inspired by an idea from chef Michael Wild, one of the pillars of California cuisine who ran a restaurant called the Bay Wolf. The combination of tender duck gizzards and red seedless grapes was a great idea. I added shiso and lime leaves, then wrapped them in a rice noodle sheet. I knew it was a hit when staff who normally did not like gizzards had no problem tasting them. You can use any herb here you wish. This dish does not need a dipping sauce.

You can use the same technique and salt mix with duck thighs to make ordinary duck confit.

SERVES 8

1 kg fresh rice noodle sheet or rice paper
500g duck gizzards
500g red seedless grapes, cut into thin slices
bunch shiso, roughly chopped
5 lime leaves, sliced into very thin slivers
Salt mixture for confit
10 tbsp salt
6 tbsp sugar
6 tbsp cracked black pepper
6 tbsp sliced garlic
4 tsp chopped ginger
4 tsp chopped lemon grass

With a paring knife, clean the gizzards of the silver skin, or have your butcher do this for you. Place the gizzards flat on a baking sheet. Sprinkle with the same salt mixture for the duck gizzards confit. Make sure that the gizzards are well coated, and then place another baking sheet on top and weight down. Marinate for 24 hours.

Remove the gizzards, and wash them clean of all the salt mixture. Dry them with a kitchen towel, cover with duck fat and cook for about 4 hours over a low heat, until the soft and tender.

In a mixing bowl, mix the duck gizzards and the grapes until somewhat homogeneous. Spread this mix over the sheet of rice noodle. Sprinkle the shiso and lime leaves over the mixture, then simply wrap and roll.

Rice Noodle Wraps with Sautéed Garlic Beef PHỞ CUỐN

This is a Hanoi original, with a very modern beginning. In fact, it was invented only in the very early '90s. Despite its relatively recent appearance on the scene, the exact origins of this famed dish are still quite hotly disputed.

The epicentres of Pho Cuon remain on the main streets of Truc Bac Island. Lined with woks and cooks, frying away, each stall has its own version. It was made to order, light, simple and very easy to make.

When I used to live down the street from these stalls, I arrived at my usual spot with the expectation of the same routine. A kid, who was the main cook, stood over a wok stir-frying meat and garlic. Once cooked, he'd throw the contents of his wok on to a bowl. His sister sat at a table of freshly made rice paper noodles, stacked up on top of each other like large rectangular lasagne. In another bowl, she would sprinkle fresh herbs ranging from coriander, shiso, mint, dill and lettuce on to the noodle. She proceeded to throw on some of the stir-fried beef and tightly wrap little cigars of the mixture.

Ten of these little rolls were sold for 14,000 dong. Once completed, they would appear on your table almost as quickly as you took your seat on a short plastic chair…well, as long as you came at the right time. And my time was well after midnight, once we closed up shop. During the day, you would not have as much luck, but the plates of Pho Cuon still came piping hot!

The lady next door, Miss Vinh, was making some of the tastiest Bun Cha I'd ever had, and the lady across the street made cha, the dessert. Next to her was a lady cooking Banh Cuon. Within six months of moving to this neighbourhood, they all gave up their individual dishes to join the bandwagon of Pho Cuon. The overflow from this one kid changed the variety of dishes served and this little unknown neighbourhood became THE place for late-night snacking.

MAKES 6

300g filet mignon, thinly sliced
2 garlic cloves, finely chopped
1 tsp freshly ground black pepper
300g fresh rice noodle sheets
½ head of lettuce, leaves separated
40g coriander
40g herbs, such as mint, dill or shiso)
Sweet-and-Sour Sauce (page 47)

Place the thin strips of beef in a bowl with the garlic and pepper, and mix well.

Place a frying pan over a medium-high heat, add a tablespoon of oil and fry the beef until cooked.

Cut the fresh rice noodle sheets into 15cm squares. On each piece, place a layer of lettuce, then herbs and, lastly, the sautéed beef.

Wrap and roll like a cigar, then serve with the sweet-and-sour sauce.

Duck and Crab Imperial Rolls CHÀ GIÒ

This dish is traditionally made with pork, but in this recipe I have replaced it with duck confit, which teams very well with the crab. On top of that I have opted to use cellophane noodles over the rice noodles as they offer more of a bite.

These imperial rolls can be made with lobster or prawns - you name it, it is a magical dish for the crispy moist textures of the spring rolls paired with the nuoc cham sauce.

MAKES 12–15

50g cellophane noodle vermicelli
1 tbsp vegetable oil, plus more for deep-frying
4 shallots, finely chopped
25g dried wood ear mushrooms (black fungus), presoaked and chopped
250g duck confit, shredded (see page 63)
200g sake-steamed crabmeat (see page 160)
4 tbsp roughly chopped coriander
4 medium eggs
salt and pepper
12–15 round rice paper wrappers
Sweet-and-Sour Sauce (see page 47), to serve
Pickled Daikon and Carrots (see page 42), to serve

Put the noodles in a bowl of hot water for a couple of minutes until tender.

Once soft, drain them and, using kitchen shears, cut them into 1cm lengths into a dry mixing bowl. In a sauté pan over medium heat, sauté the shallots in the vegetable oil until tender.

Add the shallots to the cut noodles together with the mushrooms, duck, crab meat, and coriander. Mix well. Season with salt and pepper.

Once thoroughly mixed, crack one egg and mix it into all the ingredients until well coated.

Lightly beat the remaining eggs together.

Place 3 or 4 rice papers on a slightly damp work surface. You may find a damp kitchen towel useful, but it depends on the quality of the rice paper. If the towel is too wet, it might cause the paper to rip, so be careful – or work quickly.

Spoon about 2 heaped tablespoons of the mixture into the lower third of the rice paper. Fold both ends from the side, and then roll the bottom up. Make sure that the contents are nice

and tightly rolled. Brush the end with a little of the beaten egg to ensure that it is well sealed.

Place the rolled spring rolls on to a plate, making sure that they do not touch each other, otherwise they have a tendency to stick.

In a shallow pan, heat the oil to medium hot, 190–200°C (when a pair of chopsticks submerged in it generate small bubbles at the tips). Next to the cooking area, place a plate with towels to drain off the oil once the rolls have been cooked.

Place two to three rolls in the oil, sliding them in gently. They key to frying these is to make sure that the oil remains at the proper temperature, so do not add too many at a time. Cook the spring rolls, turning them over and over again until all sides are golden. Once golden, remove with a slotted spoon and drain.

Serve with the Sweet-and-Sour Sauce and Pickled Daikon and Carrots.

Bánh Bèo

This is one of the classic imperial Hue dishes, but exists in many variations throughout Vietnam. In other regions they may be served in banana leaves. In the south, cooks are inclined to add coconut milk, while other regions keep to a clear dipping sauce accompaniment. It is refined, well balanced and easy to make.

This recipe is from chef Tuan from Hue. He has a special mould for these. If you're vegetarian, instead of prawns this dish can be garnished with cooked mung beans that have been ground up and dried a little, and served with a vegetarian dipping sauce. The real masters of the vegetarian version is Tibs restaurant in Saigon.

MAKES 10

1 kg rice flour (300g refined rice flour and 700g regular rice flour, mixed)

3 tbsp salt

4 tbsp vegetable oil

1kg fresh prawns, shelled and finely chopped

1 tbsp sugar

Garnish

8g spring onion, sliced into thin rings

20g Crispy shallots page (38)

Pineapple sauce

5 tbsp pineapple juice

5 tbsp sugar

5 tbsp soy sauce

Other optional sauces

240ml Nuoc Cham sauce (see page 43)

120ml fish sauce

Place the flour and salt in the middle a large mixing bowl and slowly pour in 1.9 litres water and the salt, until well incorporated.

In Hue they use special moulds, but you can use very small deep saucers like those used to serve soy sauce for sushi. Lightly coat them with oil before pouring in the rice flour mixture. This will make it easier to remove the rice disks after steaming. Pour a couple of millimetres of the mixture into each saucer, trying to ensure they are about the same quantity. A measuring cup with a spout is probably the best thing for this.

Place the containers over a steamer or in a bain-marie if you do not have one, and cover. Steam for about a 1 minute.

Coat a sauté pan with a little oil and, over medium-to-high heat; stir-fry the prawns until cooked, 3–5 minutes. Do not overcook, as you want them moist. Season with sugar and salt.

Remove the rice disks from the moulds and place on a plate, or keep in the moulds. Top with chopped prawns, spring onions and shallots.

To make the accompanying sauce, combine the pineapple juice, sugar and soy sauce with 120ml water. Mix and serve. Alternatively, use any other of the suggested sauces.

Salmon Cha CHA CHA HOI

This is a very quick and simple dish to prepare. I had fallen in love with Bun Cha, but I knew a lot of people that would not eat on the streets.

I decided to make these without the traditional pork and use freshly flown in salmon from Norway for non-meat eaters. The restaurant was going through so much salmon, I decided to introduce a teriyaki salmon burger for the lunch menu, as well as a Vietnamese tapas dish using close to the same ingredients. I never would have imagined that this dish would have become so popular.

The meat that remained on the bone after filleting would be scooped up with a teaspoon, leaving close to nothing on the bones. The belly, rich in fat, would be ground up with the tail of the salmon for our mini salmon burgers.

These little burgers are really tasty, as the salmon belly sweats a lot on the grill, creating wonderful smoky flavours, making them moist and tender. I cook them medium rare.

MAKES 4

600g thin rice vermicelli (bún)
5g each coriander, shiso, dill, mint and basil
120ml Nuoc Cham sauce (see page 43)
FOR THE SALMON BURGERS
500g freshly minced salmon meat
50g finely chopped shallots
1 tbsp toasted sesame oil
1 tbsp fish sauce
5 tbsp finely chopped coriander
½ tbsp Caramel sauce (see page 43)
freshly ground black pepper to taste
vegetable oil for greasing

First make the burgers: mix the minced salmon with the shallots, sesame oil, fish sauce, chopped coriander, caramel sauce and pepper to taste.

On a well-oiled surface, make little burgers. Season with salt and pepper and place on a well heated well oiled surface and sear on both sides so that they are still rare inside. These little burgers cook very quickly, so make sure that they are not overcooked, as they should be eaten medium-rare to medium – about 4 minutes in total between both sides, depending on the size and the heat source. If you can grill them, even better.

Set the noodles on a plate, next to a plate of herbs and a bowl of Nuoc Cham sauce. Place the salmon burgers on another plate.

There is a way of eating these; Each guest should be given a rice bowl. Then he or she places the rice noodles into the Nuoc Cham, then places it in the bowl and mixes in some herbs. Take a salmon burger and place in the bowl, then scoop it out with the Nuoc Cham-laced noodles and herbs.

Vietnamese Rice Noodle Soup with Chicken PHỞ GÀ

Pho Ga is another all-time favourite dish. It is not quite the same blockbuster sensation as its counterpart Pho Bo, but it certainly has a lot of oomph for a light and clear soup.

Pho Ga became popular when the supply of beef was limited in Hanoi. In one of his popular essays, the infamous Vietnamese food writer Vu Bang, reports that at one point in Hanoi, Pho Bo was not served on Mondays and Fridays.

To quell the widespread disappointment, a market grew for Pho Ga to feed avid pho eaters. Although Pho Ga was just a stand-in for people, who couldn't get their hands on another bowl of Pho Bo, many stalls cropped up to meet the demand for this great soup tradition.

Notwithstanding the common preferences of the past, this substantial soup is quite popular now, and has its own following.

This soup is possibly the closest thing to a panacea for all flu-type ailments. It has a very clean taste and its deceptively clear broth is full of the vitamins and protein you need to get back on your feet. I can vouch for that. Whenever I feel a little rundown, or if I have a late night, this is one of the best things to get into my system.

SERVES 6

3 litres chicken stock (see page 50)
20g ginger, cut in half lengthwise
20g shallots
3 whole star anise
5cm piece cinnamon stick
120ml fish sauce
30g sugar
2 poached chicken breasts
1kg dried 2mm-wide rice noodles, reconstituted in cold water
Garnishes
8 spring onions, the green stems cut into thin rings and keeping the long white stems whole
bunch coriander
20 Thai basil leaves
1 Thai bird's-eye chilli
3 limes, each cut into 6 wedges
1 tsp freshly ground black pepper

Bring the stock to the boil, then reduce to a simmer.

Under the flame, place equal portions of ginger and shallots and char them until all sides are blackened. Remove and, when cool enough to handle, remove the bitter black skin, and give them a healthy whack with the side of the cleaver. Add these to the stock and they will release the subtle complex flavours into the stock, as well as add a little colour.

In a dry pan, heat the star anise and cinnamon until they are nice and dry and start releasing their aromas. Add the spices to the stock and cook for an hour. The longer it cooks, the more subtle the broth flavours become.

Season with fish sauce for salt and a little sugar to taste. The measurements above are a guide, so add seasonings slowly to your own taste.

Shred the chicken with your fingers and set aside.

Blanch the noodles in boiling water until tender and warmed through. Drain as much water as possible from them and put in a large bowl.

Garnish with the chopped spring onion greens, coriander and basil. Top with the shredded chicken and ladle over the seasoned stock.

Serve with fresh lime juice, chopped chilli (or chilli sauce), pepper and additional herbs.

Vietnamese 'Pho' Rice Noodle Soup with Beef PHỞ BÒ

The tradition of Pho Bo is from the North, but it has travelled through to the South, in the process evolving into a sweeter and spicier dish. This dish reportedly originated in Nam Dinh Province, just outside Hanoi and was made by the Co family. If you ever make the effort to go to Nam Dinh, you will find that there are over five major (and unrelated) Co families specializing in this dish and four townships claiming expertise in the original soup. With the largest known family, Co Cu, in Hanoi, Hanoians claim this to be their own invention, or a perfected version of the Nam Dinh prototype. Despite this friendly feud, everyone agrees this is the ultimate national dish.

I was about to film with Merilees Parker for her show on the BBC 2, called *Full on Food* and I decided to revisit all my favourite pho stalls.

Unfortunately, my most favourite had become a Panasonic dealer. I love the dish and had recently seen the documentary called *Supersize Me* in which a person goes on a diet of only MacDonald's food to see what the effects would be. I did a similar thing, with only pho, and I lost weight, but eventually got bored after 2 weeks.

When you make pho, you can choose between shredded chicken, braised brisket or just very thinly sliced raw beef as the meat element. Sounds pretty simple? Well it goes further then this. You can also garnish it with beansprouts, lime juice, chilli sauce and hoisin sauce!

If you choose to make the dish with brisket, simply place the brisket in a pot, cover with beef stock and simmer for about 5 hours or until tender. Allow the brisket to cook in the liquid. Refrigerate the meat and then, once it is cold and firm, cut it into think slices.

If you prefer raw beef raw, use lean fillet.

SERVES 6 AS A MAIN COURSE
3 litres beef stock (page 50)
225g brisket of beef or beef sirloin
900g dried 2mm-wide rice stick noodles, soaked, cooked and drained
Garnishes
50g spring onions, cut into thin rings
7g chopped coriander
225g beansprouts
10 sprigs Asian basil
6 saw-leaf herb leaves (optional)
1 Thai bird's-eye chilli, cut into thin rings
freshly ground black pepper
1 lime, cut into 6 thin wedges

In a large stockpot, bring the beef stock to the boil and then reduce to a simmer. If using brisket, place it in the stock and cook for about 5 hours. If using the beef fillet, put it to freeze slightly.

Once the brisket is tender, remove the pot from the heat and allow the meat to cool in the liquid. Refrigerate the meat, and then once it is cold and firm, cut it into thin slices.

To serve, blanch the noodles in hot water so that they are nice and warm. Drain as much water from the noodles as possible and then place

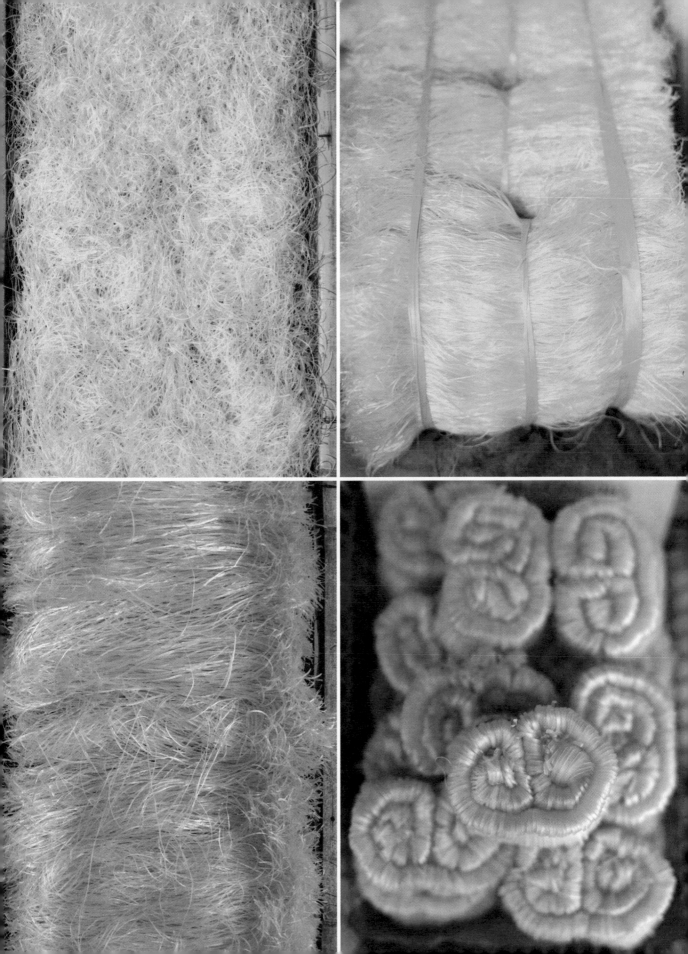

in the serving bowls. Fan the sliced brisket over the noodles. Ladle the hot beef stock over the meat and then garnish with spring onions.

If using beef fillet, once it is slightly frozen, cut it into paper-thin slices. Place these on top of the noodles and ladle the hot stock over them. The heat of the stock will cook the meat.

Scatter with the garnishes and serve immediately with a lime wedge.

Sautéed Beef with Rice Noodles and Salad BÚN BÒ

After a year in Vietnam I finally ate Bun Bo for the first time, opposite Hang Xia market in the old quarters – it was love at first bite. This one-dish wonder was all they served. Bun Bo and fermented pork in banana leaves. The fermented pork is to nibble on while waiting for the Bun Bo.

The place was run down and packed. I sat on the second floor, observing the cooking process. In the front of the restaurant, the lady sat there with two burners, one with a frying pan and one with a large vat of the sauce, which was flanked with a long rectangular table with all of her mise en place: mounds of thin slivers of meat, chopped garlic next to beansprouts, chopped peanuts, fried shallots and fermented pork wrapped in banana leaves. On the floor was a 5-litre tin can filled with oil. Behind her sat a woman with bowls stacked up high, as she filled each bowl from a basket of salads, a basket of herbs, a basket of rice noodles, stacking more and more bowls higher and higher.

If five people walked in, five bowls would be placed on the table, oil would be ladled in, garlic would be thrown in, followed by the beef, flipping it up to splatter, fire and smoke. Once it was cooked, beansprouts would be thrown in and then quickly covered with a lid. Then the ladle would be rushed over the bowls, pouring the sauce over the chilled ingredients. As soon as that was done she would throw over the beef and the sprouts. The waiter would garnish with spoonfuls of chopped peanuts and fried shallots, and rush them over.

It was magic. How I dreamed I could have a place that only made one dish!

The dish was hot, yet cold, sweet and sour, with textures and sensations that were light and clean. I adapted a little by making it a little more French as I was never able to perfect the sweet and sour balance for the beef stock.

Using filet mignon makes the dish a little more decadent, and it simply melts in the mouth.

SERVES 2

100g beef fillet, thinly sliced
5g coriander, chopped
20g shiso
50g mixed salad
100g rice noodles
1 tsp vegetable oil
1 tsp finely chopped garlic
2 tbsp Beef stock (see page 50) or water
50g beansprouts
2 tbsp Sweet-and-Sour Sauce (page 47)
Marinade
1tsp vegetable oil
1 tsp finely chopped lemon grass
Garnish
1 tbsp Crispy-fried Shallots (page 38)
1 tbsp white sesame seeds
1 tbsp Roasted Peanuts (page 41)

First marinate the meat: oil it, then coat with the lemon grass and leave for about 15 minutes.

Prepare each serving bowl by adding some herbs and salad and topping with rice noodles.

Lightly oil a stainless steel sauté pan almost to smoking point. Place the meat in the pan and sear, then let it sit a bit before shaking the pan to create a little caramelization.

Stir to ensure it is all evenly cooked, then place the chopped garlic in the pan and sauté a little more making sure that it does not brown.

Keeping the heat high, deglaze with beef stock or water, scraping the pan to release the caramelized juices, creating a brown sauce.

Throw in the beansprouts and cover for a minute while the sprouts cook a bit. Add a little Sweet-and-Sour Sauce and taste.

Spoon the beef and beansprouts, with their juices, into the bowls. Garnish with shallots, sesame seeds and peanuts.

Deep-fried Rice Noodles with Beef and Vegetables PHỞ XÀO BÒ

This is a very comforting dish and demonstrates the Chinese influence in Vietnam. A simple stir-fry, it can be made with an array of noodles, rice noodles, egg noodles or even the pre-packaged instant noodles.

Laugh if you wish, but quite often I would get this dish very late at night by my old house in Truc Bach lake. They would blanch the dried noodles in hot water and drain them once they were a little al dente. Then they would be thrown into a smoking-hot wok coated with oil and tossed several times, imparting a wonderful smoky, charred flavour to the noodles. Finally, thin slices of bok choi and wedges of tomatoes and onions would be thrown in.

Here is a dish that can be made in no time flat, with very pleasing results. If you are a little shy of using oil, my grandmother taught me a nifty trick. It turned out that my grandfather did not like the use of much oil in his food, so she devised several ways to reduce the oil in her cooking.

For stir-fried noodles, she would do the following. After blanching her noodles in hot water until al dente, she would then rinse them in cold water to stop the cooking process. From there she would then drain as much water as much as possible. She would then spray oil through the noodles working her fingers through. By coating the noodles with a little oil reduces the amount of oil that is generally used in the wok.

SERVES 4

1 tbsp cornflour

300g pho noodles (flat rice noodles)

vegetable oil for frying, plus more for spraying
    the noodles

100g beef fillet

1 tsp fish sauce plus an extra splash or two

½ tsp finely chopped garlic

½ tsp sugar

1 tsp soy sauce

1 tsp oyster sauce

100g onion, cut into eighths and segmented

100g tomato, cut into 8 wedges

40g spring onions, cut into 4cm lengths

50g celery, cut into 4cm lengths

50g leeks, cut into 4cm lengths

4 coriander sprigs

1 tsp red thinly sliced chilli pepper

Mix the cornflour with 3 tablespoons of water and set aside. Ideally you are using fresh rice noodles, if not soak them in water so they become pliable. Dry them off, spray them with a little oil and reserve.

Thinly slice the beef and then add a couple of splashes of fish sauce, then the garlic and sugar, with a little oil to coat the mixture. Set it aside to marinate.

In a small rice bowl, mix the teaspoon of fish sauce with the soy sauce and the oyster sauce.

Place a sauté pan with a tablespoon or two of oil over a high heat and bring it up to smoking-hot. Add the noodles and toss for about 1 minute, making sure that the noodles are well coated with the oil. The idea here is to get a little smoky flavour from the pan. It is also common to leave the noodles sitting in the oil to create a very crispy nest, where most of the noodles are still tender but with a crispy base.

Remove from the pan and place it out on a serving plate with the crispy bottom on top.

Into a very hot pan with a little more oil, throw in the beef and stir-fry until half cooked. Add a little water and, with a slotted spoon, remove the beef.

Quickly add the onions, and stir-fry until well coated with oil, then add the tomatoes and cook for a couple of minutes until they become a little soft.

Add the spring onions, celery and leeks, and stir-fry until all the vegetables are tender.

Add the fish sauce, soy sauce and oyster sauce mixture and toss to coat all the ingredients. Return the beef and cook further, stir to incorporate the rest of the ingredients.

Mix the cornflour mixture again and then add to pan, creating a thicker sauce.

Spoon the mixture over the noodles and garnish with coriander and chilli.

Grilled Pork Patties with Rice Vermicelli BÚN CHẢ

Bun Cha is a brilliantly simple dish that relies on something as simple as caramel sauce to make it what it is. There are two options with this dish. It can either be made out of thin strips of pork belly grilled until the meat is slightly crispy and smoky or as little burgers. I generally prefer the latter, as these burgers are quite unique.

This is a great example of the art of Vietnamese grilling. The fat content is more then that of a traditional burger, which helps it retain incredible moisture, simultaneously allowing the fat to melt, sweating the meat with drips of fat into the fire allows for a more smoky flavour. The burnt sugar aids in the caramelization, resulting in subtle crispness while achieving a light golden exterior. The contrast when paired with the fresh chilled herbs, rice noodles and dipping sauce makes this a real crowd-pleaser.

MAKES 5

200g pork belly
200g minced pork
20g finely chopped spring onion
2 tbsp Caramel sauce (see page 43)
2 tbsp fish sauce
1 tsp freshly ground black pepper
500g thin rice vermicelli
350ml Nuoc Cham sauce (see page 43)
Salad
20g lettuce leaves
10g basil
10g shiso
10g mint
20g coriander

In a mixing bowl, mix the pork belly and minced pork well, then mix in the spring onions a little at time. Season with the caramel and fish sauces. Add a couple of good twists of the pepper grinder. Let it rest for about 10 minutes.

Shape the rested meat mixture into bite-sized burgers. Grab a piece of meat, closing your hand around and tossing from hand to hand until you make a smooth ball. Slightly press each ball so that it is a pattie about 2.5cm thick.

Preferably over a charcoal barbecue (or under a preheated grill or even in a frying pan over a medium-high heat, but it would not achieve the level of smokiness of a grill), sear the patties. Do not move them around, let them get browned before making any attempt to move them. It is much easier to cook them in a barbecue cage, as it is easier to move, turn over and gauge the cooking of all the patties at the same time. Cook for 5–10 minutes, or until nicely browned and crisp on both sides.

Place the cooked burgers on a serving dish. Garnish with the salad of lettuce leaves and herbs.

In a large communal bowl, place the rice vermicelli noodles in the middle. Serve the dipping sauce to accompany the burgers.

Everyone should have their own rice bowls, which they fill with the rice noodles and herbs, then dip the hot burgers into the dipping sauce, lacing the noodles with the dipping sauce.

BC's Hanoi Grilled Fish with Rice Noodles and Fresh Herbs

CHẢ CÁ HÁ NỘI

It has been said that one of the 100 things you should do in your lifetime is to eat at Cha Ca La Vong in Hanoi. It is one of the first restaurants in Hanoi and, although the place is packed all the time, not much money has ever been spent on fixing it up or improving the décor, but with a dish like this, you really don't have to. This dish is a must try when in Hanoi as it is also fun to eat. Year after year I am asked what is the best Vietnamese restaurant in Hanoi, and this is right there on the top of the list for a 'one dish wonder'.

Firstly the dish is served in a large pot of very hot turmeric oil. The pieces of fish are fried at the tabletop and customers are basically made to cook it themselves. It is served with fresh rice noodles as well as a large selection of herbs. Roasted peanuts also accompany the herbs, with a choice of several sauces – Nuoc Cham as well as fermented shrimp pastes

I highly recommend that you stay away from the latter as they really are an acquired taste. It has literally taken me eight years finally to understand their appeal and, quite frankly, they still don't do much for me. If you can eat them, though, you will seriously impress the Vietnamese, but that encourages them to take you to a dog restaurant later! At Cha Ca La Vong, I have actually seen the fermented shrimp sauce bubble away in front of me. If you smell a rather pungent intoxicating sauce, it is probably the shrimp sauce. The proud owners of the establishment rarely offer the fermented shrimp paste dipping sauce to foreigners.

Now, although I feel compelled to warn you off the fermented shrimp sauce, I do recommend asking for the Ca Cuong, which is the pheromone (scent) gland found under the wings of the female Giant Water Bug (actually a beetle). If you are able to get over the fact it is a bug gland, you will quickly discover why it is referred to as the truffle of Vietnam. I have noticed, however, that one has to request it, and it goes for about a dollar and change for a single drop. If you ever get around to this restaurant, I highly recommend that you give the Ca Cuong a chance. It smells a little like nail polish remover, but tastes like a pear. It totally transforms the dipping sauce and puts white truffle oil to shame for its power. They now produce a synthetic version out of Thailand, but the original is much nicer. It is also very easy to detect the synthetic version, as the real pheromone juice is an oil, and when it is put into the Nuoc Cham sauce, it looks like a drop of oil in the golden water. The synthetic one is water-based and does not do this. In order to get the flavour through the sauce it is recommended to agitate the Nuoc Cham sauce by whipping your chopsticks into the bowl.

There is also a special way to eat this dish. You place the rice noodles into the dipping sauce and then into the bowl so that the noodles are laced with sauce. Pick out some of the hot crispy fish that is frying in the oil and throw that into the dipping sauce or right into the bowl. A little herbs, some peanuts, and bang! Hot fish, cold noodles, sweet-and-sour, textures from the noodles, the nuts, punctuated by herbs, and you recognize immediately the wonders of Vietnamese food. But then you might have a Vietnamese person sitting next to you, and then they would tell you that you are eating incorrectly, that you should throw the herbs into the hot oil as well, and then eat them once nice and wilted, transforming the fresh herb into a more subtle hot herb mixed in with the chilled rice noodles topped with some of the sauce. And that would be correct as well, but less healthy.

Either way, the dish is a winner and no one does it better then Cha Ca La Vong. In the recipe below I have opted not to fry the fish in the turmeric oil. If you would prefer to keep it authentic, then just make turmeric oil the same way as you make the other infused oil by cooking turmeric powder over a low heat until the oil takes on the colour and taste of the turmeric. For me, turmeric-marinated grilled monkfish would be a winner anywhere and, in Hanoi, they use a freshwater fish. The key here is use a fish that is firm. You can also use fresh turmeric, either way you will have very pleasing results.

The recipe might seem a little daunting, but there are two ways to cook this. You can either make it as above or go authentic, grilling the marinated fish then serving it in turmeric oil and frying it at the tableside. Don't be daunted by the extensive list or steps below as most of the items need very little work, it is literally just grilling the fish, the rest is a shopping list.

SERVES 4

600g monkfish fillets, cut into 5cm chunks

240ml Turmeric Oil (optional, if you wish to fry the fish, see page 172)

Marinade

2 tbsp ground turmeric or 10g fresh

20g galangal

1 tsp salt

2 tsp sugar

4 tbsp lime juice

Accompaniments

1 butterleaf lettuce, torn into bite-sized pieces

40g each Asian basil, mint leaves, dill and coriander leaves

10 spring onions, cut into 5cm lengths

600g rice noodles, soaked in cold water for 20 minutes or until tender, rinsed and drained)

150g Chopped Roasted Peanuts (page 41)

salt and pepper

4½ tbsp shrimp sauce (very stinky stuff called mam tom, sold in Vietnamese or the more serious Asian specialty stores)

125 ml fish sauce (Vietnamese nuoc mam sauce is a must)

240ml Sweet-and-sour sauce (see page 47)

240ml Nuoc Cham Sauce (page 43)

1 red chilli, deseeded and chopped (optional for the dipping sauce, if you like a little spice)

2 drops Ca Cuong (optional, this exotically aromatic additive is possibly found at the better Vietnamese or Asian specialty stores)

To make the marinade: using a grater or a food processor, extract the juice from the fresh turmeric and galangal. If using dried turmeric, simply add it to the galangal juice (traditionally this is a watery liquid, but a light paste is totally acceptable). Stir in the salt, sugar and lime juice. Add the monkfish and toss to coat the fish evenly.

Skewer the fish on presoaked wooden skewers and marinate for 1 hour in the refrigerator.

The rest of the ingredients for this dish are served at room temperature. Set the table with large individual bowls for the lettuce, herbs, spring onions, rice noodles, peanuts and any of the dipping sauces that tickle your fancy.

About 20 minutes before cooking, take the fish out of the fridge.

Preheat a barbecue, grill or griddle pan or an oven to 230°C/Gas 8. Oil the cooking surface of the barbecue or the grill or griddle pan, if using, and brush oil over the skewers to prevent sticking. Season with salt, pepper and shrimp paste.

Cook the monkfish pieces over the fire or bake in the oven for 10 minutes. The sugar in the marinade will assist in caramelization, so be careful not to let the fish overcook, or it will burn.

Remove the cooked fish from the skewers and place in the middle of the table. Have the guests add rice noodles to their bowls with herbs and peanuts, and simply dip the fish into whichever sauce(s) and dressing you choose, and then into the bowl so it laces the noodles with the sauce.

Rice Paper Wrapped Foie Gras on Apple Compote, Tamarind Apple Jus

NEM CUON GAN NGONG VOI SOT ME TAO

SERVES 4

270g foie gras, cut into 4 pieces
3 apples, peeled and cored
125g spinach
chopped shiso
salt and black pepper
4 rice papers
Tamarind apple jus
120ml tamarind pulp
240ml apple juice
ground coriander to taste
sugar to taste
Salt mixture
2 tbsp sugar
1 tbsp salt
½ tsp crushed coriander seeds

To make the Tamarind apple jus, mix the pulp and 120ml water and simmer for 30 minutes. Strain, add the apple juice and cook again until reduced by half. Season with coriander and sugar.

Make the salt mixture by mixing the ingredients and season the foie gras pieces with it.

Heat a frying pan over medium-to-high heat, place the foie gras in the pan and cook on each side for about 20 seconds – it should remain soft when lightly pressed. Don't worry about adding oil as the foie gras will release lots of fat. Remove from pan and reserve the fat left in the pan.

Dice 2 of the apples and pulse the third in a blender until finely mashed. Place a little foie gras fat in the pan and sear the chopped apples in it until coloured. Add some of the blended apples and cook until most of the water has evaporated off. Throw in the spinach and herbs, and season with salt and pepper until lightly wilted.

Wrap the foie gras pieces with rice paper and heat another pan with some fat until smoking. Place the wrapped foie gras in the pan and sear for a couple of seconds on each side until the exteriors are crisp. Place some spinach on each plate, top with apple compote and place a foie gras parcel on top. Spoon some tamarind apple jus around the plate.

79

Chicken Congee CHÁO GÀ

This incredibly simple and delectable dish was actually one of the first dishes that I ever made, or at least it was right there with the 'Top Ramen' with sliced bok choi and a poached egg in the middle.

I was in college and my lovely Chinese grandmother was teaching me how to cook over the phone. I was afraid I was going to screw it up, but she insisted that I should have more confidence and that it was very easy. She would make it with water. After Thanksgiving she would use all the bones from the turkey and call it turkey congee.

To tell you truth, it is very hard to ruin this dish and I could almost promise that it is foolproof. It is incredible comfort food for me, and when I get sick in Hanoi, and don't have Pho, my staff will make me this with a lot of fresh herbs.

Since there are Chinese communities all over Asia, the dish can be found all over the place: Vietnam, Malaysia, Thailand. In fact, name me a country in which the Chinese have a community and I will show you a country that has congee available in some shape or form.

When I was filming *World Café Asia* for Discovery Travel and Living, I was pretty much forced to do a breakfast dish in the 'How to cook' segment of the show. Time and time again, I had to eat the congee. In Singapore I ate a frogs' leg congee for dinner. In Bangkok, I made chicken congee in the early morning for the monks. I protested to the producer that I had eaten it all over the place, and that I was getting tired of the dish – and so would the viewers if they watched the entire series.

They told me that I could change it and make it my own. As an act of protest, I decided to make it ridiculously expensive! So I made it with the freshest seafood, fresh fish fumet, expensive scallops with coral and jumbo prawns. After I cooked the dish, the entire crew ate it, which is not very common with TV productions, but it was that good. I would have liked to have garnished it with caviar, but the producer Jaq, said 'Bobby, don't push it!'

Congee is one of the greatest leftover dishes of all time. It is a no-brainer. You basically keep all your leftover rice and boil it with water, that is it. Traditionally it is seasoned with soy sauce, as it is rather bland. Consider it a German oxtail soup without the oxtail. You cook it until the rice turns into a porridge. It is that simple. You cook it until it becomes thick, or you can add water to make it thin. The rice gruel is seasoned with soy sauce and enhanced with fresh herbs.

When I am sick, my staff would make me their version with shredded shiso in it, blending it in a blender so that it is a little green and somewhat sticky, or starchy by blending it in the a blender.

In the recipe below, however, I want to give you a dish that is a little more complex in flavour. You don't have to use sticky rice, as any rice will do.

SERVES 4

1.5 litres chicken stock (page 50) or water
170g rice
85g sticky rice
200g poached chicken, shredded
1/2 tsp salt or soy sauce
4 tbsp fish sauce
1 1/2 tsp finely chopped spring onion
1 tsp coriander or shiso
1/2 tsp pepper

Put the chicken stock or water in a pot and add both types of rice. Bring to the boil and then reduce to a simmer. Make sure to stir all the corners to prevent the rice from sticking – or, worse, burning. Cook for about 1 hour (if the mixture gets to thick at any point, simply add more liquid) until the rice grains are about a quarter of the size that they used to be, or where it turns into almost a purée. It is pretty much up to you.

Add the shredded chicken and mix well. Season to taste with salt or soy sauce as well as the fish sauce.

Pour into serving bowls and garnish with the spring onion, coriander and shiso. As an additional garnish, sprinkle with freshly ground black pepper.

Fixing the oven

Nha Tho Street is now known as Church Street after the miniature replica Notre Dame Cathedral that lies at the end of the road. It has become a tourist destination, filled with some of Hanoi's finest boutiques and restaurants, and claims some of the highest rents in the city. Back in 1996, however, this wide tree-lined street was a quiet residential neighbourhood and Moca Café was one-of-a-kind, bringing much attention to this then-unknown area.

Set in a converted colonial convent, the restaurant was unusually large, with sweeping views of the street and windows that slid freely from one side to the other, giving a breezy, open-air feel. It was one of the finest casual dining establishments Vietnam had yet seen. At the front, an antique brass coffee roaster stood by the door, churning out freshly roasted coffee.

Jeff, an American from New Orleans, was a managing partner and the mastermind behind the design of the place. One of the most colourful characters in the growing expat community, he was rich in experience and told stories so wide and varied that he was nicknamed Zelig after the Woody Allen movie. He had opened what was probably the best independent restaurant in Hanoi at the time, and it was an incredible achievement. Moca Café was an instant success, serving three distinctly different cuisines: Vietnamese, Indian, and Western, plus freshly roasted coffee. It was one of the first Western-managed restaurants to attract Vietnamese diners, expats and tourists alike.

A year after its opening the place was still jam-packed, but starting to look run down due to lack of cleaning and maintenance. Jeff called me up to ask if I knew anyone who could install a thermo-regulator for his Wolf range oven. I immediately suggested that I bring over Willie, chief engineer at Hanoi Towers, where I was working at the time, as well as Vu Son from the purchasing department. Willie was from Singapore, and always made a point of showing off his knowledge of everything concerning anything that touched upon engineering. He was very proud of his engineering triumphs and the Hanoi Towers operation.

As purchaser, Mr Vu Son was very close to Willie, as he needed to keep him updated on all the new fixtures, spare parts and so on that were coming on to the local market. On Saturdays they would take the company van out to source supplies for Hanoi Towers, so I decided to tag along and take them on a slight detour to Moca Café for a coffee. That would give Jeff the opportunity to show up 'coincidentally' and tell us about his equipment failure.

We arrived at Jeff's establishment on a typically busy Saturday afternoon, luckily nabbed a table by the window and ordered our coffees. Jeff magically appeared, looking a little frazzled – like he had already had more than his fair share of caffeine – and I made the introductions. After a couple of minutes of small talk, Jeff tentatively made his request. 'Hey, you wouldn't know how to install a thermo-regulator would you?'

To my surprise Willie did not know what a thermo-regulator was. Jeff looked a little perplexed and became rather undiplomatic. 'What? You don't know what a thermo-regulator is?' He quickly looked at me with his eyes blaring, confused as to how they could help his situation. Willie calmly replied: 'I know what a thermostat is, and I know what a gas regulator is, but I have never installed a thermo-regulator.'

Jeff immediately turned to me waving off Willie and Son. 'I'd be fucked if you think I'm going to let him touch my oven when he doesn't even know what a thermo-regulator is!'

Willie threw me a look of surprise and I wasn't sure if it was because my friend was rude or because I had roped him into doing a little free consulting without his consent. I focused on getting Jeff to calm down.

Clock wise from top left: Fire stew; Bikes in Saigon; Charcoal for barbecue grilling in Saigon; An iced-fruit drink vendor in Saigon

'Now slow down, tiger, we are here to help you.' With that I gave him a glacially slow nod, staring deeply in his eyes in the hope that he would remember that they were coming out of their way to assist him. Trusting that he would mellow out, I then turned to Willie.

'He is having a YIV day.'

'You're In Vietnam', or 'YIV', was a code used to remind expats that culture shock was kicking in, but the person who was experiencing it did not recognize it. It was a phrase we all learned to use. Say 'I'm going to paint my walls a Saharah sand bashe', and someone would reply 'YIV', as there are only primary paint colours available on the Vietnamese market.

Willie tilted his head and agreed reluctantly. I turned to Jeff. 'Why don't you show us the oven and then we can all see what you are talking about?' As we got up to make our way to the kitchen, Jeff explained: 'A thermo-regulator is an instrument that regulates the temperature of the oven based on the setting, which in turn regulates the gas to insure that a temperature is retained continuously. When you open the oven door, a lot of the heat is lost, so the regulator increases the gas flow to bring the heat back up to the temperature that the oven is set to.'

Moca Café's kitchen was one of the first open kitchens in Vietnam. Most operators knew full well that hygiene was a deterrent to anyone ambitious enough to even consider a display kitchen in those days. To the side lay what appeared to be a brand new six-top Wolf range oven in the midst of a lot of second-hand, locally-fabricated equipment. It worked briefly the first day, according to Jeff. Someone had installed it without checking the manual first, or without knowing what a thermo-regulator was, and within a couple of minutes the oven door had blown open with a fire and never worked again.

Everything looked copacetic until I opened the oven door to a stench that reminded me of the lion cages at San Francisco zoo. The smell was so overpowering that Willie and Son took a couple of steps backwards.

The base of the oven was a large steel plate; below that would be the source of the heat. 'The thermo-regulator is below this steel plate?' I asked Jeff.

'Yeah, I think so, that is what I need help with. I don't know as we lost the manual.'

'Okay. Do you have a screwdriver with a Phillips head?'

Willie and Son looked like they were ready to bolt. 'We can come back later if you don't have a Phillips head,' said Willie.

'No, let's do this now or it will never happen,' I replied.

I reached into my pocket and pulled out my Swiss army knife. Kneeling down on the grease-riddled floor, I took a deep breath of fresh air and, using the finger file, began to unscrew the oven's base. My head now deep in the lions' cage, I was struggling not to gag from the nauseating smell. When coming up for air, I plaintively looked at Jeff, hoping to see some recognition of the true friendship I was showing him by doing this disgusting job. But all I could see in his eyes were impatience and a caffeine haze.

Once the base was removed, the heating system was exposed: two parallel cast-iron plates designed to radiate the heat throughout the oven as well as help hold its temperature; beneath those plates ran the gas lines. From the corner of my eye, I could have sworn I saw something move in the darkness from one pipe to the other. I looked at Jeff: 'Did you see that?'

I then kicked the oven and clearly saw a rat run from one pipe back to the other, hiding beneath the shelter of the cast-iron plate, its tail exposed. I quickly jumped up on a plastic stool. 'Dude – you got a rat in the oven!' I screamed.

He quickly hushed me. 'Come on man, I got customers.' He picked up a twelve-inch chef's knife that sat on the prep table in front of the oven and fell to his hands and knees, slamming the blade down on the exposed tail of the rat as it quickly ran to the shelter of the other gas pipe. Jeff brought the knife down over the left gas pipe, where a pair of rats ran from left to right.

'My God, it's two rats!'

Frantically hacking away, back and forth between the pipes and on top of the cast-iron plates, Jeff desperately tried to kill off the rats, looking like he had lost his mind. More and more rats were sent running back and forth through the guillotine of his Henckels knife. The vermin were now bumping into each other, as more and more rats appeared.

It was apparent to me, and the rats, that their fate was doomed in the congestion of the oven. Their only chance of survival was to quickly storm the executioner, and in one sudden moment, they charged, leaping out of the oven like a waterfall. Jeff fell on his back in shock, his knife still slashing about like a musketeer.

One after the other they ran, some limping, some with bloodied bodies, some with tails, some without. Like a madman he swivelled the knife, waving it in vain as the rats literally jumped over him in their great escape.

From my place on the low plastic stool, I spoke again, but this time my words were filled with resonance and colour. 'Oh my God! You have tons of rats!'

His index finger quickly rushed to his mouth as he lay there on the floor now bloodied by the rats. 'Shhhhhhhush! I have customers!'

I turned to the dining room packed with people enjoying their food, oblivious to the present state of the kitchen.

Jeff got back on his feet and, knife in hand, turned to Willie and Son. 'Where'd they all go?'

Willie, wide-eyed, pointed to the inside kitchen. 'They went that way.' Son pointed in the opposite direction, then changed his mind and went with Willie's suggestion.

The kitchen floor was lined with trails of blood that seemed to run off in many directions. Jeff did not know what to do as the pack of rats escaped into the busy dining area.

He placed his chef's knife back on the prep table. It was dented and laced with blood from all the tails he had successfully amputated. A prep cook arrived with a bucket of peeled potatoes in water and placed a chopping board on a wet towel. He picked up the knife and proceeded to chop up a potato. Someone had to alert Jeff, so I cleared my throat loudly until I got his attention. My eyes darted towards the prep cook cutting away at the potatoes with the bloody knife.

Jeff's eyes rolled up into his head and then fell into a deeper state of despair. He slowly placed his hands on the hands of the cook, then removed the knife from him, placed it in the sink and said: 'Don't ask, please don't ask!'

The confused cook stood there staring at Jeff, then at me perched on a plastic stool, petrified from the rat attack, and in the middle of the kitchen at two horrified members of the management of Hanoi Towers.

At that point Willie decided to make a suggestion: 'Do you want to do this another time?'

Jeff propped a smile, which lacked any form of ingenuity and agreed. 'Yeah, let me fix things up here and I will give you a call when I am ready. Can you do me a favour? Please don't mention this to anyone?'

Willie agreed, but it was a tall order. They didn't ever fix that oven. I never went back to Moca Café to eat after that incident, but I also kept the story close to my chest until the day Jeff was kicked out by his partner. Four years later I hired Jeff to help me open my restaurant, where he worked as barman and trained the staff in our prolific cocktail list. He's one of the most entertaining barmen I've ever met, and we still get a giggle out of that story.

Salad Standalones

In the West, people traditionally think of salads as something leafy, but the Vietnamese will use anything from pickled vegetables and peanuts to banana blossoms and lotus roots. They're masters in the art of salad making and produce a wide variety. Vietnamese salads can be spicy, sweet, sour or sweet-and-sour; they can be hot or cold. The dishes here are all light, easy to make, and have clean flavours – all of the things that make Vietnamese food great. While the recipes may seem very modern, in reality they're classics – the wider world simply never heard of them before because this great cuisine has been overshadowed by war.

Vietnamese Salad

RAU TRON KIEU VIỆT NAM

To do justice to this very simple chicken salad it is essential to use the freshest herbs, as the recipe relies on them for its explosion of flavours.

SERVES 2

100g skinless chicken breast fillet or ready-cooked poached chicken

2–3 lemon grass stalks

50g carrots, cut into fine matchsticks

30g white onion, thinly sliced

1 tbsp finely chopped spring onion

1 tbsp thinly sliced bird's-eye chilli

1 tbsp thinly sliced garlic

3½ tbsp lime juice or lemon juice

1 tbsp chopped basil

2 tbsp finely chopped coriander

If you have not already done so, poach the chicken in water or stock until it is fully cooked, then leave to cool.

Remove the tough outer leaves of the lemon grass. Slice the remaining stem as thinly as possible then chop finely to make a tablespoonful.

Shred the chicken and combine it in a large serving bowl with the tablespoon of lemon grass, carrots, white onion, spring onions, chilli, garlic and lime juice. Toss well, then add the basil and coriander, and toss again.

Shredded Cabbage and Chicken Salad GAI XEU PHAY

SERVES 2

160g skinless chicken breast fillet, or ready-cooked poached chicken

50g white cabbage, thinly sliced

50g carrot, cut into fine matchsticks

1 tbsp finely chopped mint

4 coriander sprigs, to garnish

Dressing

2 tsp deseeded and finely chopped red chillies

3 tbsp sugar

1 tbsp rice vinegar

3 tbsp lime juice

1½ tbsp fish sauce

1 tbsp vegetable oil

100g white onion, thinly sliced

¼ tsp freshly ground black pepper

If you have not already done so, poach the chicken in water or stock until it is fully cooked, then leave to cool.

Meanwhile, mix all the dressing ingredients in a bowl and set aside for 30 minutes.

Shred the cooked chicken and put it in a large mixing bowl with the cabbage, carrot and mint. Add the dressing and toss thoroughly.

Transfer to a serving plate, garnish with coriander and sprinkle with black pepper to serve.

Grilled Prawn Salad with Green Mango and Papaya, Tamarind Vinaigrette

The textures and flavours of this salad are fantastic on a hot summer day. The contrast between the sour green mango and sweet, tangy sauce, the bite of the chilli and refreshing hit of coriander, make this a masterpiece.

SERVES 2

vegetable oil

6 raw jumbo prawns, shelled and deveined

salt and pepper

1 green mango, peeled and thinly sliced

240ml papaya, peeled, deseeded and diced

small handful of green papaya noodle strips using a mandolin on the middle blade

small handful of cucumber noodle strips using a mandolin on the middle blade

small handful of carrot noodle strips using a mandolin on the middle blade

3 tablespoons chopped coriander

2 tablespoons chopped chilli

3 tablespoons Crispy fried shallots (see page 38)

Sauce

400g palm sugar

300g tamarind pulp

200ml apple juice

Garnish

4 tablespoons chopped peanuts

10 coriander leaves

Place all the ingredients for the sauce in a pan and bring to the boil. Reduce the heat and simmer until reduced by a quarter. Pass it through a fine-mesh sieve. When cool, store in a squeezy bottle and chill.

Preheat a grill or grill pan. Lightly oil the prawns and season with salt and pepper. Cook under the grill or in the grill pan for about 3 minutes on each side until cooked through.

Line a ring mould with cling film, and place the mango slices around the sides, overlapping.

In a mixing bowl, mix the papaya concassé and noodles, cucumber and carrot noodles, chopped coriander, half the chilli and the fried shallots. Add a little sauce so everything is well coated.

Place the mixture in the mango-lined mould. Flip the mould on to a plate and remove the film. Place the prawns around the mound of salad and garnish with chopped peanuts, coriander leaves and the remaining chilli.

Banana Blossom Salad with Chicken

NỘM HOA CHUỐI GÀ

This salad is difficult not to love. When you slice the banana blossoms, place them in the acidulated water quickly or they will turn brown.

SERVES 4

100g skinless chicken breast fillet, or ready-cooked poached chicken

1kg medium-sized banana blossoms

1/2 tbsp lime juice

50g cucumber, deseeded and cut into matchsticks

50g onion, sliced paper-thin lengthways

40g carrot, grated

2 tbsp Crispy-fried Shallots (page 38)

3 tbsp chopped Roasted Peanuts (page 41)

4 coriander sprigs

Dressing

1 1/2 tsp crushed garlic

1 tbsp deseeded and finely chopped bird's-eye chillies

2 tbsp sugar

2 tbsp lime juice

1 1/2 tbsp fish sauce

If you haven't already done so, poach the chicken in water or stock until cooked, then leave to cool.

Combine the dressing ingredients in a bowl with 2 tablespoons water, stirring well. Set aside.

Peel off the coarse outer layer of the banana blossoms (usually purple) and remove the stalk. Cut the blossoms across into slices about 1.5mm thick. Rinse well and place in a bowl. Immediately cover with cold water and add the lime juice to prevent discoloration. Leave to stand for 15 minutes (you can leave the banana blossoms at this stage for hours without any problems).

When ready to assemble the salad, drain the blossoms and pat dry with kitchen paper. Shred the chicken and put it in a mixing bowl with half the dressing. Leave to marinate for 10 minutes.

Add the banana blossoms, cucumber, onion, carrot, half the crispy fried shallots and half the peanuts to the chicken and toss well. Transfer the salad to a serving plate and garnish with the rest of the peanuts, shallots, dressing and coriander.

Young Jackfruit Salad

NỘM MÍT NON

I'm not a fan of ripe jackfruit, but when young it is quite wonderful. I was introduced to this dish when I first arrived in Vietnam. My friend Joanna and I went to try Hue food at a restaurant named Tibs. One of the dishes ordered was the jackfruit salad. I immediately expressed my reservations, and we almost cancelled our order. But I have been so grateful we didn't, as I was instantly converted and the experience opened my mind to trying many foods I wouldn't normally eat.

The recipe name is very misleading, as it is not really a salad but more of a stir-fry. It can be a little bland, but an undiluted fish sauce with chopped chillies changes all that. Vietnamese coriander, or *rau ram*, punctuates each mouthful with a sharp spice that sparks an explosion of different flavours. At Tibs they use minced pork and small prawns, but we have removed the pork and use both small prawns and jumbo prawns.

An important thing to bear in mind: when you peel young jackfruit it excretes a white sticky liquid reminiscent of glue. Oil your hands and knife to ensure that this liquid is easy to remove later. If you can't find fresh young jackfruit, use the canned variety, or choose another dish – this is one of those occasions where a substitute just won't do.

SERVES 2

1 small young jackfruit, about 250–400g

1 tbsp crushed garlic, plus a few extra slices

salt and freshly ground pepper

2 tbsp vegetable oil

1 tsp shrimp paste

2 raw jumbo prawns

½ tsp sugar

10 small cooked prawns, halved lengthways

1½ tbsp toasted sesame seeds

1 tbsp Vietnamese coriander leaves (rau ram)

sesame seed rice crackers, deep-fried, to serve

Using a large well-oiled chef's knife, remove the tough outer skin of the jackfruit, leaving the flesh and seeds intact. Cut the fruit into 4 pieces.

Place in a large saucepan of water with the garlic slices and some salt. Bring to a boil then adjust the heat to a simmer and cook for 10-20 minutes or until the jackfruit is very tender. Remove with a slotted spoon and set aside until cool enough to shred with your fingers.

Heat the oil in a wok or frying pan, then add the shrimp paste and toast it a little bit. Reduce the heat and add the crushed garlic. Stir-fry until the garlic takes on a light golden colour. Throw in the jumbo prawns and cook these until just pink, then remove them from the pan with a slotted spoon.

Add the shredded jackfruit and stir-fry until it is well coated with the shrimp paste and oil. Season with sugar and a little salt and pepper, then add the small cooked prawns and about half the sesame seeds, and stir until well combined. Mix in the Vietnamese coriander.

Pile the stir-fried jackfruit mixture on a serving plate and place the jumbo prawns on top of that. Sprinkle the remaining sesame seeds over the salad and serve hot with deep-fried sesame seed rice crackers.

Lotus Root Salad with Prawns

NỘM NGÓ SEN

When planning to entertain guests, this unique salad should be one of your first choices. I love it. Sweet, sour and refreshing, it can also be spiced up to make it hot. It's extra-healthy too, especially if you need a little more roughage. If you can't find *rau ram*, substitute ordinary coriander.

SERVES 2

200g lotus root

100g cucumber, deseeded and cut into thin strips

100g peeled cooked prawns, deveined and halved lengthways

handful Vietnamese coriander leaves (rau ram)

4 tbsp Crispy-fried Shallots (page 38)

about 25 coriander sprigs, cut into 2cm lengths

3 tbsp chopped Roasted Peanuts (page 41)

2½ tbsp toasted sesame seeds

Dressing

1 tbsp crushed garlic

1 tbsp sliced bird's-eye chilli, sliced at an angle

2 tbsp fish sauce

2 tbsp lime juice

2 tbsp sugar

good pinch of freshly ground black pepper

Put all the dressing ingredients in a large bowl, stir together and set aside.

Quarter the lotus root lengthways, then cut at an angle into 5cm pieces. Place in a bowl, cover with water and stir vigorously to remove the fibres that separate from the lotus stems. Drain and add the lotus root to the dressing. Toss well and set aside to marinate for 10 minutes.

Add the cucumber, prawns, Vietnamese coriander and shallots, and toss gently. Transfer the salad to a serving plate. Garnish with the coriander, peanuts and sesame seeds.

Crab Salad

NỘM CUA

This is a seafood variation of a chicken salad. I decided to change it because the crab in Vietnam is so sweet, and steaming it in sake makes it incredibly tasty. A kilo of fresh crabs will yield 125–400g of meat, depending on the type of crabs. In Vietnam both swimming and mud crabs are available, and both generally yield less meat than most temperate species.

You could skip the sake-steaming process and use 100g lump crabmeat, or substitute shredded cooked chicken. When it comes to thinly slicing the vegetables, a mandolin will give the best results, but do watch your fingers.

SERVES 2

1kg fresh crab

900ml sake

1 lemon grass stalk, roughly chopped

20g fresh ginger, roughly chopped

50g white cabbage, thinly sliced

50g red cabbage, thinly sliced

50g cucumber, peeled, deseeded and thinly sliced

30g carrot, peeled and thinly sliced

1½ tbsp coriander leaves

3 tbsp mint leaves

100g pomelo or pink grapefruit, peeled, segmented and deseeded

2 tbsp crushed Roasted peanuts (page 41)

2 tbsp sesame seeds, toasted

3 tbsp Sweet-and-sour sauce (page 47)

3 tbsp Lemon oil (page 49)

Thoroughly clean the crab with a stiff brush. Remove the top shell and the bottom flap. With kitchen shears, cut away the gills that line the sides of the crab. Cut the crab in half lengthways, remove the legs and quarter the body. Gently crack the claws with a cleaver (this will accelerate the cooking time and allow the aromatics to perfume the dish more, and make it easier to remove the meat later).

Choose a medium saucepan with a well-fitting lid. Put the sake, ginger and lemon grass in it and bring to a boil. Add the crab and cover. Turn the heat up high and, once it comes to a boil, reduce the heat to a simmer and steam for about 10 minutes (cooking time will vary depending on the size of the crab and number used). Check to see that the sake does not completely evaporate. Remove the pan from the heat and leave it to sit, still covered, until completely cool – this will ensure that the crab remains moist and tasty.

Pick out the crabmeat. Put a quarter of it in a large mixing bowl and add the cabbages, cucumber, carrot, coriander, mint, pomelo, peanuts, half the sesame seeds, and the sweet-and-sour sauce. Toss until well combined.

Pile the salad on a serving platter and sprinkle with the remaining crabmeat and sesame seeds. Toss lightly. Drizzle with a little lemon oil to finish.

Pomelo Lobster Salad

NỘM BƯỞI

At the restaurant we like to make Vietnamese food extravagant, and there are countless lobster salads from which to choose. Pairing lobster and orange is very Californian, but the acidity provided here by the pomelo is more subtle.

SERVES 4 TO 6

100g cooked lobster or crawfish meat

100g grated carrot

100g cucumber, deseeded and cut into matchsticks

300g pomelo, peeled, deseeded and crumbled

10g mint leaves, very finely chopped

50g roasted peanuts, crushed

2 tbsp Crispy-fried Shallots (page 38)

Dressing

1 tbsp crushed garlic

1 tbsp bird's-eye chilli, sliced at an angle

2 tbsp fish sauce

2 tbsp lime juice

2 tbsp sugar

To make the dressing, combine all the ingredients in a large bowl and mix well.

Add the lobster or crawfish , carrot, cucumber, pomelo and mint, and toss well.

Cut the seafood into 2mm medallions and fan into a circle in the middle of serving plates. Pile the salad in the middle of these circles. Garnish with peanuts and shallots. Serve immediately, or chill briefly first.

Minced Meat, Crab and Pomelo Vietnamese Salad

RAU TRỘN THỊT XAY, CUA VÀ BƯỞI VIỆT NAM

SERVES 4–5

175g minced pork or beef

2 tbsp lime juice or lemon juice

2 tbsp fish sauce dip or Nuoc Cham sauce (page 43)

1 tbsp thinly sliced green chilli

1 small Spanish onion, finely diced

1cm ginger root, finely chopped

2 tbsp finely chopped coriander

100g crabmeat, thoroughly drained

1 pomelo, peeled, segmented and deseeded

lettuce leaves

100g grated carrot

large handful grated cucumber

Put the minced meat in a saucepan with 3 tablespoons of water and cook over medium heat until the meat has changed colour and is cooked but still tender. Allow to cool briefly.

Add the lime juice, fish sauce and green chilli, then set aside to cool completely.

In a large mixing bowl, combine the onion, ginger, coriander and crab thoroughly. Tear the pomelo segments into small pieces and add them. When the meat is cool, toss it into the salad.

Arrange the lettuce leaves on a serving dish. Top with the salad and sprinkle with the grated carrot and cucumber.

Vietnamese 'Caesar' Salad

A regular customer came in, plopped himself down at a table and ordered a Caesar salad. Unfortunately I had changed the menu and he was rather disappointed.

'How the hell do you take a Caesar salad off the menu?'

'I had to change the menu.'

'It's a Caesar salad! You should always have a Caesar salad on the menu. It was a good one!'

'Well, it is hard to get people to order a Caesar salad when there is bird flu.'

'You can't get the bird flu from an egg for Christ's sake! Can't you make me a Caesar salad? You have all the ingredients, don't you?'

'Everything except the anchovies.'

'Surely you can do something. Make me a Caesar salad with what you've got. I have a serious craving for one.'

As I walked through the kitchen, I checked the pantry and it was clear we had no more canned anchovies. Strangely enough a bottle of fish sauce was right in front of me. Fish sauce is fermented anchovies. Surely I could use fish sauce? The problem was that fish sauce is saltier and more pungent than anchovies. To mellow the flavours, I diluted the fish sauce with water.

I also realised we could reduce all risks of infection by cooking the eggs like a sabayon sauce. Bird flu and salmonella had made it policy never to serve raw eggs, so this was a good solution.

SERVES 4

4 thick slices bread, cubed

2–4 tbsp roast garlic oil, for drizzling

2 large Cos lettuces, leaves separated

4 tbsp grated Parmesan cheese

Dressing

3 egg yolks

3½ tbsp fish sauce

2 tbsp crushed garlic

250ml olive oil

¼ tsp Tabasco sauce

4 tbsp lemon juice

salt and pepper

First make the dressing: put the egg yolks in a heatproof bowl and set over a pan of steaming hot water. Whisk in the fish sauce and continue whisking until the eggs are at ribbon stage. Remove the bowl from the heat and carefully pour the mixture into a blender.

Add the garlic (or some roast garlic oil) and switch the machine to a low speed. Slowly pour in the oil in a steady stream. Add the Tabasco sauce, lemon juice, and a couple of tablespoons of water. Whiz until creamy – you can add more water if you want to make the sauce thinner. Taste and adjust the seasoning with pepper and a little salt, if necessary. Set aside.

Preheat the oven to 180°C/Gas 4. Put the bread cubes in a bowl and drizzle with roast garlic oil until evenly coated. Spread out on a baking sheet and bake for 10 minutes.

Tear the lettuce leaves into large pieces. Toss in a large bowl with the dressing. Sprinkle over the Parmesan and toss again. Serve with the garlic croutons.

Moroccan Beetroot Salad with Hazelnut-crusted Goat's Cheese

This is one of my quasi-Arabic-Californian dishes. It's a simple rendition of a Moroccan dish. It may seem very complicated but it really isn't.

Moroccan cuisine is pretty much defined by its generous use of sweet spices in savoury dishes – a very interesting balance – but although I love Moroccan food, I find its flavours are way too bold to pair easily with wines.

Traditionally the beetroot are served hot with the honeyed, spicy cooking juices from the pan. I decided to make the recipe more wine-friendly and somehow it has become one of our bestselling dishes.

Hazelnut-crusted Goats' Cheese

100g fresh goats' cheese, cut into 4 round discs

60g plain flour

110g chopped hazelnuts

1 egg

Beetroot

3 beetroot, brushed clean and washed

120ml orange juice

120ml apple juice

2.5cm cinnamon stick

3 cloves

½ tbsp allspice

Lemon Oil (see page 49), to taste

Salad

50g mixed salad leaves

2 tbsp Vinaigrette (see page 49)

Chill the cheese discs in the fridge until firm.

Combine 2 of the beetroots in a pan with the orange and apple juices, cinnamon, cloves and allspice. Bring to the boil, then reduce to a simmer. Cover and cook for 30 minutes or until the beetroot are tender (check with a toothpick: they should be soft with no resistance). Lift the beetroots from the liquid and set aside until cool enough to handle.

Bring the pan back to the boil and simmer until the liquid has reduced by about half. Meanwhile, put the remaining beetroot through a juice extractor. Add the juice to the pan and simmer until the liquid is syrupy. Transfer to a squeezy bottle and add the lemon oil. Shake well, then taste and add more lemon oil as desired.

Remove the cheese from the fridge. Put the flour and hazelnuts on separate plates, and beat the egg in a dish. Dust each cheese disc in flour, then dip it in the egg and roll in the hazelnuts, making sure they are evenly coated. Heat the oil in a frying pan over a medium heat. Fry the cheese discs two at a time – don't overcrowd the pan or they will be difficult to flip over once the cheese softens. Cook until light brown on both sides.

Peel the beetroot and slice thinly. Fan the slices out on the centre of 2 serving plates.

Dress the leaves with vinaigrette and pile on top of the beetroot. Place the goats' cheese on top and drizzle around the beetroot/lemon emulsion.

Stumbling to success

It was the wilder earlier years and I was in a Hanoi nightclub with a group of friends on a rather intoxicating Halloween night. I wanted to dance on the stage and as I attempted to leap on the stage, a guy grabbed me and said, 'You can't dance on stage.'

I said: 'Well, I AM going to dance on the stage.' Then he grabbed my arms and started pulling me, repeating: 'You can't dance on stage.' I was pulling away from him saying: 'Yes I can.'

'No you can't.'

'Yes I can.'

The young security guy was dressed in an orange jumpsuit like he had been a detainee at Guantanamo Bay. That's how the security guards dressed at nightclubs in the early days of Hanoi's new burgeoning clubbing scene, and you really didn't want to screw around with them because, if you did, the policy was simple – make an example out of anyone who breaks the rules or misbehaves, whether foreigner or Vietnamese, it made no difference.

As he attempted to pull me from the stage, I made the rather dubious decision just to let myself go and he fell abruptly down to the ground. Swearing at me in Vietnamese, as everyone turned around and laughed, I realized that I had made a foolish mistake. A security guard losing face meant that I would need to be humiliated, thrown out and disciplined, and as he was on his way to get reinforcement, I quickly ran to my close friend Arthur for moral support.

Hidden beneath my attempt to find a quick way to tell him that I am just about to get the shit kicked out me, I rambled off 'Dude – do you still want to open a restaurant?'

'Yes.'

'Do you think you can fix problems in Hanoi?' I asked.

'Every problem has a solution, and I am sure we fix any problems' he said with a smirk.

'Ok, well, if you can fix this problem coming up right now, then I think we can be partners.' Looking slightly puzzled, we stood there looking over the dance floor.

Arthur was a young businessman who was a significant investor in Vietnam, and a very well respected one. A soft-spoken, low-key gentleman, he was very private. We became friends over the years, when he would visit my earlier restaurant and require a special tasting menu for him and his guests. After several years and many tasting menus, Arthur eventually offered me a job that I reluctantly declined.

'I can't work for you because you're my friend. I can't work for friends, as work will eventually undermine our friendship. You're going to tell me to cook something that I don't know how to cook, or do not want to cook, and I'll tell you no. Then you'll order me to do it, and I will still tell you no, then you'll fire me because you're my boss and then our friendship would end. If you believe in me, you can always invest in me, but more importantly, I value our friendship.' I didn't need or want another boss; I needed a friend and a good partner.

A couple of minutes later, about ten security guards surrounded us, all dressed in their orange outfits ready to take me out. Arthur, made a gesture to his right-hand man, a man we nicknamed Mario for his ability to change peoples minds like Il Padrino. It was a showdown that attracted many of the other guests, as the potential spectacle was already eclipsing the shaking bodies on the dance floor.

The head security guy started off raising his voice at us, while Mario interrupted, cutting him short, responding quietly, raising his voice decibel by decibel with each passing word until he was shouting. With my lack of understanding

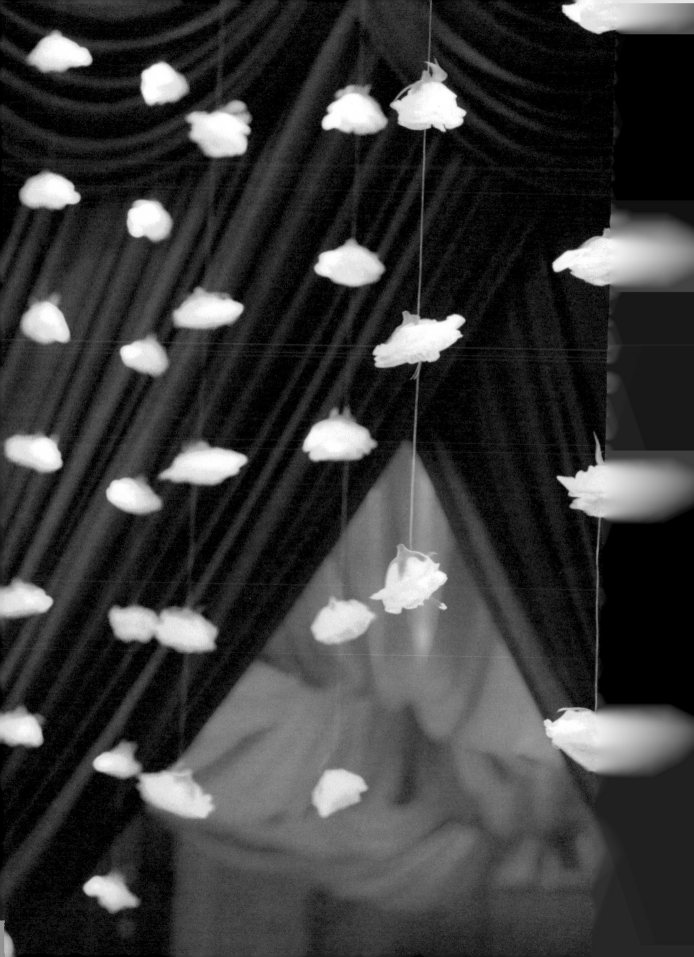

of the language, it was like watching two dogs barking, except ours was barking louder.

It seemed as though they had reached a stalemate as one of the security guards was ushered away, while the rest stood us down until the owner of the nightclub crept up from behind his heavies to find us standing there.

When he saw who he was dealing with, he quickly put his head down, bowed, took both of his hands and wrapped them around Mario's and grovelled to him, repeatedly saying 'Sorry! Sorry!'

As the guy was shaking his hands, Mario started pointing fingers at the security. All of a sudden they were not standing as belligerently as before. Arthur threw his arm around me, saying, 'My brother' as the owner introduced himself.

I have never gone back to that nightclub or any other after that if I did not have him with me. I knew right there and then, I found myself a good partner and a very good friend.

A piece of property opened up on the banks of Hoan Kiem Lake. I approached Arthur for his thoughts. 'I'll give you the money and I just want to let you know that money's not going to come between us. You're my friend. All I care about is that you don't embarrass me. You have to make sure that when I come in, everything is perfect. I don't want to be saying to people "this is my restaurant" and find it's a shit-hole.'

He had all his guys fly up to Hanoi, including his architect. We had to design the space in two days and we had it built from scratch in thirty-three days, because I wanted to use the restaurant opening as a going-away party for the outgoing American ambassador, Pete Peterson, who had given me so much support over the years.

Everyone said the timescale was impossible, but one thing I have learned is that the Vietnamese don't know the word 'impossible'. Their proud history is filled with battles and wars that were considered impossible to win, but time and time again they remained victorious. They kicked the Chinese out three times, they kicked the French out, and they kicked the Japanese out. And if it was not bad enough getting carpet-bombed with the additional use of Agent Orange by the Americans, right after they ran them out, they invaded Cambodia, and fought the Chinese on their Northern border.

The problem with the restaurant business is that anyone with money gets to open one, probably one of the reasons it is the business with the highest failure rate all over the world. Everybody has an opinion about everything, and I was not about to allow anyone to make a bad decision, which I would be forced to live with. My fate should be written by me, not by others, and my argument was short and sweet.

'You are opening a restaurant because of me, you're investing money because you believe in me. So do me a favour, let me decide. If I fail, I can forgive myself, but if you fail me, I will hold it against you. You can express your opinions, but I have final say as I have a vision.'

One of the first issues was the budget and those design elements not visible to the eye.

'I want to acoustic the entire restaurant.'

'Why do you want to do that?'

'Because it's never been done before. It only costs $4,000'

'So what? It's $4,000!'

'So what? It'll be a quiet restaurant. A noise-reduced restaurant with surround-sound music system, so that when you're sitting there talking to someone, it will have an ambience that no one else has. That's what we want. And in order to do, that we'll cover all the walls with padded foam wrapped in canvas, then covered with silk. And in doing that we can change the colours and looks of the restaurant around at any given time,

'Someone's got to get these flowers and string them with fishing line in eights, because eight is a lucky number, and I want them all the same.' Who would ask for something like that in the West? It would cost a fortune. But the Vietnamese will do it with pride and perfection.

by changing the silk.' In Vietnam it's cheaper to buy silk than it is to paint a restaurant, and there's around 1,000 metres of silk in our place.

Flowers are cheap too, so I thought: 'Let's hang flowers all over the restaurant. We will make it look expensive! Someone's got to get these flowers and string them with fishing line in eights, because eight is a lucky number, and I want them all the same.' Who would ask for something like that in the West? It would cost a fortune. But the Vietnamese will do it with pride and perfection.

We would buy the roses at the evening flower market and string them by lunchtime. We started to get rose petals for all the tables, bar tops, floor and in the ladies' toilets. The latter would bring a lavatory service unparalleled there, where the staff monitors the lavatories. If there are no rose petals floating in the lavatory it would mean that the toilet had been flushed, and required an inspection, folding the toilet paper into a 'v' shape like all the swank hotels I'd stayed in, sprinkling additional petals to ensure that they have been cleaned. To me a clean bathroom reflected the cleanliness of our kitchen.

It wasn't necessarily that my standards were high or unusual; it was just that we were doing things no one had done before in Vietnam. For instance, we were the first to install handicap-

access toilets, apart from the US embassy.

A friend of mine, John Lancaster was shot in the back in the Vietnam War, leaving him in a wheelchair for the rest of his life. He had made me aware of the lack of handicap access toilet facilities. It cost us an additional $500 to convert one of the rooms to allow handicapped access. It was essentially for one person, but when another man in a wheelchair came up to me one night to say: 'Thank you so much, it's the first time I've been able to go to the bathroom in a restaurant here,' it was worth every penny.

In those early days, while I was training staff and ordering equipment, money was tight with no real controls. I moved out of my apartment and slept in the restaurant for more then six months. My problem was I didn't really know how to set up such a business from scratch. I knew how it was supposed to work – I'd just been running a restaurant based in serviced apartments, serving breakfast, lunch, dinner, rooms service and banquets. But I needed people to help me set it all up and was forced to micro-manage out of default. Financially, I had no idea what I was doing as we had no accountant or controls. We'd count the money each day and as quick as it came in it would go out again.

One day a friend from the Ford Foundation, Michael, showed up with someone and said: 'This is Oscar. He used to be the Ford Foundation's Arts and Culture Officer. He's just come from a pagoda and he's got a present for you.' It was some money that he'd had blessed by a very well respected monk – 200 dong in notes – the equivalent of about 6 pence.

He said, 'Here's some good lucky money. Put it in the cash register.' And that was the first day we hit over $1,000 in sales. From then onwards it just kept going up and we finally became profitable after almost three years of operation.

Garden of Earthly Delights

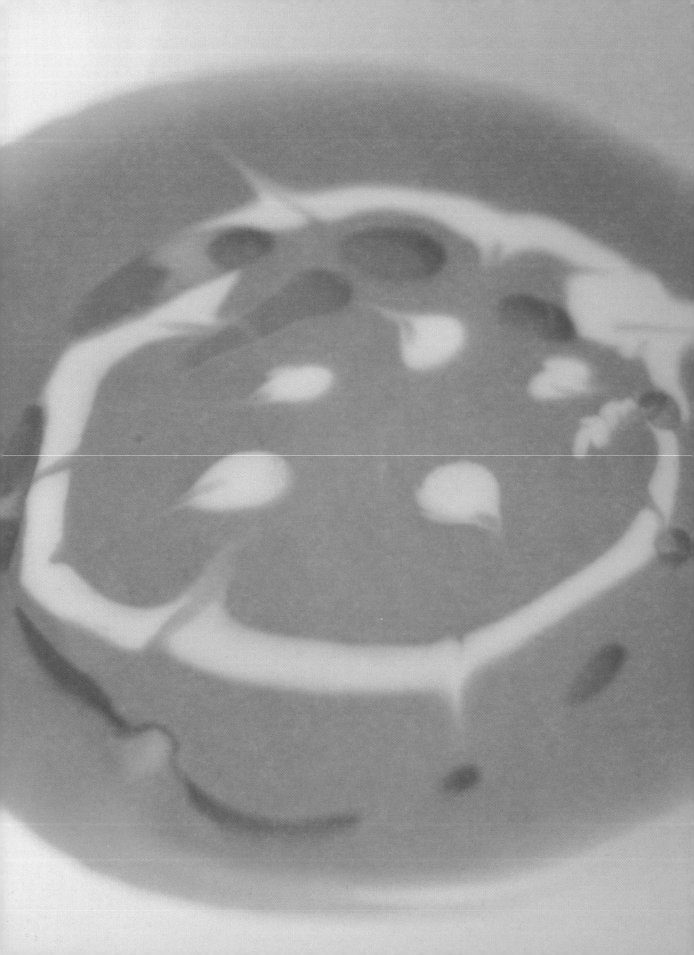

The Vietnamese have some very simple recipes for vegetables – they just pair them with a couple of condiment sauces and fresh spices. Even those cooked in soy sauce, water and sugar can taste incredible. Unlike as in Western kitchens, the Vietnamese do not use salted water when boiling vegetables. Yes, they will taste bland on their own, but then they'll be dipped in a mixture of, say, fish sauce and a little bit of sugar, to bring the flavours out. Try it with cabbage or daikon for something that's really special, but a real no-brainer. I don't like to cook all the time, so I'll prepare two or three vegetable dishes at once and eat them over the course of a couple of days.

Pumpkin Soup

SÚP BI NGÔ

Cooking over the grounds of the old prison – the infamous Hanoi Hilton – brought me a lot of publicity from the international press back in the late 1990s. The place where American POWs suffered just like the Vietnamese nationals under the French, was now a super high-rise service apartment block with an adjoining office tower.

Pete 'Douglas' Peterson, America's first post-war ambassador to Vietnam and personally selected by Bill Clinton, was a prisoner of war for six and a half years at the Hanoi Hilton. He returned as a man of peace, a bridge builder to help heal the wounds of the former adversaries, and was welcomed by Americans and Vietnamese alike. The last time he was in Vietnam he was a POW, and on his next visit his title was 'Your Excellency' – I loved that.

I heard he was being entertained at a famous restaurant and the chef made a Vietnamese tasting menu, sending out course after course all night until the pumpkin soup was announced. To the shock of his hosts, Pete had said he would pass on the soup, but the host was rather insistent.

'Your Excellency, this is one of the specialties of the chef.'

'Thank the chef, but I really do not care for pumpkin soup.'

'I am sure if you try it, you will find that the chef's version is much nicer.'

'I am sure it is, but I really do not like pumpkin soup.'

'Well chef has made it specially for you.'

'Well then tell chef that I had it everyday for six and a half years and I would prefer not to.'

The day I heard this story, I added a note to our menu that 'I refuse to serve pumpkin soup in honour of all our old tenants.'

For years I never made pumpkin soup because I felt it was old-fashioned and just too easy to make. Then last year, when I was sick, my staff made me a bowl. It was delicious, simple and visually pleasing. I decided to keep it on the menu, as it is a classic version that has all the underpinnings of a great Western Vietnamese dish. Instead of simply cooking the pumpkin in the broth, they steam it first, making it extra tender and creamy. In the restaurant we garnish this with a little drizzle of cream and herb oil.

SERVES 6

1 whole pumpkin (about 3kg), peeled, deseeded and cubed (about 1.3kg)
4 tbsp olive oil
200g onions, very finely chopped
5 tsp crushed garlic
1.1 litres chicken stock or water
2 bay leaves
5 tbsp coconut cream or coconut milk
1 tbsp salt
½ tsp pepper

Put the pumpkin in a steamer with water in the base. Bring to the boil and steam the pumpkin until tender.

Heat the olive oil in a large saucepan or pot. Add the onions and garlic and cook, stirring occasionally, until the onions are translucent. Throw in the steamed pumpkin and cook for a few more minutes. Add the chicken stock or water and bay leaves. Bring to the boil and simmer for about 20 minutes.

Remove the bay leaf and allow the soup to cool slightly. Transfer the mixture to a blender. Make sure the cover is secure, being extra careful as you're using a hot liquid. Pulse the mixture to break down the vegetables, then run the blender until the soup is nice and smooth.

Pour back into the pan. Reheat gently, adding the coconut cream or milk, salt and pepper.

Courgettes with Spring Onions

BI NGÔI XÀO HÀNH

The tender flesh of the courgettes makes this a wonderfully quick dish to make. Pumpkin is an excellent substitute as the flesh is rather sweet.

500g courgettes
30g spring onions
2 tbsp vegetable oil
2 tsp sliced shallot
2 tsp crushed garlic
1 tsp soy sauce
1 tbsp oyster sauce
1 tbsp Chinese rice wine

Cut the courgettes into 1cm pieces. Cut two-thirds of the spring onions into thin rings. Cut the remaining spring onions into 5cm lengths.

Heat the vegetable oil in a frying pan over a medium-high heat and add the shallot and garlic. Reduce the heat and cook, stirring, until tender but not golden. Throw in the courgettes, turn the heat up and stir-fry for 2 minutes, keeping all the ingredients in motion to prevent burning.

Add the soy sauce and oyster sauce and stir-fry for 30 seconds. Add a couple of tablespoons of water, then add all but a few of the spring onion rings and the Chinese wine, and reduce the heat slightly so that the courgettes simmer in the light sauce for about 2 minutes.

Remove the pan from the heat, transfer the courgette mixture to a serving plate and garnish with the remaining spring onions.

Mustard Greens with Garlic

CẢI XÀO TỎI

SERVES 2

500g Chinese mustard greens
2 tbsp vegetable oil
1 tsp crushed garlic
1½ tsp fish sauce
1 tbsp oyster sauce
a little sugar (optional)

Cut off the stems of the mustard greens and slice them at an angle into pieces 2.5cm thick. Cut the leafy parts into 7.5cm strips.

Heat the oil in a wok over a high heat. Working quickly, add the garlic and stir-fry until fragrant. Add the mustard greens, fish sauce and oyster sauce. Toss several times to coat the greens evenly in the sauce. (You may find it useful to add a little water if the fish sauce becomes over-reduced. You might also consider adding a little sugar in the event that it is too salty for your liking.) Cook for 2-3 minutes, until the leaves are done but still green and crunchy.

Transfer to a serving plate.

Stir-fried Water Spinach with Garlic

RAU MUỐNG XẠO TỎI

This is a staple dish found all over Vietnam. There are many variations and, as we often have it for staff meals, I've found each method is worth giving a chance. The simplest is to boil the water spinach until tender, then drain it and serve with a pungent dipping sauce, such as fish sauce with sugar, or Chilli lime dipping sauce (page 46). Another option is to add foo yee, a fermented bean curd that has to be used with a very light hand. In any case – without wanting to sound like Popeye – when you eat this vegetable you feel like you've done something healthy.

SERVES 2

500g water spinach, shredded
2 tbsp vegetable oil
½ tbsp crushed garlic
¼ tsp salt
1 tsp fish sauce

Bring a large saucepan of water to the boil. Add the spinach and cook for 2–3 minutes, then drain. Plunge the spinach into a bowl of cold water to maintain the colour and prevent further cooking, then squeeze as much excess water from the leaves as you can.

Heat the oil in a wok, add the garlic and stir-fry until it is just beginning to turn golden. Throw in the blanched spinach, salt and fish sauce, and stir-fry for 2–3 minutes or until all the leaves are coated with oil and garlic and warmed through. Serve immediately with rice.

Stir-fried Cabbage

BĂP CẢI XÀO

This classic dish that can be found in food stalls over the country. Once again it is quick, simple and light. I am always amazed at how many people gain weight in Vietnam when the food is usually so very light and low in fat. My rationalisation is that the food is so good, they end up overeating, and do you know what? The rice does not help!

SERVES 4 AS A SIDE DISH

500g cabbage

3 tbsp vegetable oil

1 tsp finely chopped garlic

1 tsp very finely chopped shallot

1 tsp fish sauce

¼ tsp salt

1 large tomato, about 100g, cut into 8 wedges

10g spring onion

10g coriander leaves

Halve the cabbage, separate the leaves and tear them into small bite-sized pieces. Bring a saucepan of water to the boil, add the cabbage and cook until just tender. (Be careful not to overcook as the cabbage will be cooked again in the next step.) Drain the leaves, plunge them into cold water and set aside to drain fully.

Put a wok or sauté pan over a medium heat and, when hot, add the vegetable oil. Stir-fry the garlic and shallot until translucent and tender. Add the blanched cabbage, fish sauce and salt, and stir-fry for about 5 minutes, until fragrant.

Add the tomato and cook for 5–7 minutes, stirring so that the flesh breaks down a bit. Throw in the spring onion and stir-fry briskly until wilted.

Transfer everything to a serving plate and garnish with the coriander.

Boiled Cabbage with Egg

BĂP CẢI LUỘC

Admittedly, this dish sounds terribly boring, but in fact it is the very thing that turned me on to using fish sauce as much as I do today.

The egg and fish sauce mixture adds substance to the cabbage, while the cabbage balances the sulphur and salt with a very light sweetness.

It can be made quickly with very pleasing results, but you do need an appreciation for fish sauce – make sure you use a very high quality one here. (If I run out of high-quality fish sauce at home a clever trick to get around it is to add a little sugar to the not-so-good sauce.)

I've included tomato because some traditional households prefer to eat the cabbage with a slightly tangy broth. If you prefer an austere version, remove the tomato. This is great served with white rice.

SERVES 4

700g white cabbage, cut into slices 6-7cm long

2-3 tomatoes, diced

10g fresh ginger, peeled and crushed

¼ tsp salt

¼ tsp sugar

1 egg

75ml fish sauce

Bring a large pan of water to the boil. Add the cabbage, tomatoes, ginger, salt and sugar and cook for 3–5 minutes or until tender. Drain.

Meanwhile, in a small pan of water, bring the egg to the boil and cook for 5–7 minutes, so that it is on the soft side of hard-boiled. Drain and plunge the egg into a bowl of cold water.

Shell the egg, cut it into wedges and mash it into the fish sauce.

Serve with the cabbage and some hot white rice.

Boiled cabbage with the egg prior to being mashed with the fish sauce

Roast Aubergine with Shallot Oil

CÀ TIM NƯỚNG TÂM DẦU HÀNH

I find it impossible to get bored with this, and when I'm in Saigon I don't miss an opportunity to eat it at a restaurant called Hoang Yen.

The butter-tender flesh of the smoky aubergine is sweetened with nuoc cham sauce and deep-fried shallots, to give a real gem of a dish.

Using a skewer or toothpick to pierce the aubergine all over accelerates the cooking time and helps to infuse the flesh with smoky flavour. The whole point of the dish is to actually char the aubergine, so don't be afraid if it is totally black!

SERVES 4

2 (500g) slender dark purple Asian aubergines
2 tbsp Fish Sauce Dip (page 43)
1 tbsp thinly sliced spring onion
1 tbsp Shallot Oil (page 38)
pinch of black pepper
1/2 tsp salt
1 tbsp Crispy-fried Shallots (page 38)

Ideally you would use a charcoal grill to cook the aubergine but a gas burner is a good alternative. (You can also place the aubergines directly on an electric stovetop over a moderate heat.) Pierce the aubergines all over with a skewer and use tongs to place them directly in the fire. Roast for 3–4 minutes, turning so that they are evenly charred. When the aubergines are soft on the outside but still firm in the middle, place them in a plastic bag, tie closed and set aside to cool.

When the aubergines are cool enough to handle, remove them from the bag. Reserve the juices as they will also impart smokiness, but pick out any black bits as they will give an unpleasant bitterness. Holding each aubergine by the cap, run a knife down the length to split it right open, then run a metal spoon down the inside to remove the flesh in two long strips. Place on a serving plate and sprinkle with the reserved juices.

Heat the fish sauce dip and spring onion together until the onion has slightly wilted. Pour over the aubergines. Sprinkle with the shallot oil, salt and pepper, and garnish with crispy fried shallots.

Banana Blossoms

HOA CHUỐI OM

500g banana blossoms
2 limes
Dressing
2½ tbsp sugar
1/2 tsp salt
2½ tbsp lime juice
1/4 tsp vegetable oil
4 sprigs sweet basil
3 tbsp crushed roasted peanuts

Wash the banana blossoms and remove the coarse outer layer. Quarter them and place in a large pan with 1.8 litres water. Squeeze the juice from the cut limes and add the shells and the juice to the pan. Bring to the boil over a high heat then reduce the heat and simmer for about 80 minutes. Drain the blossoms in a colander. Place a heavy object on top of them to encourage excess water to drain away and set aside until cool.

Remove and discard the tough outer leaves. Shred the rest and place in a bowl. Season with the sugar, salt and lime juice, and add the oil. Shred the leaves of the basil and add to the banana blossoms together with the crushed peanuts. Stir well and adjust the sugar, salt and lime to taste — the mix should be sweet and mildly sour.

Sautéed Chayote Squash with Beef

SU SU XÀO

The squash is quite sweet in this savoury mixture. This side dish is light, quick and easy to match with just about anything – in the restaurant we use it as a base for grilled fish dishes. The beef can be replaced with prawns or crabs.

SERVES 4

200g beef, thinly sliced
4 tbsp vegetable oil
1 tsp crushed garlic
600g chayote squash, peeled and cut into slices about 2.5 cm thick
1/2 tsp fish sauce
3 spring onions, cut into 2.5cm pieces

Ý ĐẢNG - LÒNG DÂN

Marinade

½ tsp crushed garlic

¼ tsp fish sauce

⅛ tsp salt

1 tbsp vegetable oil

In a mixing bowl, combine the beef with the marinade ingredients and let it stand for 5 minutes.

Heat the vegetable oil in a frying pan over medium heat. Add the garlic and cook until slightly golden.

Add the marinated meat and stir-fry rapidly to ensure the meat cooks evenly. When the meat is lightly cooked but still rare, transfer it to a warm bowl.

In the same pan, heat the remaining oil and add the chayote and fish sauce. Cook, stirring, for 3 minutes.

Add the spring onions, toss well, then add the meat back and cook for about a minute or until the spring onions are slightly wilted.

Daikon with Pork

CỦ CẢI KHO THỊT

SERVES 4

300g pork belly, cut into 2.5cm cubes

1 tsp salt

⅛ tsp pepper

150ml Caramel Sauce (page 43)

500g daikon, cut into 2.5cm cylinders

1½ tsp fish sauce

1 tbsp oyster sauce

1 tsp soy sauce

Put the pork in a saucepan with the salt, pepper and half the caramel sauce. Mix well and leave to stand for 5 minutes.

Set the saucepan over a medium heat and cook, stirring, for about 10 minutes. Pour in 225ml water, then add the daikon, fish sauce, oyster sauce, soy sauce and the rest of the caramel sauce. Cover and braise over a low heat for about 30 minutes or until the daikon and pork are tender and the sauce is rich and salty.

Serve with plain boiled rice.

Tofu in Tomato Sauce

ĐẬU SỐT CÀ CHUA

Like many northern Vietnamese dishes, this delightfully robust recipe is Chinese-inspired. During the seventeenth century, when there was a major exodus from southern China (Canton and Hakka) to Vietnam, much of the local culinary know-how was also exported and adapted in Vietnamese kitchens. Stuffed tofu, a popular side dish from the Hakka, is a standard in many homes and at food stalls all over Hanoi.

In the restaurant we use chicken stock for this dish, but you can get very similar results just using water. To make it completely vegetarian, replace the fish sauce with salt to taste. The sugar needs to be added to taste as well, as the amount required really depends on the sweetness of your tomatoes, which will vary with the seasons.

This dish really does not need anything more than some boiled rice served alongside.

225ml vegetable oil

400g firm tofu, cut into 2.5cm cubes

1 tbsp thinly sliced shallot

300g ripe tomatoes, coarsely chopped

½ tsp sugar

¼ tsp salt

2½ tbsp fish sauce

4 tbsp thinly sliced spring onions

3 tbsp shredded coriander leaves

Heat the oil in a frying pan. Fry the tofu cubes in batches as you want the heat of the oil to remain constant. Cook, turning, until golden and crisp on each side then remove from the pan and drain on kitchen paper while you fry the remainder.

Carefully pour most of the oil from the pan, leaving just a film. Return to the heat and add the shallot, tomatoes, sugar, salt and fish sauce. Sauté until the tomatoes break down into a light sauce.

Pour in 175ml water and bring the mixture to a simmer. Add the tofu to the sauce and allow to simmer uncovered until the liquid has evaporated. Just before serving, add the spring onions and cook they have until slightly wilted.

Transfer to a serving bowl and garnish with the coriander.

Sautéed Kohlrabi with Eggs

CA CAI KHO THIT

Kohlrabi is a light, refreshing and rather versatile root vegetable that pairs very well with scrambled egg.

The trick is to julienne the vegetable vertically from top to bottom. Duyen Kauffman, who helped to educate me on the simplicity of Vietnamese food, learned this from her grandmother.

Kohlrabi works very well with the classic nuoc cham dipping sauce.

500g kohlrabi, peeled

2 tbsp vegetable oil

3 shallots, very finely chopped

salt and pepper

1 spring onion, thinly sliced

2 eggs, beaten

2 tbsp chopped coriander leaves

225ml Nuoc Cham (page 43),
to serve

Cut the kohlrabi vertically into matchstick strips.

Heat the oil in a frying pan over a medium heat. Add the shallots and sauté until tender and translucent.

Add the kohlrabi, increase the heat to high and stir-fry quickly for 2–4 minutes, depending on the root's age and thickness.

Season, reduce the heat and add the spring onion. Cook, stirring gently, until slightly wilted.

Pour the beaten eggs evenly over the kohlrabi, shallots and spring onion. Without touching it, let it sit for about 30 seconds, then use a spatula to gently flip over the mixture as though it were a big fritter. Do not worry if it does not remain all in one piece: the water content of the vegetables makes it unlikely it will stay together, and the real aim is to cook the eggs gently and quickly so they are still soft on the inside.

Plate the dish by simply sliding it out of the pan and garnishing it with the coriander. Serve with the nuoc cham or fish sauce dipping sauce on the side.

Bitter Melon Stuffed with Prawn

MƯỚP ĐẮNG NHỒ TÔM

The first time I ever tried bitter melon, my Chinese grandmother had cooked it in a soup. As the name implies, it is bitter – tremendously so. The dish stood out for me as my grandmother's food was always light, clean, and leaning towards a sweeter side of Chinese food. I figured anything tasting like that just had to be healthy! Bitter melon stimulates digestion and has been associated with the prevention of malaria and improving immune function.

My grandmother was pleased to see that I immediately acquired an appreciation for such a thing. You'll also find it in Indian cuisine, in curries.

SERVES 2

400g bitter melon

Filling

2 dried shiitake mushrooms

200g prawns, peeled and finely chopped

1/2 tsp very finely chopped shallot

1/4 tsp soy sauce

1/8 tsp salt

pinch of pepper

Soup

20g shiitake mushrooms

1/4 teaspoon salt

20g spring onions, cut into 7cm strips

For the filling, soak the shiitake mushrooms in hot water for 20 minutes or until soft.

Finely chop enough of the rehydrated mushrooms to fill 1 teaspoon and put in a mixing bowl with the prawns, shallot, soy sauce, salt and pepper. Mix well and let marinate for 5 minutes.

Cut the bitter melon into 2.5 cm slices and remove the soft centres with a melon-baller or cookie cutter. Pack the prawn mixture firmly into these space, ensuring there are no air bubbles.

In a large pan, bring 900ml water to a boil over a medium-high heat. Add the stuffed melon plus the shiitake mushrooms and salt. Reduce the heat to a simmer and cook for 30 minutes.

Remove the pan from the heat. Transfer the soup to serving bowls and garnish with spring onion. Serve with boiled rice on the side.

Rancid Tomato Juice (or Learning When to Buy a Customer a Drink)

It was early evening and, except for a few people at the bar, the restaurant was empty. It was my habit that, as Hanoi settled into the dark of night, I would keep bright lights on at the front of the restaurant, causing it to glow from the dark bustling Hang Kay Street, showing off the beautiful interiors. Red silk curtains and a well-appointed bar beckoning the weary tourists, expats and business people alike.

Once customers flowed in like moths to the flame and were settling down for their dinner, I would start slowly dimming the lights. As evening led on, with people moving from cocktails to wine and dinner, the restaurant would be transforming its ambience from the bright lights of come hither baby to the most romantic spot in town.

I was also now in the habit of not wearing my chef whites, to avoid appearing available for compliments and complaints, giving me more freedom to hang out with friends and chat undisturbed at the bar. Sitting on the left side of the bar were two of my favourite drinking guests, Hank and George. They were regulars and appeared to be just getting started on their first beers. More to the centre of the bar and separated by several empty bar stools, sat a woman I had never seen before. She was seemingly drinking on her own and her demeanour was such that I imagined that this was not unusual; she was not unattractive but had a very stern air about her. As I emerged from the silk curtains at the back of the restaurant, I smiled at the lads and sidled up to the bar.

'Gentlemen, I have a great story to tell you!?'

All ears, they eagerly smiled waiting for what would be a funny story. I sat in the empty stool closest to them and swivelled in their direction,

giving my back to the lone lady at the bar. As I turned my attention to by friends, I continued:

'Your gonna love this one!'

Behind me a loud demanding nasal voice caused my attention to move away from my buddies, now listening to what she was saying.

'Excuse me, sir, this pineapple juice tastes stale?'

Jeff, bartender extraordinaire, who doesn't do well with complaints, was at the washing station polishing wine glasses. I slowly rotated my chair in his direction; there was something in her tone of voice that I feared he might react badly to.

Sure enough, though she spoke loud and clear, Jeff merely gave her a quick stare as if looking over the top of non-existent reading glasses, then chose to ignore her, going back to his business with the wine glasses.

I could now see that he was in rough shape, dark bags under his bloodshot eyes and that 'I haven't had enough caffeine' look. His curly hair looked wild and unkempt as if he had just fallen out of bed minutes before work, not even having enough time to take a shower. He looked done in and fed up, and the night was just beginning.

'Excuse me, this pineapple juice tastes stale?'

She squawked more emphatically this time, now commanding the attentions of every one at the bar except Jeff.

Catching Jeff's eyes and with a pleading, sympathetic, smirk I hoped to get him to attend to our guests needs. Jeff had no smile for me or for her, his face was tight and aggravated, as if he had just been asked to perform a duty that offended him to his core. Putting down the wine glass and towel he slowly walked towards me, now sporting a forced smile, instantly dropping the smile as he confronted our complaining guest. He approached her in a deliberately slow manner, his gruesome leer a tight slash that scarred his bedraggled face. He moved into his position directly in front of the woman who, unfazed, stared right back at him with equal animosity. He picked up the glass and took a big exaggerated whiff of the frothy yellow juice.

'Funny, I just squeezed it.'

We all erupted with laughter and as I laughed, I protested.

'Come on Jeff! Lets be nice to our guests as we don't have many! Let's try just a wee bit!'

'Well, I just squeezed it!' He said with not the slightest note of apology, his gaze fixed firmly on the now intransigent woman.

Jeff then whips out a straw and proceeds to place it into the pineapple juice, then slowly, with his eyes still fixed on the guest, starts to stir the juice in slow motion.

That's when Hank, who also likes to stir things up, pipes in with, 'WHAT? You think that's going to make it tastes better?'

Jeff now turns his obstinate gaze to Hank and, with a tone dripping in disdain, asks, 'What? You never worked in a bar before?'

Placing his index finger over the top of the straw, he pulls it from the glass creating a vacuum to hold the collected juice; Jeff tilts his head back, releasing his index finger allowing the juice to spill into his mouth.

The woman shakes her head and, with a mocking tone, spits, 'What are you afraid of? Do you think I have cooties?'

Eyebrows raised and lips pursed, Jeff throws a look that says, 'Yes, absolutely!'

More peals of hysterical laughter from bystanders George and Hank, who are thoroughly enjoying the public showdown.

"Hank and George are now raucously laughing and the woman turning purple. Realizing she is now about to lose her cool, I step in and say. 'Oh come on Jeff! Let's try and be nice to our guest!'"

Jeff, placing the drink back in front of the lady and looking her straight in the eye says, 'Tastes fine to me!' He turns and walks back to the washing area and resumes polishing glasses.

Hank and George are now raucously laughing and the woman turning purple. Realizing she is now about to lose her cool, I step in and say. 'Oh come on Jeff! Let's try and be nice to our guest! Come on! You are like a New York bartender, but we have no customers! If we are really busy and the place was packed, I could understand, but we are practically empty!'

My identity as proprietor has now been given away, I throw her my most conciliatory smile.

'Madam, I am so sorry. Please let me make it up to you by getting you a drink. Please. It's on the house. Anything that you want!'

Jeff immediately throws me a displeased look, with venom filling his bloodshot eyes, and proceeds to come back slowly towards us, still polishing the red wine glass in hand. He places it on the bar next to her and with his arms spread wide across the bar top as if he was about to perform a push up, he leans towards her and says:

'How about some rancid tomato juice?'

We are now all howling like hyenas, any notion of telling a funny tale to the boys overshadowed by Jeff's sparring with the irate guest. I had to spend the rest of the evening making nice and plying her with free booze.

On the Ground
and In the Air

Probably the most widely consumed meat in all Vietnam is pork, as it is both cheap and abundant, whereas the consumption of red meat in particular is very much a demonstration of one's wealth. Even poultry was a sign of luxury for quite some time and up until not that long ago. Today it is often taken for granted that when ordering pho, one can order it with or with or without meat, depending on the budget. To this day, no part of the beast or bird goes to waste, and a quick stop at any wet market and you can find the entire anatomy of an animal displayed for sale. From the nostrils to tail, via the intestines, all the way to the hooves, you will find by the end of the day that it has all been sold.

Bisteeya with Steamed Pigeon

I learned this Moroccan speciality from my Egyptian grandmother, who made some of the tastiest North African food I've ever eaten. When I gave up working on Wall Street, I found hanging out in her kitchen very therapeutic and spent hours closely observing everything she did.

She'd take thin slices of onion together with stems from the herbs and lay them at the bottom of a pot to act as a base for the birds, which were then placed in it on their backs. She would then douse the pan with a little water to produce steam, sprinkle a very generous helping of cinnamon over the birds, cover and steam them over a very low simmer for about 30 minutes. She then turned off the heat and let them rest, still covered, until cool enough to handle.

She would strain the steaming juices, mix them with a beaten egg, then carefully work her way through each bird, stripping it of its tender meat and shredding this into smaller pieces until she had a large mixing bowl of the meat.

In a Pyrex pan, she would brush a layer of filo pastry generously with clarified butter and then sprinkle it with almonds, icing sugar and ground cinnamon. Then she covered this with another buttered filo sheet and top with an even layer of shredded pigeon and drizzle some of the egg over the meat. This was covered with another buttered filo sheet, then several similar layers of flavourings and meat, and a final sheet of filo. The package was baked until crisp and golden brown and served garnished with more icing sugar and cinnamon.

Crispy light filo with moist shredded pigeon perfumed with cinnamon was a real treat. I had to figure a way to serve it in individual portions. Here I was inspired by Greek *spanakopita*. I use the *bisteeya* either as an hors d'oeuvre or as a small first course, but by making more parcels, it can be used as a main course, topping these with grilled butterflied pigeons.

Bisteeya is a really easy dish to make, and it was an instant hit on the menu. I deviated from the classic recipe by using pigeon fat between the layers of filo instead of the classic clarified butter. (I would render the fat from the neck etc; you can always ask your butcher for any trimmings to make a stock - or indeed some of the fat.) To ensure the meat didn't dry out, I would add some of the braising liquid or throw in some chopped cooked spinach, with a very light hint of nutmeg, together with corn kernels, then top this with the shredded pigeon perfumed with the cinnamon.

Although I have made it a little more complicated, it is basically a simple dish to prepare. In Vietnam, however, there were many times when things did not turn out to be that simple. The *bisteeya* was on a tasting menu and all the mise en place was pretty much ready when sous-chef Huong, nicknamed 'Phuc Ka', showed me the last of the filo, which was mildewing at the edges. As there was no way we could use it, I asked him to call the supplier and get more – no more was to be found in Hanoi. 'What about rice paper?' he asked. We had no other option and necessity being the mother of invention, the recipe below resulted.

The only drawback of using rice paper is that I

find it can be rather salty, but since the dish is a cross between sweet and savoury, the sugar pretty much wipes out the saltiness. On the plus side, not only is rice paper easier to work with than filo, it is a hell of a lot quicker to cook. So, instead of baking these rice paper bundles, we actually cook them on the stove top, shortening the cooking time. You can used filo or rice paper, both taste great, but griddled rice paper is never quite as tender as baked filo.

SERVES 6

20g fresh whole coriander leaves
10g fresh dill
50g spring onions, sliced
100g celery, cut into strips
10 pieces pigeon or 300g boneless skinless pigeon
2 tbsp ground cinnamon
500g spinach
½ can corn kernels, drained
pinch of salt
pinch of freshly ground black pepper
3 tbsp icing sugar
20 sheets of rice paper or filo pastry
125g clarified butter or pigeon fat (see above)
150g shelled pistachio nuts, a quarter chopped very finely to a powder, the rest coarsely chopped
vegetable oil for frying

Scatter the coriander, dill, onions and celery evenly over the bottom of a pan. Place the birds on their backs on top of the herbs, with their breasts facing up. Add a couple of tablespoons of water, generously sprinkle with the cinnamon and put over a medium heat. Once the steam starts to rise, reduce the heat to low, place the cover on top and steam for about 30 minutes. Remove from the heat and let cool to room temperature, covered.

Once cool enough to handle, remove the meat from the bird, starting at the breast, stripping it away from the breastbone. I usually don't keep the skin, but some people like the additional fat as it adds moisture to the dish. Keep on stripping the birds until left with bare bones.

Blanch the spinach briefly in salted boiling water. Remove, then quickly refresh in a bath of cold water. This will help it retain its vibrant green colour, as well as stopping the cooking process. Remove from the water and squeeze out as much of the residual water as possible. On a chopping board, chop the spinach roughly. Throw it into the mixing bowl with the shredded meat. Add the corn kernels and fold these into the mixture. Taste and season with salt and pepper.

On a flat surface, lay out 4 pieces of rice paper and spray with a little bit of water. Once the paper becomes pliable. Brush 2 of the rice papers with clarified butter or pigeon fat. Sprinkle with the finely chopped pistachio, cinnamon and sugar, and then place the other rice paper on top.

Depending on the shape of your rice paper, you can pretty much make the bisteeya any shape you want. If the paper is square, it is easy to make rectangular bisteeya; if round, it is easy to make round bisteeya as well as rectangular ones. I like to use square rice paper and cut it so it becomes more rectangular. I place the long length of the paper running away from me, then put 10–20g of the mixture on the bottom left-hand corner a little in from the edge. Then I fold the bottom right hand corner over it, making a triangle. Then I repeat alternate foldings of left and right hand corners up, squeezing the mixture to ensure that it is nice and tight, until you have a nice triangle of rice paper stuffed with pigeon. Repeat with the remaining rice paper and mixture to make 10 parcels in all.

Cover these with a damp towel and be careful not to make them too wet, or the papers will stick and rip (so don't let them touch each other). If you cook them immediately, there should be no problem. You can either shallow-fry them in some hot oil, or roast them in an oven preheated to 180°C/Gas 4 for 2 minutes.

If using filo, I would brush them with more butter or pigeon fat and roast them to get a crisp golden finish, but when I use rice paper I like to sear the bisteeya as the rice paper is much quicker to cook and it is easier to gauge the doneness of the dish.

Small bite-sized bisteeya, make great hors d'oeuvres or just serve larger ones on a plate.

Barbecue Pork Ribs

When it comes to cooking, I learned just as much from a well-read amateur foodie as I have done from the master chefs. My childhood friend, David Bransten and I would cook at weekend baseball games for many of his other friends. It was a lot of fun. Through the years, the recipes we tried became more and more complicated, and in order to show off our culinary skills, we started trying more and more technically difficult food with ever more expensive ingredients.

We went from BBQ chicken, to lobster risotto, and learning to cook with a pressure cooker. Daniel Boulud, Alain Ducasse, Charlie Trotter, you name them, we read the cookbooks of the greatest chefs we could get our hands on, then did our very best to duplicate the hardest dishes imaginable. We would look at the picture, read through the recipe, and then decide which dishes we would do. We grew as cooks, with both of us imparting ideas, as well as opinions of the best way to cook a particular cut of meat, or a soft shell crab or whatever.

After several years in Vietnam, I returned to San Francisco incredibly proud of all the new techniques and dishes I had created as well as the Vietnamese dishes I knew David loved. But when I eventually I got the opportunity to share my secrets with him, he cut me short and started to tell me how he was the greatest barbecue master in the Bay Area. I smiled, as this was coming from one of the humblest people I knew.

'Dude, I am embarrassed to say it - I do not want to say it - but Leon [the best BBQ joint in San Francisco] has nothing on me! This Jew can cook better then any of the BBQ places here in the city!'

'Dude, I believe you.'

David had just finished filming a one-off documentary on barbecue, based on a book by Lolis Eli, 'Smoke Stacks and Lighting', which had taken him more than a year to make. In the process he had learned the many different styles of barbecuing, from Texas to South Carolina, filming the masters of the craft as they shared their secret recipes.

'Dude, you have to use pork! I know you're a Muslim, but it's an incredible piece of meat and by using spice rubs and different types of wood, it has the ability to develop incredible flavour.' So the Muslim got to learn to cook pork from the Jew.

So we have a brine, a mixture of salt or vinegar and sugar in water, in which we marinate the meat. Brining meats seems to make everything just a little juicer. A sugar vinegar brine with some spices was already made and in the fridge. We dumped the pork shoulders in this and marinated it for 2 days. Meanwhile, we made a spice rub, consisting of numerous different dry spices all whipped into a mixture quite different from anything I'd known before. After 2 days of brining, the meat was marinated in this dry rub for another 2 days in the refrigerator. Then we'd cook it, and that took literally an entire day.

I figured this wasn't such a big deal, as cooking for an entire day to me meant just letting it simmer for that time. Not with barbecue. We needed to make sure the temperature remained the same throughout the cooking process and this requires constant attention, as the heat of the wood could vary over the day.

An important element is the type of wood used. We would change the woods constantly, as the different types of woods imparted different types of flavour, plus some woods would drive the temperature higher. So there we were, moving wood to the fire throughout the day, switching between apple wood and hickory.

I sat there staring at the meats that now rested on the countertop in the kitchen, waiting for them to be cool enough to handle, rather like waiting for the turkey to be carved on Thanksgiving.

'It's called 'pulled pork sandwich',' said David. 'You pull the pork, shredding it like it's string cheese.' More work? Five days and still nothing to eat.

While the meat rested, we made the sauce by simply mixing vinegar, ketchup and molasses with the leftover dry rub. There was no measurement, it was all about tasting and adjusting. One taste made me wonder why the hell we ever bought proprietary BBQ sauce. It was just that easy, as well as much tastier.

Once the pork was cool enough to touch, I started stripping away the meat, pulling pieces into small strands. I was so curious to taste it that I put a piece straight into my mouth, flabbergasted at how

it took on all these different flavours, while remaining juicy and tender. I had never experienced such incredible flavour development or change in anything like that in barbecuing.

The Jew had taught the Muslim, and the Muslim now wanted to add pork to his repertoire, without all the work. I did eventually come up with a method that was pretty simple, and I was able to create smoke a little less traditionally, without the time and the wood. It was another technique I had picked up from my Chinese grandmother and is the one used in the recipe here.

I liked the results so much I started to smoke many different pieces of meat, from pork to lamb, to birds, to fish, it was a new flavouring technique that would generate wide attention.

The barbecued pork ribs were very well received and considered better then those of my arch rivals. Nina Simons from *Gourmet* magazine loved them so much that she added them to the prestigious October Restaurant Issue. One busy night, I received a call from someone claiming to be calling from New York on behalf of *Gourmet*. It was Nina and she proceeded to tell me that she had heard that I made a wicked pork rib and wanted the recipe. There I was at the other end of the line from the most popular food magazine getting asked how to cook pork! My mind quickly concluded that the culinary world was in dire straits. If Gourmet has to call Vietnam to ask for a pork recipe from a Muslim who had learned it from a Jew, then things just weren't right in the food world.

SERVES 2

1 kg pork ribs
1 litre brine (see page 145)
Asian slaw of shredded cucumber, daikon, carrot and red cabbage, to serve
Dry rub
75g brown sugar
15g ground paprika
25 garlic salt
1 tbsp ground black pepper
1 tbsp onion powder
1 tbsp chilli powder
½ tsp ground dried sage

1 tbsp yellow mustard powder
¼ tsp cayenne powder
¼ tsp dried thyme
Vinegar-based barbecue sauce
125ml cider vinegar
250ml apple juice
5 tbsp tomato ketchup
5 tbsp molasses
10g chilli flakes
black pepper
For the smoking
dry rice
sugar
green tea

First marinate the ribs in the brine for 3 hours.

To make the dry rub, combine all the ingredients well. Store in an airtight container in a cupboard for use as required.

To make the sauce, combine the ingredients in a saucepan. Bring to the boil, then reduce the heat and simmer for about 20 minutes. While the sauce is cooking, throw in about half the dry rub. It is pretty much up to you how much you use.

Clean the ribs and trim off excess fat. Cut each in half (to about 6 cm lengths), then steam over a pan of simmering water until cooked through and tender. I cook them until tender enough to pull the bone from the meat freely. Cover and leave to cool.

Make a thick layer of dry rice in the bottom of a large pot, create some indentations in that and sprinkle sugar into these. Put the pot over a high heat until the sugar starts to burn, then scatter dry green tea on top. When that starts to smoke, rub the ribs with the some remaining spice rub until nicely coated and set on a steaming rack over the smoking tea, cover the pot and take off the heat. Leave to smoke for at least 20 minutes. Get a barbecue good and hot.

Cook the smoked ribs on the barbecue for about 4 minutes on each side.

Place the cooked ribs on a cutting board, sprinkle about a tablespoon of dry rub over them and chop through every 2 ribs. Drizzle some sauce on top of the ribs and serve them with Asian Slaw.

Grilled Lemon Grass Beef

BỜ NƯỚNG SẢ ỚT

This is a very simple dish to make and we usually serve these rolls with chicken satay or prawns on sugar cane or the seafood satay. They do very well at cocktail parties. The only issue I have with barbecue dishes is the use of marinades or basting sauces containing sugar as it is then easy to burn the meats - not to mention the mess they end up leaving on a grill. I like to throw on my sauces at the very end, where they will help caramelize the meat and add smoke but give less of a risk from burning. I also like to use fillet steak here as it is incredibly tender and I also like to serve it medium-rare. For better presentation at VIP functions, etc, I also use the lemon grass stalks as skewers.

SERVES 2

3 tbsp sugar

4 bamboo skewers or 12–15 lemon grass stalks, plus 3 tbsp finely chopped lemon grass (white parts only)

200g lean fillet steak, cut into 1 cm cubes

2 tsp finely chopped shallot

2 Thai bird's-eye chillies, finely chopped

2 tbsp finely chopped garlic

5 tbsp vegetable oil

¼ tsp salt

¼ tsp freshly ground black pepper

20 lettuce leaves

15 rice papers

250 g herbs, such as coriander, shiso, Thai basil or dill

125ml Nuoc Cham sauce (see page 43)

In mixing bowl, combine the sugar with 3 tablespoons water and reserve for later use.

Soak the bamboo sticks in hot water. If using lemon grass stalks as skewers, cut away the top leafy part of each and trim the base to resemble the tip of a pencil.

In another large mixing bowl, place the beef, lemon grass, shallots, chilli, garlic and 1 tablespoon of the oil. Mix well, making sure that all of the ingredients are well incorporated. Cover and marinate for 30 minutes in the refrigerator.

Preheat a hot grill or barbecue. Pierce the meat cubes with the tip of the skewer, threading them through so you can fit about 3-5 pieces on the top two-thirds of each skewer, or however many you feel comfortable cooking at one time. If you are using lemon grass, keep it to no more than 2 pieces on each stalk.

Once all the meat is on the skewers, quickly season them with salt and pepper and brush the skewers with the remaining oil to prevent sticking. Cook, turning them over every 1–2 minutes, depending on the thickness.

When they are close to being done, as a final touch, finish the skewers with a splash of the sugar water. This will help achieve additional smoke and caramelization so the meat is a little crisp in places without getting too burnt. Alternatively, you can just brush them with the sugar mixture without them returning to the grill, to give it a sweet finish.

Serve with lettuce, rice papers and herbs. Just remove the meat from the skewers and make your own spring rolls with or without the rice paper – just wrap them in the lettuce leaves. Serve with Nuoc Cham sauce for dipping.

Braised Short Ribs of Beef

One of my suppliers wanted me to add short ribs to my menu. I had previously been invited to host a dinner using many cuts of meats from GOP – not the Grand Old (Republican) Party but the Greater Omaha Packing. The guest chef was introducing us to many different cuts of meats that were not readily available in Vietnam, one of the them being the short rib of beef.

This was usually found in Korean barbecues, where the ribs are cut through the bones into smaller pieces and then, using a zigzag cutting technique, through the thick marbled beef down to the bone, so that it could then be rolled out thinly and barbecued. The meat is very flavourful.

I didn't want to duplicate the Korean grilling technique, and instead opted for a long slow cooking method. I decided to cook the short ribs in the same seasoning as used in the Vietnamese version of beef jerky, and braise them in a mixture of nuoc cham sauce, sugar and water.

SERVES 8 AS AN APPETIZER OR 2 AS A MAIN
COURSE

8 short ribs of beef, cut about 5cm thick
Salt and freshly ground black pepper
3 tbsp vegetable oil
750ml Nuoc Cham sauce (page 43)
2 star anise
5cm piece of cinnamon stick
1 daikon, peeled and cut into pieces about 5cm
long
1 lotus root, boiled until tender, refreshed in cold
water, cut into 2.5cm slices and kept under
cold water
100g spinach
5 tablespoons finely chopped coriander

Season the ribs with salt and pepper. In a hot pan
over medium-to-high heat, sear the ribs in a little
oil until the skin is lightly coloured.

Place the ribs in the Nuoc Cham sauce in a
saucepan and bring to the boil, then reduce the
heat to a simmer. Add the star anise and
cinnamon stick, and leave to braise until the meat
is tender, 2–3 hours. After about 1 hour of
cooking, add the daikon slices.

In another pot filled with boiling water, boil
the lotus root until tender, about 1 hour.

Just before serving, add the spinach and lotus
root slices to the hot broth in which the ribs are
cooking until the spinach leaves are just wilted.

Arrange the lotus root slices over each plate,
spoon the spinach over them and arrange the
braised daikon on the outer rim of the plate. Pour
the broth over the vegetables and top with the
ribs. Garnish with coriander and a little pepper.

Minced Pork Omelette

TRUNG DUC THIT

This is a classic Vietnamese dish that is another
one of my favourites for staff meals, as it is simple
to prepare. Although I do not eat pork, this can
be easily replaced with minced chicken or
prawns. Simply put, this is another one of the
many dishes that I consider 'comfort food' and is
rather like a Vietnamese take on a frittata. In this
recipe you can also use crab and oysters in place
of the pork with very pleasing results. Fish sauce

is often used this dish, but I have taken it out, as I
don't find it necessary. I generally feel that the
saltiness of the fish sauce is a way to encourage
the eating of rice.

There is a scene in the movie 'Scent of a
Green Papaya' where the wife turns to the
housekeeper to inform her that her husband has
run off and lost all their money gambling. As a
result they were left with very little funds. She
gives the housekeeper the limited money
remaining and tells her that it has to last the rest
of the month. She requests that she add more fish
sauce and salt, which would ensure copious
amounts of rice were eaten to dilute the saltiness
of the dish. This is still common practice. For
some staff meals, I get complaints that the food is
too salty. When I check, the usual excuse from the
kitchen, is, 'Sorry, there wasn't enough food so we
had to make it salty. Delivery man show up late.'

Should you want to make it a little salty, just
add a tablespoon of fish sauce to the mix below.

SERVES 4

250g minced pork
4 spring onions, chopped
6 eggs
2 tbsp vegetable oil
bunch of fresh coriander, to serve
2 tbsp fish sauce, to serve
1/2 tsp chopped chilli, to serve

In a large bowl, mix the pork, spring onions and
eggs well, breaking up the pork into smaller
pieces – a fork is quite useful for this task or
chopsticks are traditionally used, whichever
tickles your fancy.

Place a sauté pan over medium heat and coat
it well with oil. Slowly pour in the egg mixture.
Move the mixture around by tipping and the pan,
ensuring that it cooks equally. Turn the heat
down to low, cover the pan and cook for about
5 minutes more. The eggs should be cooked, but
check by putting the fork into the mixture: if it is
still soft and undercooked, remover the cover and
cook for another 2–3 minutes.

Using a spatula, free the eggs from the
bottom and sides of the pan from all round. It is

key to make sure that nothing is sticking, so that it will be easy for you to flip it over on to the other side. If the eggs stick, just pour a little more oil into the pan to help it cook a little more, making it easier for you. If you do not have enough confidence to flip it over, simply place a plate above the pan and turn both pan and plate over together, and then slide the eggs on the plate back into the pan, to cook the top side of the omelette. Continue to cook until both sides are golden brown and the sides are firm.

To plate, simply slide it out of the pan, and cut across in 5 slices and then again at right angles to the first cuts. Serve scattered with coriander and chilli, and sprinkled with the fish sauce.

Chicken Wings Cooked in Caramel Sauce and Ginger CÁNH GÀ KHO GỪNG

These chicken wings are quite addictive and, with the combination of the smoky bitter-sweetness of caramel and the spiciness from the ginger, you really can't say no to another wing.

The sauce here is quite strong and in the South, they have a tendency to take the sauce and reduce it even further, requiring it to be diluted with rice, vegetables or anything else you can get your hands on.

Either way, these wings are ridiculously tasty and I always find myself licking my fingers, so I can just be undisciplined and grab yet another one.

SERVES 3

700g chicken wings
20g fresh ginger, finely shredded
3 tbsp Caramel Sauce (page 137), at room
    temperature
½ tsp salt
3 tbsp sugar
2 tbsp fish sauce
1 tsp freshly ground black pepper
Asian slaw of shredded cucumber and daikon
    (optional)

Cut each wing into its 3 main pieces: the main wing joint, the second joint and the wing tip. I usually save the tips for stock, unless I am totally famished or serving some cheap-ass friends.

In a saucepan, add the chicken wing pieces and shredded ginger to the room temperature caramel sauce. Add the salt, sugar, fish sauce, pepper and 500ml water. Over high heat, bring the mixture to a rapid boil, then reduce the heat to low and simmer, stirring occasionally, for 30-40 minutes, or until the chicken is very tender. Skim off any excess fat.

Serve on a bed of Asian Slaw if you like. Note: You can grill these wings as well, but the high sugar content makes them liable to burn, plus it makes a mess of the grill, which is always a pain to clean. The option is to brush the sauce over the wings once the wings have been grilled.

BC's Grilled Chicken Wings

CÁNH GÀ NƯỚNG BOBBY CHINN

This dish was learned by total and utter luck, as well as two years' perseverance. I used to drink at a bar called the 'Relax Bar' on the corner of Le Trung Kiet Street, after I got kicked out of Miró's. It was a watering hole that attracted a lot of beer drinkers, especially among the Australian fraternity, as their old diplomatic compound was right around the corner.

It was one of the first bars that expats would hang out at, as the beer was cheap, they played pretty good music and it was a pretty good place to get the gossip on what was going on back then.

It also however had a sleaze variable attached to it, as the bar was attached to a salon where you could get your hair washed for $3.00 from pretty sexy women. What I always loved about the place was that a haircut costs less then the hair washing! A haircut was only $2.00!

So I'm in the bar and I am watching this woman that has a Beer Hoi next door to the bar (Beer Hoi's are cheap locally produced beer that sells relatively cheap but very good Vietnamese food that is generally served at room temperature) The lady dressed in her pyjamas would reach into the side of a lamp post and proceed to remove large wooden skewers from the side of a lamppost that was left out overnight from the night before. She proceeded to pierce chicken thighs and chicken wings one by one, placing them in a bucket that sat on the sidewalk. It would sit there in glaring heat marinating in finely chopped lemon grass. She has a little rectangular grill that was locally fabricated. And then proceeded to grill them as she sat on the side of a tree fanning them by hand. As I watched this I tuned to the guy sitting next to me and asked:

"Do you know anybody that has ever eaten this women's chicken?"

He looked at me somewhat dumbfounded and asked me, "You mean to tell me that you have never had chicken from her?"

"I am not about to eat chicken from the side of the road that are skewered with wooden skewers from the night before and have been stored in the side of a frigging lamp post! Especially in this heat!

He proceeded to tell me that those were most probably the best-grilled chicken I would ever eat in my life. I immediately ordered them and was addicted. They were perfectly cooked, moist in the inside and crispy on the outside, but what makes these chicken wings so good is the out-of-this-world sauce that was spicy hot with just the right amount of sweetness... not to mention the little bites of lemon grass.

I made it a mission to find out the recipe! Several other chefs who frequented the bar told me different recipes. Each one had their interpretation, but none of them actually knew it or tried to duplicate it. I would order chicken thighs and wings close to 3 times a week. I would get a little bag of sauce and go back to the restaurant and try to recreate the flavour without any success.

One day I ordered the thighs and she didn't have any sauce left. I started to make faces and grunt and moan until she gave me some sauce. The next minute she made some right in front of me. It was so simple I started laughing. She, of course, did not find it amusing to be making a small batch of sauce just for me at the end of the night.

I went back to the restaurant and made it myself, and it was perfect. The lady then stopped making her chicken, as her Beer Hoi really took off and she focussed more on the beer.

If you love chicken wings, here is another alternative to consider. These are grilled and what

makes them great is the execution and the subtle balance of the sauce coupled with the punctuation of the lemon grass, as opposed to the sweeter, almost braise-like Chicken Wings Cooked in Caramel Sauce with Ginger on page 133.

SERVES 1 HUNGRY AMERICAN OR 4 VIETNAMESE

15 chicken wings
3 lemon grass stalks, finely chopped
4 tbsp oyster sauce
4 tbsp chilli sauce
2 tsp honey
1 cucumber, cut into ribbons using a potato peeler
3 carrots, cut into ribbons using a potato peeler

Place the chicken wings in a bowl with the lemon grass. Cover with cling film and leave to marinate for about 3 hours.

Whisk the oyster and chilli sauces together with 2 tablespoons water and the honey, then set aside. Preheat the barbecue.

Score the wings with a knife to ensure they cook evenly and help create more smoke. Place them on the barbecue and cook for 5 minutes on each side until just cooked.

Then brush with some oyster sauce mixture. It is important not to put the sauce on until the wings are completely cooked or the high sugar content will cause them to burn and get bitter.

Place the cucumber and carrot ribbons on a plate and top with the chicken wings. Serve with a drizzle of the remaining sauce.

Caramel Ginger Chicken

GÀ CARAMEN SỐT GỪNG

I am often asked why I moved to Vietnam, and after many tellings, the truth is boring and too long. One day, therefore, I decided to say, 'Because I like the smell of fish sauce first thing in the morning.' It was, of course, a sarcastic response, but years of living here, and of being in countless eating establishments where a passing clay pot steaming out pungent wafts of caramel fish sauce, had made me realize that I don't mind the smell of fish sauce any more.

I am sure this dish had something to do with my change in attitude. It is one of the most

common dishes in Vietnam, where the flavours can be dramatically different from north to south, where the saltiness and sweetness vary depending on where the influence is from; southern influences being usually much bolder, with the sauce more reduced to intensify the sweet and salty flavours, while in the North everything is much more subtle. It is not uncommon for pieces of pork fat or lard to be used to enrich the sauce in both the North and South, but due to my Islamic upbringing, I have omitted the pork to redeem myself just a bit.

As it does not go bad, my suggestion is that you make a lot of caramel sauce at one go, and you then have it for use over a long time.

You can make this dish with anything, substituting pork, prawns or even fish for the chicken. This is one of my all time favourite dishes: when served in a clay pot, I literally go gaga over it. It is an example of great Vietnamese food, as it provides incredible layers of flavours, from sweet and salty, mild spice from the chilli and the addition of ginger giving it a real lift.

SERVES 4

900g boneless, skinless chicken thighs, cut into 5 cm cubes

2 tbsp vegetable oil

steamed rice , to serve

Marinade

1 tsp sugar

2 tbsp fish sauce

2 tbsp chopped shallot

2 tbsp finely chopped garlic

freshly ground black pepper

1 green chilli, finely chopped

juice squeezed from 5 cm (40 g) ginger, which is then finely chopped

Caramel Sauce

200g brown sugar

4 tsp fish sauce

750ml hot chicken stock or water

1 chilli, cut in half

1 tsp lime juice

1 small cinnamon stick or 1 teaspoon ground cinnamon powder (optional)

1 tsp black peppercorns (optional)

Garnish

2.5cm ginger, cut into julienne strips

2 spring onions, cut into 5 cm lengths

5 sprigs of coriander

Combine all the marinade ingredients in a mixing bowl, reserving the chopped ginger, and mix in the chicken well. Cover and marinate in the refrigerator for an hour.

Make the caramel sauce: put the brown sugar in a pan (ideally with high sides) over medium heat and cook it slowly until melted, making sure it does not burn at the edges. Once fully melted, turn the heat up and stir, making sure the sugar browns equally and uniformly. Be very careful, as the sugar can cause a wicked burn.

Once the sugar is just a little bit darker, turn the heat off to prevent overcooking of the caramel, remove your hand and spoon from the pot, and quickly pour the fish sauce into the caramel. (The sauce should be at room temperature, not chilled). Do this very carefully, as it will splatter violently. Add the 500ml of hot stock or water to thin the sauce, then add the chilli and lime juice. The hot liquid will prevent the sugar from crystallizing, but if it already has, just cook it longer until it dissolves. Reduce the heat and add the reserved chopped ginger. You can also add the cinnamon and peppercorns if you wish a little heat.

In a separate pan, place the vegetable oil over medium-to-high heat and wait until it is close to smoking point. Add the marinated chicken mixture to the saucepan; stirring well to prevent burning (the sugar helps caramelize the chicken, but it is at risk of burning if it is not stirred). This is a quick stir-fry, as you only cook the outside of the chicken in the pan for approximately for 2 minutes, and the majority is cooked in a pot.

Transfer the chicken to a pot (ideally a clay pot) and deglaze the pan with the remaining stock, transferring all the caramelized juices to the pot. Simmer the chicken in the pot until cooked and the liquid has reduced by one-quarter to a half. You may also reuse the sauce, but store it in the refrigerator and bring it to the boil again first.

Serve garnished with ginger julienne, spring onions and coriander, and accompanied by rice.

Chicken Curry, Vietnamese style

CÀ-RI GÀ

When I first arrived in Vietnam in 1996, I slowly worked my way through the restaurants. When I lost my job, though, I had to ration my money but, in fact, great food could be found very cheaply on any street corner. Although there was a huge selection from which to choose, it would get tiring at times, when the summer heat and humidity started to determine where one would eat, more for the presence of a fan than for the food.

Air-conditioned restaurants came at a premium, and an open restaurant's fan would also come at a premium in relationship to the street stalls. The cheaper restaurants could be found in the back-packing district of Pham Ngu Lao. There was a long restaurant by the name of Kim Café that was packed with locals, expats and tourists alike. On the outskirts of the room were oscillating fans that would swing a welcomed breeze for a couple of seconds at a time.

There was something very comforting about curry on a hot day, but the Vietnamese curry is very different from all the other curries I have ever had. Although I love the gee-enriched curries of the Punjab, as well as the coconut-rich curries of Malaysia and Thailand, the Vietnamese curry is light and sweet, yet retaining the fine spicing characteristic of a curry. The spiciness is more mellow, almost passive, in comparison to the curries of its neighbours.

I was a regular at Kim Café, usually ordering the curry for consistency and speed – they served it literally in 3 minutes from the placing of the order. Served on an oval plastic plate, a mould of steaming hot rice from an inverted bowl, with a quarter of a potato and a breast of chicken, cooked tenderly and served warm, drenched with a light curry sauce and garnished with star anise.

This was not the place to get a recipe, but it was clear to me that the curry spice mixture was something very special. You just can't buy any curry spice or paste. It really needs to be Vietnamese and there are some types that are worth searching for, like Three Bells brand.

My first attempts at making a curry were very ill-fated. Attempting to make an Indian curry in college, I failed miserably. I then tried it again before venturing into a professional kitchen and that almost killed my confidence completely. Eventually, moving to Asia, I got to observe the early morning Thai markets and watched them over and over again.

The Vietnamese curry is a cross between the Indian and the Thai. In many Indian curries, the base is the mixture of dry spices that are ground and sautéed with onions and garlic over ghee: whereas in Thailand, they would make a fresh spice mixture by grinding the chillies, lemon grass, galangal, peppercorns, and shrimp paste as a base. In Vietnam, it is a combination of the two, sautéing some of the ingredients in their fresh form and then adding the dry spices which are introduced exactly the way it is in Indian Cuisine.

If you prefer a thin curry, you can use more water or stock instead of the richer coconut cream. Many of us expect our curries to be rich and hearty, but the Kim Café version is light and well balanced, and a nice departure from the traditional rich curries that I grew up loving. Although it is a classic, it is modern and light, perfumed with star anise. Try this dish when it is summer. I have not added much chilli as the Vietnamese don't go for very spicy, especially up north – you can use as much as you feel like.

SERVES 2

6 fresh lemon grass stalks (about 100g)

½ onion or 12 shallots, thinly sliced

1 tbsp finely chopped ginger

1 tbsp crushed and finely chopped garlic cloves

5 tbsp vegetable oil

3 tbsp curry powder

2 tsp chilli powder

2 skinless chicken thighs, cut into 2.5cm pieces

salt and freshly ground black pepper

1 litre water or chicken stock

250g (2) potatoes, pared and cut into 2.5 cm cubes

250g (2) carrots, peeled and cut into 2.5cm pieces

3 star anise

125ml coconut milk

sugar to taste

8 coriander sprigs, to garnish

steamed rice, to serve

First prepare the lemon grass by discarding the outer leaves and cutting off the coarse upper half of the stalks to retain the lighter-coloured lower stalks. Chop these finely and reserve. Finely chop the onion or shallots, ginger and garlic. Using a mortar and pestle, or a food processor, purée all these to a paste, adding a little water if necessary.

Put 3 tablespoons of the oil in a pot over medium-high heat. When close to smoking-hot, sauté the fresh spice mixture in it until the pan is dry. Then add the dry spices. Cook, stirring, until these are well incorporated, about 3 minutes.

Season the chicken with salt and pepper, and sauté until it is completely sealed and browned all over, and well coated with the spices. Remove from the pan and set aside.

Add the stock or water to the pan, first drizzling it in just a little at a time to deglaze the bottom of the pan and then pour in the rest.

Add the potatoes and carrots, and bring to the boil. Add the star anise and reduce the heat to just simmering. Cook for 15–20 minutes or until the carrots are tender. Add the browned chicken to the simmering curry and cook for about 8 minutes, until the chicken is cooked through.

At this stage your curry will still taste bland and potentially rather horrible – don't freak! Stir in the coconut milk and season one more time with salt and then sugar. Stir well, garnish with the coriander and serve with steamed rice.

Poached Chicken in a medicinal broth GA TAN

This recipe really is one of a kind. The ingredients can only be found in one place, and that is a Chinese herbalist. One of the issues with a cookbook like this is availability of ingredients, but I made this dish for a press dinner in London and picked up the essentials on the streets of Soho.

This medicinal soup originated in China and can be found in many Asian countries with a Chinese community. Although I have yet to see it in Ho Chi Minh City (Saigon), there is a street in Hanoi known as 'Food Street' or Tong Duy Tan Street where it is served at night. I have also seen a packet version on sale in a Saigon supermarket.

I was introduced to the soup by a friend who had a serious case of hepatitis and he told me that it was a very good for headaches and your blood as well as for women menstruating (when was the last time you opened up a cookbook and found a recipe where hep and menstruation are in the same sentence?) One sip of the almost black broth converted me. There were pieces of ginseng that just tasted healthy, while a reddish-looking fruit that they called a Chinese apple about the size of a date, imparted a little smokiness.

In the middle of the bowl lay a baby chicken cut into pieces. The chicken is usually picked out of the broth and dipped into a salt, pepper and lime mixture, where chillies can be added for additional spice.

I was taught to make this dish by my sous-chef Huong (Phuc Ca), after struggling to figure out how to source the ingredients. There were no words for them in English. For years, neither the vendors that sold it nor my foodie friends could tell me any of the ingredients. I could not find them in any of the Vietnamese cookbooks that I own and the market was not helpful either. I was pretty much lost. Then it occurred to me that maybe I should just go to a Chinese herbalist and ask for the soup that gets rids of headaches, etc.

There he stood, weighing ingredient after ingredient, and one by one he would dump them into a brown paper sheet. Rolling it up, he instructed me to boil them up and then drink it like a soup. I walked away with a bunch of nameless ingredients to make a dish that I simply adored.

I have perfected this dish over the years, and it did not faze me that I could not list out the ingredients, as I understood the dish and the flavours. To tell you the truth, the only reason I know the names now is because of writing this book. I had to send one of my staff out to get the exact names. Doctor Hieu at the East West Medical Center gave me the answers that had eluded me for more then a decade.

This dish is often made with pigeon, and I later learned from another vendor that you can stuff the pigeon into a coke can that has had the top removed with a can opener, leaving a closed end cylinder, and cook it in the can with its liquid - one way to sell it 'to go' as well as retain the

wonderful shape and juices of the bird. The cooking technique varies from vendor to vendor and I prefer my way, although it is more labour-intensive and more costly, but the presentation is refined and the flavours are more intense. In the recipe below, I just give the basic recipe as my more complex method might deter you from making this otherwise rather simple, easy dish.

In my version I bone the pigeon, removing the carcass and leaving a 'jump suit' of chicken meat. I stuff many of the ingredients into this and add some roughly chopped mushrooms, lotus seeds and precooked barley into the hollowed-out bird, so that it is totally boneless except for the tibia (lower leg bone) and the first segment of the wing (humerus), making it very easy to eat. I also like to make the broth with chicken stock rather than water. I marinate it in a dark stock as made below, and use the dark stock to make an even darker stock.

The proportions given here are those specified by the Chinese herbalist. He had a different method and also added dried lily petals. I also like to add more libosch, which is a dark, tar-like ingredient that imparts all the colour. The Chinese mugwort is a rather fibrous green and is supposed to reduce fatigue and stimulate the nervous system.

SERVES 5

5 baby chickens, pigeons or quails
25g oppositifolius yam (Hoai Son)
25g ginseng (Cu Sam)
3 tbsp lotus seeds (Hat Sen)
3 tbsp medlar seeds (Ky Tu)
25g adenophoro (Sa Sam)
25g dried lily petals (Bach Hop) (optional)
50g libosch (baccar)
100g Chinese mugwort or rocket or spinach
5 tsp salt
pinch of freshly ground pepper
juice of 1 lime

Clean the chicken thoroughly under cold running water. Place it in a pot with all of the other ingredients except the Chinese mugwort or greens and the salt, pepper and lime juice, then cover the chicken with water. Bring to the boil and then reduce the heat and simmer for 20 minutes. Skim off the scum that rises to the top. After the 20 minutes, remove it from the heat and allow to return to room temperature.

When the chicken is cool enough to handle, remove it from the broth and cut the bird into smaller pieces, leg, breasts etc.

Take the broth and reduce it by a quarter of its volume for a more intense flavour.

When you are ready to serve, bring the broth back up to the boil and then add the Chinese mugwort or greens and blanch until they are wilted.

Serve with a pepper-lime-salt mixture.
Note: The one ingredient that makes the broth dark is libosch. It is called 'Thuc' in Vietnamese. I like to add more of this to get the lovely rich dark colour.

Duck à la Banana

This dish owes its origins to the movie 'Four Weddings and a Funeral' with Hugh Grant. During the funeral scene, when the eulogy mentioned that the deceased had invented dishes like 'Duck à la Banana', I laughed out loud. My challenge was to make a dish called 'duck à la banana' work. It came to me very quickly, with the idea of using banana blossoms, a classic Vietnamese salad generally made with shredded chicken. In this dish I decided to change it around, making the salad a little more unconventional, with shredded duck confit, duck prosciutto and a light ginger sauce.

Duck prosciutto was the real twister in Vietnam and getting people to eat house-cured duck meat was a challenge, but once someone tried it, they would go back to it again and again. I picked up the prosciutto idea from renowned San Francisco chef Gary Danko, although Mark Franz from Stars was probably one of the first chefs to introduce the idea there way back when. I had eaten it at Stars and I just thought it was a real great flavour and texture, clueless of why no one else was making it. Years later, hanging out with Gary Danko, when he had me in to do a cooking demo, he talked about duck to an audience of 70-odd paying guests attending this high-end cooking demo at Draeger's in Palo Alto. I learned everything I wanted to know about duck that evening… That the ancient Egyptians were the first to domesticate the over-fed ducks that migrated from Europe during the winter months. That they discovered the oversized livers (foie gras) were such a delicacy that they decided to force-feed them figs. Then the later development of the idea of preserving and storing duck for months, by confiting them and storing them in duck fat. How to render fat from the breasts and the rest of the bird to preserve livers and gizzards, and obviously, curing the breast like Parma ham to yield a wonderful cured meat that has now been dubbed duck prosciutto.

Gary marinates his duck with traditional herbs from the West like dried thyme and bay leaf. What I do is add Asian spices, then give it a little smoke to impart a wonderful Asian flavour - star anise, nutmeg, coriander and peppercorn. You could just as well as use a little coating of Asian five-spice mixture with very pleasing results.

What I do is freeze the duck breast before I do this dish. The reason is that I want to render the additional duck fat, and it is easier to cut the fat when it is frozen. The key is to give the breast a very thin sheet of fat over the breast.

SERVES 5

Duck Prosciutto

1 large frozen breast of duck (about 500g)
1 tsp sea salt
1 tbsp sugar
1 star anise
1/4 tsp freshly grated nutmeg
1 bay leaf
1 tsp coarsely ground coriander seed
1/2 tsp coarsely ground black peppercorns
5 lemon grass stalk, finely chopped
1/2 Duck Confit (page 63), torn
À la Blossom Banana Salad
250g banana flower, sliced
50g cucumber, cut into julienne strips
25g carrot, cut into julienne strips

2 lime leaves, thinly sliced
1/4 tsp fragrant knotweed (rau ram)
pinch of salt and freshly ground black pepper
4 tbsp Nuoc Cham sauce (see page 43)
Optional garnish
1 tbsp ginger syrup
1 tbsp Lemon Oil (see page 49)

You need to start making the prosciutto about a month ahead. While the duck is still frozen, cut the fat from the skin side (it is then much easier to do – but do take care, as the knife can easily slip on the frozen fat). Make sure to leave a thin layer of the fat on the duck breast. On the flesh side, remove the connective tissue.

Once the duck breast has thawed out, place it in a roasting pan, skin side down. Mix the salt, sugar, star anise, nutmeg, bay, coriander seed, pepper and lemon grass, then spread this over the duck, making sure it is completely covered. Cover with cling film, then a baking tray and weight down with cans or similar (the more weight the better) and leave to cure for 48 hours.

When cured, remove the covering and wash off the mixture with water, then pat dry with until well dried.

Use the green tea smoking technique as described on page 128, with lemon grass instead of the tea, smoke the duck lightly for 5 minutes. Once smoked, wrap the duck breast in cheesecloth and refrigerate for 21–30 days.

At the end of this time, place in a freezer and, when ready to serve, use an electric slicer to cut it into very thin slices. If you do not have an electric slicer, then it would be easier to omit the freezing and just cut the duck as thinly as possible using a very sharp knife.

In a mixing bowl, toss together all the salad ingredients. Once well incorporated, throw in about half the duck confit and half the prosciutto. Mix well and dress with the Nuoc cham sauce. Season with salt and pepper if necessary.

Place the mixture in the middle of the plate. Mix the last of the duck confit and prosciutto, and mix well, and then place on top of the mound as garnish. If you like, encircle the dish with a little ginger syrup and lemon oil.

Green Tea Smoked Duck with Breast Black Sticky Rice Parcels, Baby Bok Choy and Pomegranate Jus

I am sometimes quoted as saying 'If you don't have a chicken, try a banana'. The point is keeping the idea of creativity very open, to the point of ridiculousness. This is an example of the creativity and the flexibility in cooking. A dish that has a level of sophistication in flavours that seems very difficult, but is really quite easy. So allow me to break it down.

Reading over the steps needed to make this dish, it can be a little off-putting, but the results are worth it. The techniques that are required to make this dish are so simple that it is actually a foolproof dish to prepare. It is also unique, as it uses techniques and ingredients from all over the globe. This is another favourite dish of mine – to make as well as to eat. I like to make dishes in which I can collaborate with my chefs, and get them to like and appreciate the dish, as it then makes it easier for them to prepare it, cook it, manage it and understand the final product.

Rice is a staple in Vietnamese cuisine, but black sticky rice is not really seen on many menus. Such rice is more of a dessert ingredient. To impart a little Asian flavour, my chef suggested that we cook it with a pandan leaf, which perfumes the rice. We also decided to add a little charred ginger skin to give a more complex flavour. For a little Middle Eastern twist, I wanted to add nuts and dried fruit, but there was not a reliable source for nuts, so we opted for lotus seeds and sultanas that we reconstituted in water. To give the dish a little finesse in terms of portion control, presentation and ease of plating we wrapped the steamed rice in steamed cabbage, making it a very simple to cook in a busy kitchen.

The duck breast is scored on the skin side, and cooked in order to render as much fat as possible, which is reserved for confit duck or gizzards, as well as cooking French fries. Once the duck breasts are seared, we place them in a brine, which will help keep the duck tender and moist. We cold-smoke the duck with green tea, but you can literally use any type of spice mix to impart the flavours you wish - used vanilla pods, five-spice powder, you name it, the flavour of the smoke make this a flavour to remember.

The sauce is a typical French sauce reduction with a gastrique or a sweet-and-sour sauce. We use whatever is in season or whatever we have. I like to use pomegranate juice and reduce it down, then season it with sugar or vinegar to get the perfect sweet/sour balance, then add the duck sauce. When pomegranates are out of season, you can actually use pomegranate molasses or syrup with pleasing results.

I also like to serve this with a cherry brandy sauce, flambéing with cherry brandy and adding dried cherries that have been reconstituted in the cherry brandy. I reduce this and then top it with duck sauce and call it a cherry brandy sauce, but it needs to be balanced for sweetness and sourness by adding a sugar vinegar mixture to the brandy sauce before adding the duck sauce; you can get a perfect sweet-and-sour sauce. I could take it further and use fruit jams are jellies, like blueberry jam, or raspberry.

Finally, to make sure our guests get their fair share of vegetables, we pair this dish with stir-fried green leafy vegetables, from pak choy to mustard greens.

SERVES 4

4 duck breasts

4 tbsp uncooked rice

2 tsp sugar

4 tsp green tea

50g spring onions, chopped, to serve

Brine

125g sugar

4 tbsp salt

450ml water

2 pieces of star anise

2.5 cm cinnamon

Black Sticky Rice

2 cups black sticky rice (soaked in cold water overnight)

3 cups water

5cm ginger

1 pandan leaf

5 tbsp sultanas

4 tbsp lotus seeds

salt and freshly ground black pepper

4 tbsp vegetable oil

8 Chinese cabbage leaves

300g pak choy

Sauce

475ml pomegranate Juice

240ml duck sauce (reduction of the duck stock)

50g sugar

1 tbsp rice vinegar

Vegetables

4–6 heads of pak choy

First make the brine: put 500 ml water in a large pan and add the sugar, salt, star anise and cinnamon. Bring to boil then set aside to cool completely.

Score the duck breast with a lattice pattern and, in a hot dry pan, sear the skin side only. Reduce the heat; the goal here is to render as much duck fat as possible. Once most of the fat has rendered, remove the duck breast and place it in the brine. Make sure the brine is nice and cold before submerging the duck in it. Leave for about 2–4 hours.

Transfer the duck to a plate, rinse and drain. Place foil in a pot fitted with a steamer. Place the rice on the foil and make a well, sprinkle the well with sugar. Turn the heat on high and cook until the sugar has melted and begins to burn. Add the green tea on top so that it smokes. Place the duck breast in the steaming basket with the skin side up and cover tightly to ensure that no smoke gets out. Turn the heat off, transfer the pot to the sink and submerge the base of the pot to reduce the heat. Keep the duck inside the pot, tightly covered until the smoke dissipates – 10 minutes would be a nice smoke. (In the event that your steamer can only fit a couple of fillets of duck breast, you can always add more duck breasts on top of the ones that you steam, but make sure the skin side is down to expose the meat to the smoke.

Prepare the rice: rinse it in water and set aside to drain. Place the rice in a steaming basket with the ginger and pandan leaf if you are using it. Cover and steam over medium-to-high heat.

Check occasionally and stir the rice to make sure it cooks equally. Reduce the heat and continue for about 30–40 minutes, until the rice is tender. Once cooked, spread it out on a baking sheet and cover with a damp cloth.

Bring a large pot of water to the boil. Once it reaches boiling point, ladle some of the water into a container with the sultanas and another with lotus seeds and let them stand until at room temperature.

In the remaining boiling water, blanch a couple of cabbage leaves at a time until tender. Blanch in iced water to prevent discoloration as well as to stop the cooking process. Remove from the water. Pat dry and cut the thick stem that runs through the cabbage, to make it easier to wrap the rice in.

Put the lotus seeds in a pot of cold water, bring to the boil over medium-to-high heat and cook for about 30 minutes or until tender, then drain.

In a large mixing bowl, mix the cooked rice, drained sultanas and drained lotus seeds. Add pepper, salt and the remaining oil then mix well again. Remove the ginger and pandan leaf.

To make the cabbage balls you will need plastic wrap and a teacup rinsed with a little water. Line the teacup with the plastic wrap and it will naturally stick to the sides due to the water. Then line the cup with cabbage leaves on top of the plastic wrap so that it completely covers the sides of the cup, making sure that there is a bit of an overhang of the cabbage over the rim of the cup. Spoon the rice mixture into the cabbage and fold the overhang of cabbage on top of the rice. Then grab the ends of the plastic wrap and pull the cabbage parcel out of the cup, turning it until the tightening plastic acts like an embryo cord. Press and shape the cabbage into a ball. Place inside a steamer and, when ready for cooking, just steam for about 5 minutes or until hot

Make the sauce: in a saucepan over medium heat, reduce the pomegranate juice to a few spoonfuls of glaze. Take care that the heat is never too high as the juice has a high sugar content and it can easily burn, especially on the side of the pan, which could impart a bitter taste.

Once it is much darker and close to syrup stage, add the duck sauce. Reduce and season with sugar and/or vinegar if too sweet.

Remove the duck breasts from the brine and rinse under cold running water to get rid of as much salt as possible. Pat them as dry as possible.

In a pan over a high heat, melt a little duck fat. When it is smoking-hot, place the duck breasts in the pan, skin side down, and cook. The heat should be high, but be careful not to burn the duck, as sugar residue from the brine will make it very easy to burn. Reduce the heat and continue cooking for about 5 minutes. Turn the breast over and cook for another 4 minutes, then remove. Place on a cutting board and season with salt and pepper, then let it rest for about 5 minutes. Reserve the cooking fat and the pan for the vegetables.

Stir-fry the pak choy in the reserved fat until just wilted. Transfer to a serving plate.

Remove the cabbage rice balls from the steamer. Holding the tip of the plastic cord, unwind it. Turn a plate upside down and place it on the bottom of the cabbage ball. Flip the plate and ball over and remove the plastic.

In the reserved cooking fat from the duck breast in the pan, stir-fry the pak choy until wilted and tender. Transfer to a plate.

Once the duck is well rested, cut the breasts into 5–8 slices and fan these out over the the pak choi. Arrange the cabbage balls to one side and drizzle the sauce around the edge of the plate and sprinkle with the chopped spring onions.

Red Wine Braised Lamb Shanks with Apple Risotto

This is one of my favourite dishes to cook and one of our signature dishes. It's a dish that I can make consistently anywhere in the world with the same pleasing results. When people taste these shanks they usually attribute it to my Middle Eastern background. Although I appreciate the idea that I have some sense of instinctive spiritual understanding of lamb, the truth of the matter is that it is a simple cooking technique that yields very pleasing results regardless of the lack of kitchen facilities and equipment.

At The Red Onion we were without a functional oven for over 9 months, and we still were able to confit and braise to very high quality, by cooking it over the stove top in hotel pans covered with foil. I really enjoy braising and confiting foods because I enjoy all the steps and the process of making it. It might be considered time-consuming, but with final dishes like this, it is worth it. I like to make this dish the day before I serve it, as I am a bit of a perfectionist, but it can be made and served on the same day.

This dish was inspired by some of my favourite chefs in San Francisco, from whom I have borrowed techniques and styles that are very Californian. What makes this dish so pleasing is simply a couple of additional steps that do not require much skill, just a little more time.

Simply marinate the lamb shanks for 30 minutes before searing. This will yield a wonderful purple colour on the shank. You really do not want to over-marinate the lamb as it will take on a little too much of the acidity and flavour of the wine, overpowering the flavour of the lamb. Instead of braising in water or stock, we use red wine. In this recipe I borrowed a technique from Hubert Keller. He would finish his Merlot red wine sauce with a vanilla bean. It was said that oak barrels can give off a vanilla character, so Hubert would reintroduce the flavour in his sauce, leaving haunting flavours at the end of every bite. For me I would not finish the sauce with vanilla, as I wanted something a little more subtle. I use cocoa powder during the braising period, as the cocoa gives additional colour and subtle flavour to the stock.

After the braising, I would chill the lambs in the stock, and refrigerate overnight. The solidified fats would be skimmed off, yielding a fat-free stock. I would reserve half the stock in which to reheat the lamb shanks and reduce the other half for a richer flavourful sauce, all to be finished with a little brown sugar to balance out the acidity of the red wine reduction.

The risotto was inspired by Arnold Wong at EOS and Baccar in San Francisco. I found that the sweetness of the apples with the lamb and rice made a wonderful combination, almost Middle

Eastern with the use of sweet fruit and savoury meats. I like to add a little spinach for colour and flavour, and finish the dish with rosemary oil. Regardless, the trio of lamb, risotto and sauce will win most people over.

SERVES 4

4 lamb shanks

3 bottles red wine

3 tbsp vegetable oil

salt and freshly ground black pepper

2 tbsp cocoa powder

seeds from 1 vanilla pod or 2 tsp essence

¼ tsp ground cinnamon

1 carrot, chopped

2 celery stalks, chopped

1 onion, chopped

4 tbsp tomato paste

4 garlic cloves

1 tbsp black peppercorns

2 bay leaves

1 tbsp rosemary

50g brown sugar

Risotto

2 apples, skinned, cored and cut into big cubes

a little butter

6 cups precooked risotto

2 cups chicken stock (see page 50)

24 spinach leaves

Have your butcher clean the excess fat and outer membranes of the lamb shank. Marinate the lamb shanks in the wine for 1 hour.

Remove the lamb shank from the wine, pat dry and rub with oil so evenly coated. This will help the salt and pepper adhere to the meat. Heat a frying pan with oil and season the shanks with salt and pepper. Place shanks into the pan, and make sure that you do not overcrowd. Sear the lamb shanks, not moving them once in the pan. Leave to sear and develop colour, browning somewhat, then turn over, and rotate the shanks until all sides are nicely browned.

Remove the shanks one by one as they are nicely browned, and place in a pot with the reserved marinating wine. In the event that you burn parts of the shank, simply remove the burnt parts by rubbing them off with a knife as these will otherwise give a bitterness to the stock as well as the sauce.

Bring the marinating liquid with the shanks to the boil, making sure that the liquid covers the shanks. (If there is not enough liquid, top up with wine, chicken stock or water.) Just as it reaches the boil, reduce the heat to a simmer. Do not let it actually boil, as this will cloud the stock and the flavours will not be as clean or as good. When it reaches a simmer, add the cocoa, vanilla, cinnamon, carrots, celery, onions, tomato paste, garlic, peppercorns, bay and rosemary. Bring to the boil and reduce the heat to a simmer again.

Place a cover on top and braise in an oven on low heat until the lamb is tender and falls off the bone, 3–4 hours. (If you have any Muslims at the table, let them know that the alcohol has burnt off over the duration of cooking.) Remove the shanks from the liquid and place in a container. Strain the braising liquid over the shanks and place in the fridge overnight.

Next day, use a large spoon or spatula to remove as much of the fine layer of solidified fat on the top as you can. This way you have an almost fat-free sauce. The braising liquid will be a little gelatinous. Once all the fat is removed, take three-quarters of the remaining liquid and bring to the boil. Reduce to a simmer and reduce by a quarter. Season with the remaining brown sugar to taste.

Add the carrot, celery and onion. Once they are tender your sauce is pretty much ready. Season the sauce with brown sugar to your own taste.

To prepare the risotto: first sear the apple cubes in the melted butter until they are nicely browned on all sides. Reserve in a bowl.

Throw the rice, 120ml of water and the chicken stock into a large pot. Once warmed through, toss in the cooked apples and the spinach.

Heat the remaining reserved lamb stock and, when your guests arrive, dump the shanks in it to reheat them.

Spoon the risotto in the middle of the plate, place a lamb shank on top, then drizzle the reduced lamb sauce over the lamb and spoon the vegetables on the outer part of the plate.

Hair of the dog

A friend of mine, Mark McDonald, a regular at my last restaurant in Hanoi, knew a young tour guide whose father cooked dog for a living. A regular dog caterer, in fact... grilled, braised, kebabs, schnitzel, soup, satay, stew – you name it, he cooked it.

The kid was regaling my friend with his father's tales of hardships during 'The American War': living in the jungle, suffering from malaria, lack of shelter, shooting tigers and other wild animals for food, that kind of thing. The war, of course, was a living nightmare for everybody who went through it, whether they were in the jungle or the city.

Eventually he got on to the subject of how his father, a common Viet Cong foot soldier, had come across a dead American pilot who was caught hanging in a tree by his parachute. Since the old man was doing the cooking for his troop, and since they were suffering from serious fatigue and a lack of protein, he decided to cut a piece of flesh from the pilot's thigh. He simply dropped it into the soup he was making that night. When the troops ate the soup, many of them didn't like the flavour. 'Too strong', they said. 'Too gamey.'

Now, twenty-five years later, the father is one of the great dog chefs of Vietnam. The kid invited us over for dinner with the promise that his father would prepare dog the customary and legendary seventeen different ways – a full-on buffet, doggie-style.

My pal, a reporter, asked his photographer and me to come along. He suggested I ask culinary questions during the dinner so it would appear that the story was about canine cuisine, although his real interest was in the gory tales of the war. What better way to talk about eating a side of man than over a little dinner of dog?

The dinner took place in the old man's house in a working-class district on the outskirts of Hanoi. The house was hidden behind a bunch of storefronts that were selling cheap pottery, electrical gadgets and various plumbing supplies that were laced in a thin layer of dust. I arrived late, and had to walk through a maze of scattered pots, PVC pipes, an array of coils and wires, and Soviet electrical gizmos that would best be described as really bad junk.

Everyone was waiting patiently, quietly sipping cups of bitter green tea. As I entered, I apologised for being late, but could not figure out why my friends were looking so tense. The faint sound of traffic was punctuated with the sound of two dogs – one howling, one barking – in the backyard.

'With all seriousness, I have to ask, is that dinner?'

'With all seriousness, I have no idea,' Mark responded, blushing either with nerves or embarrassment, I could not really tell. Dining on man's best friend is a strange emotional dilemma and the three of us were petrified.

While the food was being prepared out of sight, in a kitchen out back, I started to run through all the culinary questions that I could muster in my head. We sat there speechless as the sound of a moaning dog filled the air like a cruel winter wind.

After about twenty minutes our host finally arrived and greeted us. He apologised for not having enough time to prepare all seventeen versions of dog. I think it's fair to say he was a real expert. You know how people always say there are ninety-nine ways to skin a cat, but nobody can tell you 'the way' to skin it? If anyone could, it would be this guy.

The table was graced with sliced boiled dog, stir-fried dog with lemon grass, and a dog soup, which contained what appeared to be the shank of the dog.

Like many Vietnamese dishes, dog is

accompanied with a dipping sauce to complement the flavours and tie the dish together. Eating dog without the dipping sauce is rather like eating sushi without soy sauce and wasabi. Unfortunately this light purple sauce with the consistency of watery ketchup smells bad and tastes worse. It is the closest thing to fermented shrimp shit you can get and seems to continue fermenting in front of you eyes as fine white bubbles coat the inside of the dipping bowl. It has taken me eight years to acquire a taste for it, and I still do not really like it.

As we sized up the dishes, we darted looks at each other, knowing that the moment of truth had arrived. Wondering which one of us would start, visions of my first dog started to run through my head. Then all my friends' dogs. They say that when you die, you watch images of your life hurtle by. When you eat dog, the experience is rather similar. You think about every dog you've ever been close to. The thought struck me: What the hell am I doing? Have I lost my mind?

Our host, wanting to honour his foreign guests at Tet, the lunar New Year, graciously pointed out the three boiled pigs' eyes. They were sitting in a bowl, like three Cyclops – a real treat here, especially during Tet. Tet does that to people – they are generally much more generous and thoughtful during this very special time. But having these three eyes – with detached retinas – staring at us was more than a little eerie and I quickly retreated to my Islamic upbringing.

It was me who started eating first, under the pretence that I was the most adventurous one, when in fact I was just quickest to detect the smallest portion of boiled dog available. It sat there in front of me on an oval plastic platter – thinly sliced and fanned nicely over the plate, free of garnishes and vegetables. It was nothing, I reasoned, but beef.

I proceeded to remove the fat from the meat, peeling it away and placing it on the side of the plate. It reminded me of the fat from a breast of duck, except it was slightly charred. I turned to our hosts, gave the most superficial smile I could muster, then dropped the meat in my mouth and started to chew quickly. As the flavours released, the tastes took me right back to English boarding school. The dog tasted exactly like the roast beef they used to serve every Sunday with Yorkshire pudding: dry, overcooked, and chewy – except the dog had no large exposed blood vessels.

I quickly washed it down with beer, but the taste lingered heavily on my palate. I needed to reassure the other guys that the dog was actually edible and we are all just facing an emotional barrier. 'Tastes a little like roast beef,' I said, 'but if you put roast beef next to it, I am sure I would be able to tell the difference.'

Next was fried dog. Just as I put it into my mouth my friend frowned and complained that it was very strong, which it was. It was hard to spit it out, so I manipulated it to the back of my tongue, reached for the beer and tried to wash it down. Gamey would be an understatement: 'doggie' would be a better description.

Then we went for the soup. Our hosts were both feverishly chowing down. As I watched them shovel up pieces of dog, like famished construction workers with a limited lunch break, I could only think to myself that we (the Americans) never had a chance here. The meal for us was pretty much over within three minutes. We were like three anorexics just doing face time at a dinner table.

Conversation during a Vietnamese meal is usually very limited. The table usually falls into silence, with the exception of slurps and the ploughing of rice bowls and chopsticks. This was the opportune moment to ask all my questions and thereby avoid the food. I would learn that the

Next was the fried dog. Just as I put it into my mouth my friend started to frown and complained that it was very strong, which it was. It was hard to spit it out, so I manipulated it to the back of my tongue, reached for the beer and tried to wash it down.

best dogs for eating are six months to one year old, and the young females are best of all. The Chinese and Koreans, true connoisseurs, buy a lot of dogs from Vietnam.

When I asked our host if there was any part of the dog that couldn't be eaten, he didn't miss a beat. 'The hair,' he said, without the slightest trace of humour or irony. Surely the paws couldn't be eaten? No, they're savoured in soups and stocks. There is no prized cut from a dog, apparently, although cooking technique and execution are critical.

The normal diet for a dog is rice and leftovers, which sounds perfect for a Vietnamese pet, but the dogs raised for eating are special. They're a strange half-breed that's older and fatter than the normal Vietnamese house-dog, but strangely favoured by expatriates. I know some who have gone out of their way to save a dog, which they will then feed and fatten up only for the poor thing to be dog-napped by someone.

Curiously, those who eat dog only eat a certain type – an intellectual justification for those who regard the little darlings as part of the family. The chef said other dogs do not taste like the mutts he cooks. He made a point of telling me that 'the German dog' is not good for eating. What? When was this guy in Germany? It sounded like he must have eaten a German

shepherd. I imagine that during the hardships of war, they were forced to take on the K-9 corps of the US army. Hell, if he could eat a piece of leg from a dead pilot hanging from a tree, then dogs that were wounded or dead on the battlefield must have seemed like fair game.

On the Yin-Yang chart of hot and cold foods, dog makes you hot. It is a winter dish, eaten in northern areas, where the winters get very cold. When you eat dog in summer, it's said that you release a strange smell when you sweat. Dogs, apparently, can pick up on the scent, and I suspect they think you're some kind of werewolf.

Dog meat is more expensive than chicken, but cheaper than beef, and the price fluctuates according to the whole lunar calendar of karma and superstition. It is eaten for good luck during the last two weeks of a calendar month. Our dinner took place around Tet, when dog is in very high demand, and costs about $1.25 a pound.

There were just five of us at dinner that night, so the neighbours were given the dog's head. Others were awarded the intestines, liver and stomach. Thank God for neighbours. The chef asked us if we had a problem eating dog, which was very difficult to answer given that the guy had not only eaten a piece of American pilot, but had also cooked him.

As our hosts continued to work their way through the dog dishes, the rest of us were content to eat the bread and drink the warm beer. A small cat began to rub up against us, mewing and whining and twitching. When our hosts finished their meal and cleared the table, they fed the leftovers to the cat, which sent the scrawny feline into a kind of sexual rapture.

Yes, indeed, it's a dog-eat-dog world. Actually, it is worse then that. Man eats monkey brains, cat eats dog, cows eat sheep, and vegetarians are starting to make much more sense to me by the minute.

Under the Sea

Vietnam has a thousand-odd miles of beach-front property and the people go nuts for seafood, especially those living in coastal towns. Think about it: here's a country supposedly earning $1,000 per capita per year, but if you go to most restaurants you'll find people spending $45 a head to eat fresh seafood. Now that Vietnam is part of the World Trade Organization and exporting a lot, we are not getting the best seafood on the local market as it is snapped up by Japan. In addition to the wide variety of sea and freshwater fish, Vietnam produces great, great tiger prawns, and the soft-shell and mud crabs are fantastic. You can see the Chinese influence in dishes such as steamed fish and sweet-and-sour fish, and in the use of dried fish products.

Chawan Mushi à la Vietnam
TRỨNG CHƯNG CÁCH THỦY

One of my all-time favourites, this Japanese savoury custard is delicate, light and allows a lot of room for creative variations. It is enriched with dashi, the Japanese stock, rather than the traditional method of making custard.

I first encountered chawan mushi in Saigon, thanks to my friend Alex, and asked him for the recipe. He smiled and said: 'Very easy, 411.' Unbeknownst to him, '411' is the number for phone information in San Francisco, so I thought he was being sarcastic, but he continued: 'four eggs, one tablespoon mirin, one tablespoon soy sauce.' This mixture was then blended with dashi.

Traditionally chawan mushi is made with chopped chicken, chopped prawns, and thin slices of shiitake mushrooms. I started using crabmeat, lobster, and eventually added lemon rind, which made it taste clean and refreshing.

Once I had this dish on a tasting menu for 20 guests and ran out of dashi. I used diluted fish sauce instead and the results were rather pleasing.

We usually steam this in eggshells – you'd need around twelve for this volume of liquid. Put just a tablespoon of crabmeat and a couple of pinches of lemon zest in each one.

MAKES 8–12

4 medium eggs
2 tbsp fish sauce
1 tbsp mirin
200g crabmeat
finely grated zest of 1 lemon, finely chopped

In a large bowl, beat the eggs, fish sauce and mirin together with 530ml water. Pass through a fine-meshed strainer into a jug to remove any strings or eggshell.

Divide the crabmeat evenly between 8–12 ramekins, then pour the custard evenly into them and sprinkle with the lemon zest.

Steam in a water bath, uncovered, for about 10 minutes, depending on the size of the bath, with the water coming halfway up the sides of the ramekins. If serving in eggshells or espresso cups, steam for only about 6 minutes.

Sweet-and-Sour Fish Soup
CANH CHUA CÁ LÓC

This is the first Vietnamese soup I ever made. I was visiting the sleepy town of Nha Trang and sat there at the Sailing Club, strapped for cash, hungry and with nothing to do (literally, as tourism was non-existent).

A young Australian by the name of Peter owned the Sailing Club. He let me hang out in the kitchen observing. I saw frozen chicken being thawed in oil for a steamed chicken dish, and burgers deep-fried to order. The cooking of Western dishes in particular was pretty horrifying in those tender years.

Someone ordered a soup. I had never seen anything like it: so tasty, so simple, so new. Who would have thought such a flavourful dish could be made in seconds? I felt compelled to cook more Vietnamese food in my own kitchen. When I returned to work I described this sweet-and-sour soup that had been such a revelation to me.

Everyone laughed and made it for me right there and then. I was even scolded for wanting to cook it. 'Why are you making Vietnamese food? You're paid to make Western! No one is coming here for your Vietnamese food!'

Those words run true to this day. Few customers get past the name on the menu, but those that do can experience the difference of having this soup made with fresh fish stock or a splash of clam juice rather than water. Dishes this simple are really about freshness and execution, after all. You can also use prawns, scallops, squid and other types of seafood in this recipe.

SERVES 6

2 litres Fish Stock (see page 51) or water
½ fresh pineapple, peeled, quartered and cut into slices 2cm thick
2 finger-length red chillies, deseeded and sliced
4 okra, sliced
2 ripe tomatoes, cut into wedges
large handful celery leaves
240ml Tamarind water (see page 26)
1kg barramundi fillets, cut into large cubes
handful beansprouts
6 tbsp fish sauce
1 tbsp sugar
4 tbsp finely chopped mint leaves
1½ tbsp coriander leaves

Put the stock or water in a large pan and bring to the boil. Add the pineapple, chilli, okra, tomatoes and celery leaves, and simmer for 4–5 minutes until the ingredients are tender. The stock should taste of fish and pineapple.

Add the tamarind water gradually, constantly tasting to ensure the broth is mildly sour, but not so much that it actually tastes of tamarind. The amount required will depend on the quality and type of tamarind paste you use.

Reduce the heat to a simmer. Add the fish and simmer very gently for about 5 minutes, until just cooked.

Add the beansprouts. Season with the fish sauce and sugar, then remove from the heat.

Pour into serving bowls and garnish with the mint and coriander leaves.

Caramelized Prawns

TÔM RIM MẮN

This is a dish to try when you're feeling adventurous: people either love or hate it. You can't get around the fact that you have to eat the whole prawns, head, shells, body and all. That I'm including it in the book gives you a sense of my appreciation for it – I always ask for it to be put on the staff meals and might even serve it as a bar snack one of these days.

In Vietnam it is made when tiny prawns are in season – the minuscule morsels have a count of 100 or more per 500g. When prawns are that size, you eat the whole thing, giving a sense perhaps of what a whale's diet is like. The texture of the shells is actually quite enjoyable, as in their small stage they are tender. If you opt for larger prawns, you can remove the heads but there is still no way of getting around eating the shells – that is where the flavour is trapped, yielding a wonderful reduction of sweet and salty sauce amid the crisp shell and firm flesh of the prawn.

It is important that all the ingredients are prepared in advance, as this dish is cooked quickly over a high heat. Be organized with the oil as it makes two appearances: once at the beginning for the spring onions, and then later when frying the prawns to give a nice crisp finish. If you do not want this dish to be as salty as they like it in Vietnam, just reduce the amount of fish sauce, or increase the sugar.

SERVES 4

1–2 spring onions
350g small or medium raw prawns, unpeeled
3 tbsp vegetable oil
1 tbsp sugar
2 tbsp fish sauce
1 tbsp coriander leaves, cut into 2cm pieces

Take the white part of the spring onion and finely chop enough of it to measure 1 tablespoon. Cut the green stem into 5mm pieces, measure 1 tablespoon of them and set aside separately.

If the prawns are on the large side, make an incision in the back of each and, keeping the shells on, use a toothpick or skewer to remove the dark 'vein' or digestive tract. (When the prawns are very small, you don't have to worry about this.)

To a sauté pan over a moderate heat, add 1 tablespoon vegetable oil and sauté the white part of the spring onion until golden brown.

Add the prawns and cook until dry, tossing and turning them all the time. (You might want to reduce the heat to low at some point.)

When all the liquid has evaporated, add the sugar and fish sauce, and cook, stirring, until the sugar has dissolved and the fish sauce is reduced. Ensure the prawns are evenly coated with sauce.

Turn the heat up to medium, add another 2 tablespoons of oil and continue to cook, stirring, to make sure the prawns are evenly cooked, about 2 minutes. The goal here is here is to make the prawns crisp and glazed.

Throw in the green parts of the spring onions and toss lightly until they are tender and wilted.

Garnish with the coriander and serve immediately with steamed rice.

Tamarind-Glazed Crab Cake with Chive Flowers

BÁNH CUA

This is one of our signature dishes. When using fresh crab we usually get three dishes out of a crab. I use the stock for the wonderful classic Asian crab corn soup, and I also use the meat for the Crab salad on page 95 and these crab cakes.

My first recollection of eating crab was with my sister and I must have been about five and she was six. We were eating Dungeness crab in Fisherman's Wharf and my dad asked my sister Nina, 'Do you like the crab?' and she replied, 'I like the meat, but the skin is pretty tough', which reply left a lasting impression on me.

I love crab, but I hate doing all the work. I would often cut my fingers trying to pick the meat. Then there are the small pieces of shell that always seem to get caught between the teeth, like corn off the cob. So nowadays crab is one of those things that I shy away from in restaurants, simply because of the amount of work required to eat it. How the Chinese can eat it with two sticks has always amazed me. Then there is always the issue of what part do you want when

you split it. Who gets the top shell? Who wants the claws? I usually end up with the legs! The crab cake is the way to make it uniform, homogeneous and a hell of a lot easier to eat.

On my first trip to Vietnam in 1993 we toured up to Da Lat, Nha Trang and on our way back to Saigon we stopped off to get a bite to eat in a small restaurant on the river ten kilometres out of District 1. Freshwater prawns the size of lobsters were grilled live over an open flame, and mud crabs were hand-picked from the larder and stir-fried with tamarind. It could be a national dish, but it was one of the best crab dishes I have ever had and gives the Singaporeans' national dish of chilli crab a run for its money. Sweet-and-sour crab was a revelation to me and it inspired me to make a crab cake with tamarind glaze. This would be a lighter version and I would borrow techniques from Hubert Keller who borrowed it in turn from his sous chef Rick at Fleur De Lys, who was from Maryland.

Many customers think that my crab cakes are the best they've ever had, and since I pretty much ripped off the idea from one of the best chefs in the country, I would also have to agree. They are light, have a wonderful texture and are very meaty. You can use fresh live crab or crab from a can. If you use canned, wrap the meat in a napkin and squeeze out as much water as possible otherwise the cakes will be too mushy.

In Vietnam I use the larger mud crabs that are the most evil I've ever come across. They are usually wrapped in what looks like a plastic rope. I weighed this and it costs in weight $3.20, which seems pretty expensive considering I'm not going to eat it. I was told I don't have to have the rope, but it would be even more expensive as no one dares to handle the crab without it.

If using live crabs there are some additional steps you have to take. Firstly, you have to kill them. This is not as difficult as it sounds, and you don't appear to be so cruel, as they die instantly. Hold the crab in a kitchen towel and rip the side of its top shell from the body. You then have to remove the bottom of its rear end. I forgot to do this once and my entire stock tasted as close to crab shit as it could get.

5 live crabs, each about 700g

725ml sake

2 lemon grass stalks, smashed

**2 pieces ginger, charred in a naked flame and
    blackened skin removed, for additional flavour**

2 garlic cloves

Crab cakes

200g shelled scallops, chilled

4 tbsp double cream, chilled

2½ tbsp finely chopped fresh ginger

2 tbsp finely chopped coriander leaves

Tabasco sauce to taste

salt and pepper

2 tbsp Tamarind Sauce (see page 49)

Sautéed chive flowers

**about 180g chive flowers, each trimmed of the
    fibrous bottom quarter**

1 tbsp soy sauce

½ tbsp sugar

1 tsp finely chopped garlic

Crab Corn Soup (Sup Ngo Cua)

2 litres water or Fish stock (see page 51)

**5 cans of corn kernels, drained (about 1kg), or
    kernels from 5 fresh corn cobs**

2 tbsp finely chopped chives

4 tbsp skinned and diced tomato

3 tbsp white truffle oil

Despatch the crabs as described earlier. Clean thoroughly with a brush. Peel the top of the shell off and reserve the tomalley and membranes for the stock. With kitchen shears, remove the feathery lungs on both flanks. Cut off the back flap (digestive tract). Pull off the claws and cut off the legs. Cut the body in half and, with a cleaver, crack open the shell of the claws to shorten cooking time as well as help flavour the meat when steaming.

Bring the sake to the boil in a pot. Tilt the pot slightly, ignite the liquid and burn off the alcohol. Once all burnt off, add the lemon grass, ginger and garlic. Bring the liquid to a simmer.

Place the crabs on a steaming rack, cover and steam for about 30 minutes. The time will depend on the size of the crabs.

Once cooked, remove from the heat with the cover and top, and let cool to room temperature.

When cool enough to handle, pick out all the meat from the shell and chill until needed. (Reserve shells and steaming liquid for the soup.)

For the crab cakes, place 2 cupfuls of steamed crab meat in a mixing bowl. Place the scallops in a blender, and add half of the cream. Pulse in the cream and then slowly pour in the rest until you have a nice thick purée. Spoon into the bowl of crabmeat. Add the ginger, coriander and a couple of drops of Tabasco. Season with salt and pepper. (I always cook a spoonful until browned on both sides and nibble to test the seasoning. If seasoned to your liking, start the production.)

Roll about 100g of the mixture at a time with both hands into smooth balls, then flatten them out so you have round discs like burger patties. You should be able to get 35–40 such patties in this way. You can, of course, make these any size you wish, as they may be served as appetizers or even as hors d'oeuvres.

Spray a skillet or frying pan with oil and place over medium-high heat. Brown the crab cakes on one side before attempting to move them, otherwise the meat might stick to the pan. Once nicely browned, flip them over. You can tell if they are cooked by the amount the springiness of the patty: if soft, it means they need to cook more. Once cooked, remove and place on a plate.

Turn the heat to high, add more oil and throw the chive flowers into the pan. Sauté, adding the soy sauce, sugar, garlic and a tablespoon of water. Once wilted but still firm, remove and place on a serving plate. Top with the crab cakes and add a little tamarind sauce on top, rubbing over the surface of the crab cake.

For the crab corn soup: remove the ginger, lemon grass and garlic from the steaming liquid. In a large pot, add the reserved shells and trimmings, and enough water or stock to cover. Bring to the boil and simmer for 10 minutes. Remove from the heat and strain. Add the corn and cook until tender. Remove from the pan and purée in a blender. Strain again, return to the pot and season with salt and pepper.

To serve, add the reserved crabmeat and pour into serving bowls. Garnish with the chives and tomato, and drizzle with white truffle oil.

Marinated Grilled Squid

MUC NUONG

We do several squid dishes at the restaurant and rotate them on the menu. When we are ridiculously busy or the menu has several complicated dishes, I often put on this very simple dish.

Squid is a very common ingredient in Vietnamese cuisine as it is cheap, nutritious and readily available.

SERVES 4

500g medium squid tubes
½ tbsp salt
coriander sprigs, to garnish
Nuoc Cham dip (see page 43)
Marinade
2 tbsp vegetable oil
1 tbsp soy sauce
1 tbsp lime juice
1 tsp sesame oil
2 garlic cloves, crushed
1 tbsp finely chopped lemon grass
1 tsp curry powder
1 tsp five-spice powder
1 tsp sugar
½ tsp ground white pepper

Cut lengthways along each squid tube to open it out flat. Rinse and pat dry, then use a knife to make diagonal criss-cross slits across the surface. (This allows the squid to cook evenly and quickly, as well as making it a little more attractive.) Cut into large bite-sized pieces and rub with the salt. Set aside for about 15 minutes. Rinse, drain and pat dry again.

Combine all the marinade ingredients in a large bowl and mix well. Add the squid pieces, stir until well coated and set aside to marinate for at least 1 hour.

Preheat a grill or griddle pan to high. Lift the squid pieces from the marinade and cook for about 2 minutes on each side, or until just done. Arrange the grilled squid on a serving platter and garnish with coriander.

Serve the grilled squid hot with the fish sauce dip on the side.

Prawn and Sweet Potato Cakes

BÁNH TÔM

In the West Lake area of Hanoi (Tay Ho), you'll often find people bundled up over this rather hearty dish – a sort of alternative to Kentucky Fried Chicken but with prawns. I eat them during the cold winter months when I feel the need for a little fried food.

The sweet potato should be cut into very thin strips. I use a mandolin with the middle-sized blade. The sweet potatoes have a high sugar content, so you want to cook them fast or they burn. You can use regular potatoes as well.

MAKES 10

36 raw prawns
1½ tbsp fish sauce
1 tbsp crushed garlic
freshly ground black pepper
450g plain flour
3 tbsp sugar
1½ tbsp salt
1½ tsp baking powder
1 tsp ground turmeric
300g sweet potato, peeled and finely shredded
5 spring onions, thinly sliced
500ml vegetable oil
225ml Sweet-and-Sour Sauce (see page 47)
450g Pickled Carrot and Daikon (see page 42)

Leaving the tails on the prawns, remove the shells from the bodies, then devein them by cutting along the back and picking out the black 'vein' thread with a toothpick or skewer.

In a mixing bowl, combine the prawns, fish sauce, garlic and a pinch of black pepper, stirring to make sure that the prawns are well coated. Marinate in the refrigerator for 20–30 minutes.

Choose 10 prawns for presentation, leave the tails on and butterfly the bodies along the belly. Remove the tails from the remaining prawns and chop the bodies to give a lumpy paste retaining some of the natural texture of the prawns – you do not want a purée.

Sift the flour, sugar, salt, baking powder, turmeric and a pinch of black pepper into a mixing bowl. Whisk in 275ml water, pouring it in a steady stream to give a smooth batter. The amount of water needed will vary, but the consistency of the batter should be like thick double cream.

In a separate mixing bowl, combine a couple of tablespoons each of the sweet potato, spring onion and prawn paste, then pour in some of the batter to make a patty. Press a butterflied prawn into the mixture so that the tail stands out a centimetre (to use as a handle when eating).

In a small deep-fryer or heavy-based saucepan, heat the oil to about 200°C. Carefully slide the patty into the oil, making sure it does not splatter. Fry for about 2–3 minutes, spooning the hot oil over the patty and turning it to ensure even cooking. Remove when crisp and a little golden in colour, and leave to drain on paper towels while you repeat with the remaining ingredients.

Season the patties with a little salt and pepper and serve tail-side up with the sweet-and-sour dipping sauce and pickles.

Prawns on Sugar Cane

TÔM BAO MÍA

This dish traditionally includes pork meat but I have removed it with pleasing results. It is easy to prepare and great for cocktail parties – the sugar cane is enjoyable to chew once the meat has been eaten. You can substitute squid, chicken or any white meat for the sea bass.

Shape a little of the prawn paste into a patty and grill it in advance to check the texture and seasoning before cooking the rest of the mixture.

SERVES 4

300g raw prawns, shelled, deveined and chopped
5 tbsp chopped and crushed shallots
1½ tsp crushed garlic
1 tsp sugar
1 egg white
50g skinless sea bass fillets, minced
½ tsp fish sauce
½ tbsp five-spice powder
salt
½ tbsp freshly ground black pepper
1 tbsp chopped coriander leaves
4 pieces sugar cane, about 7–10cm long
4 tbsp vegetable oil

To serve

16 rice papers, 16cm diameter
¼ lettuce, leaves separated
3 large handfuls fresh herbs, such as shiso, coriander, dill, mint, basil
225g extra-thin rice vermicelli (banh hoi)
small handful Crispy-fried shallots (see page 38)
1 tbsp roasted peanuts, ground
2 tbsp chopped spring onions marinated in 2 tbsp vegetable oil for an hour
Peanut Sauce (see page 46) or Sweet-and-Sour Sauce (see page 47)

Rinse the prawns thoroughly under running water, then drain and pat dry using paper towels.

In a food processor, blend the shallots, garlic, sugar and egg white to a paste. Add the chopped prawns and sea bass, and pulse until fine. Add the fish sauce, five-spice powder, some salt and the pepper. Stir in the coriander.

Peel away the rough outer skin of the sugar cane. Cut off the outer round segments so you have a long rectangular block. Split each section lengthways into quarters to produce 16 pieces.

Preheat the grill, griddle pan or a barbecue. Take 2–3 tablespoons of the prawn mix in one hand, push the top 5cm of the cane into the mix and roll the prawn mixture back and forth until it is smooth and evenly distributed around the cane. Repeat with the remaining paste and sugar cane.

Brush the prawn sticks with oil and place on the barbecue or griddle pan or under the grill and cook for about 5–8 minutes over/under medium heat. Make sure you turn them over and keep the prawn paste well oiled to prevent sticking.

Serve them as they are with the dipping sauce, or wrapped in rice papers.

If using dried rice papers, rehydrate them according to packet instructions or dip them in a little water, place on a moist towel and cover with another damp towel while you are working.

Pull the prawn paste from the sugar cane. Spread out a towel and lay a moistened rice paper on top. Add a little lettuce, herbs, vermicelli and prawn paste. Sprinkle with shallots, peanuts and spring onion oil. Roll as fresh spring rolls (see page 58). Serve with Peanut or Sweet-and-Sour Sauce.

Deep-fried Dover Sole

CÁ RÁN GIÒN

There is something magical about Vietnam's fried fish. In Hanoi, freshwater fish is typically used for frying as it is readily available. Grass carp, a common choice, has been introduced to US waters, where savvy anglers can find it in many states. My only reservation with freshwater fish is the high number of small bones they contain, so in the recipe below we have used a flat fish, which is delicate and flaky.

I do not eat many fried foods, but this dish is one of my favourites. The presentation can be a lot of fun. In fine dining restaurants the skeleton is often deep-fried so that it is bent like a basket with the small fillets sitting inside. It can be transformed from a main dish to a very pleasing appetizer by presenting the fried fish like a spring roll with dipping sauce, or rolling the pieces up in lettuce leaves with herbs and rice noodles. Any dipping sauce will work here: sweet-and-sour, chilli lime, or even just fish sauce.

SERVES 2

500g Dover sole, filleted
½ tsp crushed garlic
4 tbsp fish sauce
150g plain flour
450ml vegetable oil
125ml Sweet-and-Sour Sauce (see page 47), or
    125ml Fish Sauce dip (see page 53)
salt and pepper
Rice paper rolls
15g coriander sprigs
15g mint leaves
15g dill leaves
25g spring onions, green parts only, cut at an angle
    into 5mm pieces
5 large lettuce leaves or 10 rice papers

Have your fishmonger fillet the fish. Flat fish give 4 fillets each. Cut into pieces of the same size so the cooking time will be the same – I like big chunky pieces, but it will depend on the size of your fish.

Put in a bowl with the garlic, fish sauce and salt, and stir to coat evenly. Leave to marinate for 5 minutes.

Remove the fish from the marinade and lightly coat with flour, tapping off any excess.

Heat the oil in a deep-fryer or heavy-based saucepan. Working in batches, slide the fish into the hot oil and fry until golden brown. Remove with a slotted spoon and drain on kitchen paper.

Season with salt and pepper and serve immediately with your choice of dipping sauce. In the event that you opt to serve this as a spring roll or lettuce roll, make sure that all your herbs are available and ready to roll as soon as the fish has finished cooking.

Stuffed Squid

MỰC NHỒI

Far too frequently I find guests are moving away from meat, so I try my best to keep seafood dishes with just seafood and avoid mixing them with meat. Although the original recipe for stuffed squid, which features minced pork, is very good, here I have substituted prawns and scallops.

SERVES 4–6

25g cellophane noodles
1½ tbsp dried wood ear mushrooms
6 medium whole squid with tentacles
5g shelled, deveined and finely chopped prawns
30g shelled scallops, finely chopped
1 small onion, finely chopped
1½ tsp freshly ground black pepper
2 tbsp fish sauce
4 tbsp vegetable oil
2 small tomatoes, cut into thin wedges
3 large spring onions, cut into 5cm pieces

Soak the noodles in a bowl of cold water until they are pliable. Drain well, then cut them into 2.5cm pieces and set aside.

Meanwhile, in another bowl, soak the mushrooms in hot water until softened. Drain and rinse them, then cut off the hard knobs in the middle. Roll up each mushroom and slice thinly, then cut them across so that they are very finely chopped and almost like mince. (This will act as a binder for the stuffing as well as provide extra taste and texture.) Set aside.

Finely chop the tentacles of the squid and set

aside in a large bowl. Clean the bodies, removing the cartilage and ink sacs if necessary, then rinse well under cold running water. Use the point of a knife to pierce the closed end of each squid tube so that it won't inflate during cooking.

Add the chopped prawns and scallops to the noodles, together with the mushrooms, onion, 1 teaspoon pepper, 1 teaspoon fish sauce and the chopped tentacles, and mix well.

Pile this mixture evenly into the squid tubes so that they are about three-quarters full – do not overstuff them. Use a wooden toothpick to pierce both sides and close the opening.

Place a large skillet or frying pan over a medium-high heat and add the oil. When it is hot, lay the squid in the pan and either cover with a splatter-screen or part-cover with a lid. Fry the squid for about 5 minutes on each side or until golden brown. Don't worry if some of the filling spills out – it will become part of the sauce.

Drain the oil from the pan. Add the tomatoes and the remaining fish sauce and pepper. Simmer for 2 minutes.

Serve scattered with the spring onions.

Hanoi Calamari Salad

NỘM MỰC HÁ NOI

SERVES 2

100g whole squid, preferably small, cleaned
2 bird's-eye chillies, sliced at an angle (about 2 tsp)
2 tbsp lime juice
2 tbsp fish sauce
½ tsp sugar
¼ tsp salt
large pinch pepper
1 tsp crushed garlic
5g fresh ginger, peeled and finely shredded
5g white onion, very thinly sliced into rings
5g celery, strings removed and finely shredded
1 tbsp basil leaves, for garnish
Tamarind sauce (see page 49)
Salad
1 avocado, peeled, stoned and cut into large dice
2 large tomatoes, skinned and cut into large dice
bunch of rocket
2–3 tbsp Vinaigrette (see page 49)

Cut the squid bodies open lengthways and score with fine criss-cross cuts. Bring a pan of salted water to the boil and prepare an ice bath.

Blanch the squid in the boiling water for 20–30 seconds. Once curled, remove with a slotted spoon and put in the iced water to stop the cooking.

Meanwhile, in a small bowl, mix together half the chillies, the lime juice, fish sauce and sugar to make a marinade and set aside.

When the squid is cool, drain it and pat dry. Put the squid in a bowl with the salt, pepper, garlic and ginger, and stir. Add the white onion, celery and remaining chilli, and mix together lightly. Pour the marinade over the squid and leave to stand for at least 15 minutes.

Make the salad by tossing the ingredients with the vinaigrette until lightly coated.

Arrange the salad on a serving plate or in a shallow bowl and top with the squid. Spoon the tamarind sauce around the edge of the plate and serve garnished with the basil leaves.

Steamed Whole Fish

CÁ HÁP

The Chinese influence is all over this dish but the Vietnamese have made it their own, using fish sauce, tomatoes and herbs.

There is a lot of room for personal interpretation by replacing different ingredients. I've eaten this dish all over Vietnam and it's fair to say there is no one way of doing it. It is simple to prepare and the results are always pleasing.

A little trick I learned on my recent trips to China while shooting *World Café Asia* is to salt the fish for a couple of hours before cooking. It improves the texture of very flaky fish as well as seasoning the flesh.

The Vietnamese use both fresh and dried mushrooms for this dish, for example little button mushrooms along with dried Chinese mushrooms (just a few because they have a strong – and sometimes musty – taste). Use wood ears if you can find them – they have a very short shelf life. Fresh and dried shiitake are extremely good here too.

Vietnamese soy sauce is preferable: if you only have the stronger-tasting Japanese version, reduce the amount to 1 tablespoon.

SERVES 4

2 whole white fish such as sea bass or grouper (1-1.5kg in total), cleaned and gutted

4 tbsp coarse salt (not fine salt)

50g spring onions, cut into 4cm pieces

30g coriander leaves, coarsely shredded

1 tsp fresh dill fronds

1 large cinnamon stick, cut into 4cm pieces

Steaming liquid

1 tbsp fish sauce

1½ tbsp sugar

50g fresh ginger, peeled and crushed

1 tsp black peppercorns

1 red chilli, deseeded and sliced at an angle

50g dill, shredded

To serve

2 tbsp vegetable oil

6 mushrooms, stalks removed and the tops cross cut

30g celery leaves, cut at an angle into 4cm pieces

2 tbsp soy sauce

1 tomato, sliced

2 red chillies, flower cut

4 dill sprigs

Starting at the head, score the fish on each side with crisscross slices about 2.5cm apart. Sprinkle the coarse salt into the incisions and the cavity of the fish and let marinate for 1 hour. During this time the fish will release quite a bit of water.

After the marinating, rinse well under cold running water, then pat dry with paper towels, making sure it is totally dry.

In a mixing bowl, combine all the ingredients for the steaming liquid. Pour over the fish, inside and out, and marinate for another 30 minutes.

Prepare a large steamer with boiling water. Lay the fish on a heatproof plate. Lay the spring onions, coriander, dill and cinnamon on top of the fish and place in the steamer basket. It should take approximately 10–15 minutes to cook, depending on thickness.

Meanwhile, heat the vegetable oil in a sauté pan over medium heat and stir-fry the mushrooms for about a minute. Then add the celery leaves and cook for another 30 seconds. Season with soy sauce.

To check whether the fish is done, insert the tip of a pointed knife into the thickest part of the fish, then place it against your hand to gauge the temperature: it should feel warm, not cold.

Once the fish is ready, remove it from the steamer. Arrange the tomato slices around the perimeter of the plate, top the fish with the mushroom and celery mixture, then garnish with the chilli flowers and dill sprigs to serve.

Fish Simmered in Caramel Sauce

CÁ KHO TỘ

This is one of our restaurant's takes on caramel fish. Some people find the traditional recipe too pungent. Quite frankly I prefer the simple bold flavours of the original, but this is a good alternative for those who are looking for more complexity of flavour.

SERVES 8

½ aubergine

450ml Caramel sauce (see page 43)

4 red chillies, deseeded and finely chopped

30g roughly chopped fresh ginger

1 tbsp black peppercorns

200g fresh galangal, thinly sliced

125ml sake

4 tbsp fish sauce

4 tbsp honey

1 tsp salt

1kg catfish fillets, cut into 12.5 cm pieces

freshly ground black pepper

julienne of fresh ginger, for garnish (optional)

Char the aubergine by roasting it directly over a charcoal grill, gas burner or electric hob, turning frequently. When the skin is black, place the aubergine in a plastic bag until cool. Peel away the charred skin, then chop the flesh finely.

In a clay pot or casserole, combine the caramel sauce with 2 litres water and bring to the boil.

Reduce the heat and add the chillies, ginger, peppercorns, galangal, sake, fish sauce, honey and salt. Add the fish and return to the boil. Reduce the heat to a low simmer, cover and simmer for about 2 hours, turning the fish occasionally.

Transfer to a clay pot for serving and add the

aubergine, a couple of pieces of fish, and some of the sauce with the chilli. Reheat the stew and, just before serving, sprinkle with black pepper, and garnish with the julienne of ginger if desired. Serve with steamed rice or fried rice.

Whole Fried Fish with Fried Rice & Cucumber Salad

CƠM RANG VỚI CÁ RÁN VÀ NỘM DƯA CHUỘT

I might get a lot of flack from friends who worked with me at Elka in 1994 for including this dish in the book, as it is not one of my 'originals'. It's not an Elka original either, and can easily be found on the streets of Thailand, though the introduction of coriander seed does make it a little different. It's still a favourite dish, as it's very simple to make, and in a restaurant it is easy to manage – or so I thought.

When I opened the Red Onion Bistro in 1997, I needed a dish that would be easy to execute on the hot line when it got busy. This recipe seemed a no-brainer, but we ran into problems at the preparation stage because I wanted to use the freshest fish available. I would order live catfish in the morning, and kill them three hours before service to marinate them. Unfortunately, the killing part was the problem.

It had always been my understanding that the kindest way to kill a live fish was to whack it over the head with a mallet. Or better yet, break the neck, if you can hold the damn thing down and know how to kill with your hands. But catfish have a claw next to the dorsal fin that makes holding them a bit tricky. If this scratches you, infection is guaranteed. So I put on my metal Michael Jackson glove (a butcher's glove) which still did not instil any sense of comfort or security. Fearful of being pierced by a toxic thorn, my lack of confidence showed to all who watched.

The catfish is a real fighter. I tried holding it down while feebly trying to puncture the head with a sharp knife, but the head was like rock, and the fish would forcefully shake away. After several attempts, I tried whacking it with a mallet, but the humanitarian in me cringed at the sight of this fish doing its powerful best to swing out of danger.

My staff looked on dumbfounded. I could see from their eyes that they knew I'd never killed a live catfish and that I had no idea what I was doing. They asked that they take responsibility for executing the fish. I gladly passed on the task to the first person to take my Michael Jackson glove.

Many of our cooks took pride in finding new, creative methods to 'improve' on the techniques I had taught them. They would deviate from the methodology over and over again, which would drive me nuts. It would either result in a brilliant new method or another problem – more often than not it would be the latter.

One of their first methods was to wrap the catfish in a kitchen towel, then jump up in the air, and slam-dunk the fish on the ground like they were playing in the NBA. When the dazed catfish was unwrapped on the floor, a nervous wriggle ran through its body and the whiskers pulsated randomly in bewilderment. It was clearly still alive. The young cook grinned at me, his face cracking into a fully-fledged smile that sought approval for his unconventional method. I looked at him with a stern face and told him he would have to do better than that. 'It was not particularly nice for the fish to be slammed on the kitchen floor, and now the fish will be bruised, ruining the flavour by the time it is cooked.' His smile was reduced to a frown, but he agreed.

Twenty minutes later I returned to the kitchen and noticed that all the catfish were hanging dead in the sink. I walked past the sink several times and eventually noticed a pattern of splattered blood on my clean Braggart chef jacket. I could not figure out how I got blood all over myself, as I did not do any butchering.

Taking a closer look at the catfish, I noticed that they were not actually dead – just hanging there dying. The staff had somehow managed to puncture the sides of the fishes' mouths, loop a piece of very tough plastic rope through them all and hang them from the faucet in the middle of the empty sink. They had also slit both sides of the bodies below the head, and at the tail. There the poor fish hung, bleeding to death and giving the occasional violent wriggle in search of freedom, which would splatter yet more blood all over the place.

I turned to the cook responsible for the new technique. 'What are you doing to the poor fish?'

With a wide smile he responded: 'I am bleeding it to death, chef!'

'Why the hell are you doing that?'

'Because last time you complained that we bruised the meat. This way, the meat is very clean because all the blood goes out.'

'Okay, I understand that, but you are going to have to find another way to kill it. This is way too cruel. Aren't you people Buddhists?'

I became a chef in denial. I didn't want to see the poor creatures die in such horrible ways, so I just made sure I was never around to see the killing of the catfish.

Weeks later, I opened up the freezer in search of some puff pastry. As I moved deeper and deeper into the dark cabinet, shifting items from side to side, I reached towards a plastic bag that suddenly jumped violently. I quickly jumped back, freaked out.

'Hey, there is something moving in a plastic bag in the freezer!'

The cook jumped up with glee. 'It's the catfish, chef!'

'The catfish? What's it doing in the freezer?'

'We are freezing it to death.'

I took catfish off the menu after that. Some time later I learned that, being a freshwater fish, catfish cannot handle salt. Salt water, and they are dead in seconds.

SERVES 2

1 catfish or sea bass, about 500g
10g fresh ginger, sliced
10g garlic cloves, crushed
2 tbsp coriander seeds, crushed
20g coriander sprigs, for garnish
4 lemon grass stalks, pounded
vegetable oil, for deep-frying
150g plain flour
Fried rice
400g cooked rice
1 egg
½ tbsp soy sauce
4 tbsp frozen peas
20g spring onion, sliced in 3cm pieces

Salad
200g cucumber, cut into noodle strips
¼ tbsp vinegar
¼ tbsp sugar
¼ tsp chopped chilli
¼ tbsp salt
1 tsp toasted sesame seeds

Starting at the head, score the fish on each side with criss-cross slices about 2.5cm apart. Rub the ginger, garlic, coriander seeds and half the coriander all over the fish, spreading it into the incisions and the cavity. Put the lemon grass in the cavity and marinate for 2 hours.

To make the fried rice, coat a wok lightly with oil and heat until almost smoking. Throw in the cold cooked rice and stir-fry it, leaving it occasionally until you can hear it crackling a bit as this will give it a little bit of extra flavour.

Reduce the heat under the wok and make a well in the middle of the rice. Crack in the egg. Allow the white to cook a bit, then break the yolk and work into the rice. Toss back and forth, breaking the egg into smaller and smaller pieces.

Once the egg is nicely cooked and evenly mixed in, season with soy sauce. Stir in the peas and spring onions, and cook until tender.

Remove from the heat and garnish with the remaining fresh coriander.

Combine the cucumber, vinegar, sugar, chilli and salt, and marinate for 10 minutes.

In a deep-fryer or large heavy-based pan, heat the oil. Lift the fish from the marinade and dust it in the flour, ensuring it is nicely coated (don't worry about marinade sticking to the fish). Gently slip the fish into the hot oil, being careful to avoid splashing. Fry for 10–12 minutes, depending on the size of the fish, turning to ensure both sides are evenly cooked and lightly golden. Remove the fish from the fryer, allowing the oil to drain back, and pat with towel to remove excess oil.

Place the fried rice in a bowl, patting it down tightly. Invert on to a serving plate so that the mound of rice sits in the middle of the plate. Lay the fish on the edge of the plate and the cucumber salad to one side. Sprinkle the cucumber with toasted sesame seeds before serving.

Sake Steamed Clams

NGAO HẤP RƯỢU SAKE

I've based this on the French way of steaming mussels or clams in white wine with garlic, but given it an Asian twist by using sake, ginger and lemon grass. I don't use butter, so it is a pretty light dish, but I do like to reduce the cooking liquid by half, making it a little too salty, then add cream and reduce again to give the sauce a wonderfully rich seafood flavour. This offends many Italians who tell me that in Italy you do not mix cream and seafood – then I remind them I'm Chinese Egyptian and we are in Vietnam.

One of the best ways to purge live clams is to soak them in water with one crushed chilli, a trick I learned in Vietnam. The clams go crazy and spit everything out. I asked a vegetarian friend if it was okay to purge clams like this, or if it would be viewed as inhumane, and she assured me it was okay because clams do not have eyes!

SERVES 2

2kg live clams
5 red chillies, pounded
125ml sake
20g fresh ginger, half smashed and half finely
**   chopped**
2 lemon grass stalks, pounded, plus 2 tbsp crushed
**   lemon grass**
2 tbsp crushed garlic
2 tbsp skinned and diced tomato
2 tbsp coriander leaves
2 tsp thinly sliced kaffir lime leaves

First purge the clams by soaking them in water to which you have added the pounded chillies.

Heat a wide, shallow pot big enough to accommodate the clams on the stove. Add the sake, smashed ginger, lemon grass stalks, garlic and 400ml water, and bring to the boil.

Add the clams, cover and steam for 3 minutes, or until they open. Lift out the opened clams, placing them in serving bowls. Repeat at 20–30 second intervals, until all are cooked.

Pour the hot stock over the clams. Scatter with the ginger, lemon grass, tomato, coriander and lime leaf. Serve immediately.

Seared Alaskan Day Boat Scallops

DIEP ALASKA ÁP CHẢO

In Vietnam, scallops are generally small and not as sweet as cold water ones. Donald Berger from Vine restaurant imported scallops from Alaska and served them thinly sliced, sashimi style. They were amazing. I ordered a bunch, played around with them and came up with this simple yet decadent dish. I cook the scallops in duck fat, but any vegetable oil will do - except olive oil.

SERVES 1

110g frozen peas
1 tbsp truffle oil
salt and pepper
sugar
a little duck fat or vegetable oil
3 king or jumbo scallops
40g shelled edamame
1 tsp lemon oil

Blanch the peas in a pan of boiling salted water for about 10 seconds, drain and tip into ice-cold water. Peel by hand or (if making a larger amount) push through a ricer to remove the skins. Put the peas in a blender and whiz until smooth, adding a little water and finishing with a little truffle oil. The consistency can vary: if you want it thick, add some more truffle oil for an emulsified sauce, or more water for a thinner mixture. Season with salt, pepper and a little sugar if bitter.

Heat a frying pan with a little duck fat or vegetable oil until it is almost smoking. Season the scallops, place them in the pan and sear for about 20 seconds. With a pair of tongs or spatula, move them around a little, making sure there is enough oil to coat them and give a nice brown colour. Flip the scallops over and cook for another 10 seconds. The exact cooking time depends on the thickness of the scallops as well as the frying pan – they should be medium-rare.

Blanch the edamame in a saucepan of boiling salted water to heat them up. Drain them, then place them in a bowl and season.

Spoon the pea purée in the middle of a serving plate. Place the edamame on that, then top with the scallops. Garnish with a little lemon oil to serve.

Seafood Ceviche with Mangosteen Vinaigrette GỎI HẢI SẢN

I have always been a fan of ceviche, but one chef really blew the idea wide open for me. He has a restaurant in the Mission District of San Francisco by the name of Alma, and I guess worked in Peru and picked up lots of tricks. His ceviche has the perfect balance of spice, acidity and complementary flavours that do not detract from the seafood. My problem has always been balancing sweetness with acidity, but this dish, I think, answers the question.

I love mangosteen, it has the right amount of sweetness yet it is a little tart. To smooth out the tartness we use coconut milk. To add an extra flavour dimension, we sprinkle on a little white truffle oil. (If you can't find mangosteens, fresh rambutans or lychees are appropriate, but will add a slightly sweeter taste to the ceviche.)

An additional step I take may offend purists: I blanch my seafood in a hot aromatic liquid 'just in case'. Because of the bacteria build-up in the tropics, I try to kill any form, especially on seafood. If you want you can just marinate the seafood.

SERVES 2

60g sea bass fillet, thinly sliced
60g prawns, cut into 2.5cm rounds
60g squid, tentacles or body, scored
5 king or jumbo scallops, quartered
4 tbsp orange juice
5 tbsp lemon juice
4 tbsp mangosteen purée
4 tbsp coconut milk
4 tbsp each chopped red and yellow pepper flesh
4 tbsp chopped onion
truffle oil, for sprinkling
8 sprigs coriander, finely chopped
Cooking broth
2 tbsp lime juice
1 tbsp salt
4 lemon grass stalks, pounded

In a saucepan, combine the broth ingredients with 500ml water and bring to the boil over a high heat.

Working with one variety at a time, blanch the seafood in the broth for 10 seconds, then remove with a slotted spoon or spider and place in a bowl of cold water.

In a bowl, combine the orange and lemon juices. Drain the seafood and add to the juices. Leave to marinate in the fridge for 30 minutes.

Meanwhile, in another bowl combine the mangosteen, coconut milk, peppers and onion.

Drain the seafood and stir it into the mangosteen dressing. Season and sprinkle a little truffle oil on top. Garnish with chopped coriander and serve.

Oyster Brûlée

HÀO BÒ LÒ

This lighter take on Oysters Rockefeller was inspired by my days at Fleur de Lys and is one of my favourite ways to cook oysters.

Oysters Rockefeller is so called because it is so rich, not because Rockefeller invented it or ate a lot of it. The oysters sit on a bed of mashed potatoes and are topped with a bacon, spinach purée and hollandaise sauce. It is put under a salamander or grilled until the top is golden brown.

SERVES 3

12 oysters
48 spinach leaves
salt and pepper
5 egg yolks
7 tbsp sake
3 tbsp crushed ginger
125g extra-creamy mashed potato

Shuck all the oysters, reserving the juices, and place in the fridge. Strain the juice to remove any chipped shell and set aside.

Blanch the spinach in a saucepan of boiling salted water for a few seconds, just until wilted. Remove with a slotted spoon and place in an ice bath to stop the cooking process and preserve the bright colour. Drain thoroughly, squeeze out all the water from the leaves and chop them finely.

Preheat the oven to 230°C/Gas 8.

Put the egg yolks and 5 tablespoons of cold water in a large heatproof bowl and set it over the pan of hot water. Whisk quickly and thoroughly to ensure that the eggs are cooking evenly and not scrambling. Continue until the mixture has doubled in size. Add the sake and the reserved oyster juice to the bowl and continue whisking until the sabayon reaches ribbon stage. Dip a spoon in the mixture – it should be thick enough to coat the back of the spoon. Season to taste.

Spread some rock salt (or dried beans) over a baking tray and press the base of the oyster shells into the salt so that they sit flat. Put 1–2 teaspoons of mashed potato in each shell and sit the oysters on top of the mashed potatoes.

In a small bowl, mix the spinach, ginger and a little of the sake sabayon together. Spoon this mixture over the oysters.

Bake until golden brown (alternatively, place them under a salamander or brown with a blowtorch). Serve immediately.

Kasu Sea Bass with Tamarind Rice Cake, Beet Jus and Vegetable Noodles

CÁ VƯỢC TẨM RƯỢU NẾP CÁI ÁP CHẢO

Walking through the Benton market I was introduced to an array of dessert dishes I had never seen before. One of them was fermented rice. The rice is part-cooked, then yeast is added and the mixture ferments, creating a little bit of a sour alcoholic taste. I was told it was good for an upset stomach and one bite immediately made me think that would be so. The combination of sweet alcohol and yeast flavours with the texture of rice was very interesting. It reminded me of kasu, the leftover rice lees of sake.

I bought a bag and returned to my kitchen to play with it. I threw the rice mixture into a blender and puréed it with a little sake. Strangely enough, I liked it more than the kasu. The flavours were more complex, although the sugar content was much higher, making it theoretically more difficult to cook, as a high heat could easily burn it. In the end that turned out to be a blessing, as it allowed me to cook the fish very slowly over a low heat.

Although many components are similar to the dish produced at Elka, I've altered the recipe so the tastes are totally different. The dish is light and healthy, and people usually remember it long after eating it.

SERVES 2

150g fermented rice, or kasu (rice lees)
125ml sake
300g sea bass
300g cooked white rice
3 tbsp black sesame seeds
vegetable oil, for frying
salt and pepper
200g greens, such as spinach
100g cooked beetroot, peeled and cut into slices
    2mm thick
1 tbsp Tamarind Sauce (see page 49)
handful vegetable 'noodles', such as carrot,
    cucumber and daikon
2 tbsp Lemon Oil (see page 49)
3 tbsp chopped chives
4 tbsp strained puréed beetroot

In a blender or a food processor, pulse the fermented rice or kasu with the sake. Pour the mixture over the fish, turn to coat, and leave to marinate in the fridge for 24 hours.

Next day, mix the cooked rice with the black sesame seeds. Use a Japanese rice mould, 7.5cm ring mould or similar device (such as a clean can) to shape the mixture, dampening it with water to prevent the rice sticking.

Heat a frying pan. Season the fish with salt and pepper and lay it in the pan, making sure the pan is not too hot, otherwise the marinade will burn. Keep the heat up for a couple of minutes, then reduce the heat to low and continue cooking without touching the fish, otherwise it will stick. Cook until the fish becomes a little opaque at the sides, about 3–4 minutes.

In a separate frying pan, heat a little oil and sear the rice cakes until lightly browned and crisp.

Heat some oil in another pan and sauté the greens until wilted. Season with salt and pepper.

Place the beetroot on a serving plate and top with the sautéed greens. Rest the sea bass on top. Place the rice cake on the fish and drizzle a little of the tamarind sauce on top of the rice cake.

Toss the vegetable noodles in the lemon oil. Season with salt and pepper and throw in some finely chopped chives and place on top of the fish. Drizzle the beet jus around the plate and serve.

Blackened Barramundi on Braised Banana Blossoms with a Turmeric Balsamic Vinaigrette

CÁ VƯỢC ÁP CHÀO VỚI HOA CHUỐI OM

This dish is one of my favourites as it took me six years to get it to the stage it is now. It is hot, cold, sweet and sour, and has the balance of ying and yang… It has interesting contrasts of textures and flavours that have never been brought together before. It is a dish that evolved and changed as I learned and found inspiration.

The sauce and the presentation were inspired by a movie. I had always done reductions of balsamic vinegar, but when I saw the movie 'Jackson Pollack', I decided to use his painting technique with the reduction. Each dish is very different, like a painting.

The braised banana blossom is not very common, but makes a refreshing salad. I learned this from my chef from Hue. I had heard about the technique, but it took me a good seven years to find someone who actually knew how to cook a banana blossom. We tried to take shortcuts, but we later learned that there is no real substitute for time.

A filet of barramundi is coated in the sort of spice mixture that they would sell on the streets of Cairo when you bought a couple of bread sticks. You would lick the bread stick and then dip it into the package of spice. I have added a little chilli to add some spiciness.

SERVES 3

150g barramundi fillets
1 tsp vegetable oil
Spice mixture
4 tbsp chillies, lightly charred over a flame
2 tbsp coriander seeds
2 tbsp mustard seeds
2 tbsp cumin seeds
Banana blossom
1 banana blossom
3 tbsp lemon juice
2 tbsp lime juice
2 tbsp sugar
2 tbsp basil
2 tbsp crushed peanuts

Turmeric vinaigrette
350ml balsamic vinegar
125ml vegetable oil
4 tbsp ground turmeric

Place the banana blossom in a pot of cold water with the lemon juice and bring to the boil. Lower the heat to a simmer, and cook for 1 hour or until tender. You need to weigh the banana blossom down as they have a tendency to float, imparting a darkish colour. You can do this with a kitchen towel or a plate or bowl that will fit over the blossom.

Remove from the water and, when cool, discard the outer leaves. Shred the inner leaves into bite-size pieces. Remove the small flowers that would end up being the banana, as these are both bitter and stringy. Place in a cool place and season with the lime juice, sugar and the basil.

Preheat the oven to 180°C/Gas 4.

In a dry pan, roast all the spices and then place in a spice grinder and pulverize to a powder. This can be done in batches. Reserve (it can be kept for a month in an airtight container or freezer).

Reduce the balsamic vinegar in a small pan until it is reaches a syrupy consistency, making sure you don't burn it at the sides. Once reduced, pour it into a squeezy bottle.

Put the turmeric in a pan with the vegetable oil and heat until it bubbles. Remove from the heat and leave until the oil takes on a good colour of the spice. Strain through a coffee filter and pour into a separate squeezy bottle.

Place a teaspoon of oil in a sauté pan. Coat the fish with the spice mixture. Once the oil starts to smoke, place the fish in the pan with the coating side down and sear. Reduce the heat to medium.

Once the fish is slightly blackened, turn it over and put in the preheated oven for 6 minutes.

While it is in the oven, take the chilled blossom and mix in the crushed peanuts. Place in the centre of the plate. Drizzle the balsamic reduction around the banana blossom, then drizzle the turmeric oil around the balsamic reduction. Place the fish on top of the blossom and serve.

Cooch and Bobby during an uncharacteristic quiet moment in the restaurant

Blackened Barramundi on Braised Banana Blossoms with a Turmeric Balsamic Vinaigrette

Pan-roasted Salmon on Wasabi Mashed Potatoes, Grilled Vegetables, Ginger Demi-glace

This is the dish that propelled me to 'rock star' status in Vietnam. I have never been able to take it off my menu, and although I get sick of making it, it has become second nature to all of the kitchen staff. Whenever I take it off my menu and offer another salmon dish, I still sold more salmon with wasabi-mashed potatoes then I did the other salmon or the other dishes on my menu! I see the dish all over the place now.

I made the dish by accident. At a restaurant in the San Francisco Mission District called Valencia 25, I ate this wonderful salmon dish that was served with a wasabi cream sauce. So I thought I would make it, and I accidentally added the creamed wasabi to the mashed potatoes.

For the sake of simplicity, I have given here a very simplified version of Demi-glace sauce.

SERVES 5

5 salmon fillets, each about 150g, skin on, scaled
shoestring potatoes, to serve (optional)
Sauce
225g sugar
240ml rice wine vinegar
5cm piece fresh ginger, peeled and finely chopped
2.5 litres Fish Stock (see page 51), boiled to reduce by half
Wasabi mashed potatoes
900g potatoes, peeled, quartered and those pieces cut into 4–6 pieces roughly the same size
2 tbsp wasabi powder
240ml double cream
Grilled vegetables
1 thick carrot, sliced an angle about 1–2mm thick
1 thick courgette, sliced at an angle about 1–2mm thick
vegetable oil

To make the sauce, put the sugar in a pot and place over a very low heat until it melts. Cook it slowly. Once the sugar takes on a rusty colour on the sides of the pot, with a wooden spoon stir it around. You want to cook the sugar until it takes on a caramel colour, just like you are making caramel.

Once it gets to the caramel stage, throw in the ginger. A wonderful steam will rise, so do not keep your hands in the pot! The ginger will release its juices. Let it cook until those juices are almost gone. Throw in the vinegar and reduce the liquid by half. Throw in the reduced stock, bring to the boil and reduce until it coats the back of a spoon. The taste sensation should be sweet, sour, and then ginger. If you need to adjust the flavour of the sauce you can do by simply adding the ingredient that is not strong enough. Need more ginger? Add more. Too sweet and not sour enough, add a little vinegar. Strain the sauce and keep warm.

Place the wasabi in a bowl, add 2 tablespoons of water and stir in. It should be more liquid than the wasabi served in Japanese sushi restaurants. Add the cream so you have a wonderfully light green sauce. Season with salt and pepper.

To make the mashed potatoes, place the potatoes in cold water with a little salt. Bring to the boil and then reduce the heat to simmer. Cook for about 20 minutes or until tender. The quick test is to remove a potato, cut it and, if there is no resistance, then it is ready. Pass the potatoes through a food mill and purée.

Grill the vegetables: preheat a medium grill, toss the vegetable slices in a little oil and season with salt and pepper. Grill for about 2 minutes on each side until tender. Carrot's high sugar content makes it burn readily, so take care.

Season the salmon on the skin side. Place a frying pan over high heat and coat with oil. Once the oil gets close to smoking-hot, reduce the heat and place the salmon in, skin side down. Cook for about 5 minutes (the skin should be crispy), season the top side of the salmon and flip it over, then reduce the heat to very low. Continue to cook for 4 minutes. Remove and pat off excess oil.

Pour a little wasabi cream into the potatoes, folding it in so that they are nice and creamy and the wasabi cream is well distributed. The flavour should be subtle and not overpowering.

Place the wasabi potatoes in the middle of the plate and the vegetable slices around that. Place the salmon on top and drizzle the ginger sauce around the plate. Top with the shoestring potatoes if you like and serve!

Saigon Joe's and the fish botherer

The heat and humidity was starting to weigh me down: unemployed, broke and disgruntled, my father, Frank and his childhood friend, Ronnie and I went for a quick bite down in Pham Ngu Lao, the grungy backpacker street, at Kim's Café, where the Western and Vietnamese food was good, quick and cheap. Heading into the café, we bumped into an Irish gentleman, 'Paddy', a long time expat who seemed to know everything going on in Saigon at the time.

'Listen, we're interested in opening a restaurant... know any that might be available?'

'Funny you should ask. I know a fantastic place. Great location! It's off of Ngyuen Hue and Ham Nghi. The two guys that run it have absolutely no idea what they're doing. It is called "Fashion Café" supposedly to attract models and people in the fashion industry. One of the owners is a model, and he... well, the other partner who is American, well he bankrolled it.

'They've had this place for about six months and they have not attracted a single customer since the grand opening party. They put a bit of money into the place and it looks brand new. You can most probably get a deal out of them because I think they would be more then happy to cut their losses – they have been bleeding for a while.'

It all sounded too good to be true. We quickly ate and sped over to the café. There it sat, three houses down from a large tower under construction on Ngyuen Hue called Harbor View Tower. On a one-way street stood this three-storey classic glass-front building, narrow and tall. We went in for a cup of coffee. David, the American co-owner was there, but was not prepared for customers, so it was going to take some time for his non-English speaking staff to boil water and all the other necessary preparations for a Vietnamese iced coffee.

The interiors were bland and the eyes quickly got tired of the black-and-white colour scheme. All the chairs were painted black, to match the black granite tables, black-painted floors and the black glossy frames filled with black-and-white photographs by Ansel Adams. In vivid contrast, the walls were painted bright white. As we waited for the coffee, I asked David if I could see the rest of the place.

David was gracious and provided us with a tour. At the back of the restaurant, was a lavatory that smelt like a sewer. There were no ventilation or extraction fans, so the air movement was non-existent, making it extremely hot and humid, with smells that permeated up the back of the black-painted staircase bringing us up to the first landing, a replica of the downstairs but without the bar. This wide-open floor space was very springy. It appeared that the frame of the room was being eaten away by termites.

There was yet another floor above this, but this was David's personal space. The top of the building was unfinished, with a skeleton of a floor that wobbled and shook when walked on.

The place was a potential gold mine – sitting next to a future high rise in the middle of burgeoning District 1, on two major crossroads, around the corner from a wet-market and the convenience stores where all the expats shopped. I wanted it. The thought of being able to cook and design my own place without any interference from anyone else felt very liberating.

Within a week, Frank had negotiated everything. 'Gentlemen we have ourselves a sweet deal. This is what we have. We have a turnkey restaurant for free! The rent has been pre-paid for the next 9 months with a remaining 5-year lease; all we have to do is pay operational costs. I told David that we would close the restaurant for a couple of weeks to make improvements and then we would reopen it. We would give him 90% of our sales.' The logic being that we didn't have to commit a lot of capital and if it made money we would keep it, and pay for part of his investment. If it didn't

make anything, then we could simply hand it back. Anything we made would be more than David was presently making. David's Vietnamese partner had signed the lease over to Ronnie's girlfriend, who dropped her Vietnamese name and went by the name of Kathy.

The only problem with the deal is that the people with all the money pulled out, leaving just Ronnie and I, and neither of us had the resources to honour the deal with David.

Ronnie and I agreed that he would sort out construction and I would work on everything else. I would go out of my way to source equipment and supplies. What was not available would be fabricated.

The front of the house did not need as much work as the back, as David did not have enough equipment to do any real volume. He did not have enough pots and pans, and what he did have was not very good quality.

Staff in the old days would do anything for a job. You could hire them as a cook, but make them do your laundry without complaints. I asked Laura, my girlfriend at the time, who had followed me out to Vietnam and was working at the Camargue, if I could borrow some money from her, as well as to check if one of the better guys in the kitchen of Camargue would be interested in working with me again.

She arranged a meeting with Vinh, a talented chef who was a little too close to the chef I'd fired immediately when I joined the Camargue. I would have liked him to join but, politically, I was thinking that he could be there as a spy.

After the interview he did return to Camargue to tell them what was happening and within three days they fired Laura. The only beauty of that was that we both now had an axe to grind. She was on board and we were now without an income, with very limited savings and facing huge expense. Now we had to show Alexander, the Camargue's owner, our true capabilities.

Laura had run the front of house at Wolfgang Puck's Postrio restaurant in San Francisco, as well as Aqua and Charles on Nob Hill under Michael Mina. She was one of the best floor managers in the business, as she is a third-generation hotelier, being brought up in a two-Michelin-star restaurant in Bordeaux.

Day after day I would run around Saigon telling all my friends about my new venture. I went to see Alex, a Malaysian chef trained as a sushi chef who was running one of the top Japanese restaurants in Saigon called Sekitei on Nam Ky Khoi Nghai. Alex was having a difficult time. He was not getting paid, but he was eating and drinking well. We were both in the same boat, and we would go out of our way to help each other whenever possible.

'Alex I need your help.'

Sitting on top of 50kg gas canisters overlooking his line, he would suck on his cigarettes like a dope smoker hitting on a joint that was being passed around for the first time.

'Give me a couple of your weak guys that have potential. Or, better yet, swap some shifts around and give me your best guys.'

'Toy Boy!' he demanded.

Toy Boy was a good-looking Vietnamese member of his staff who could speak English fluently. Then – in semi-Vietnamese coupled with pigeon English or what is generally referred to as Singlish – he asked him to find out from the staff who'd like to come learn Western food.

Mr Hung was a small man. He had a piece of hair growing out the side of his neck that stretched a good 8 inches. He was keen and almost cried when he came to join. I was very touched. He would oversee construction and seemed to have a lot of knowledge of electricity. He would help on the installation of an extraction fan, while hanging half his body out of a window in the middle of a torrential rainstorm.

The pressure started to mount. We were

three months into construction with no end in sight. The kitchen was completed, but without much of the equipment. The middle floor had one of the best banquettes I'd ever seen, but it was so far from completion I was going nuts.

'Ronnie, how long is this going to take?'

'Hey man, these guys are working their ass off for you and all you do is complain.'

'Because it's taking them forever. It would have been completed by now if we paid them by the job, and not by the day.'

'Great workers won't work by the job.'

I did not know construction costs here, but everyone I talked to told me that $5 per person per day was a lot of money, and that they were most probably working slowly to kept their jobs.

Later that day I returned to the restaurant to find all my Van Morrison CDs missing. It was now war!

'It is really simple. If my CDs are not returned, everyone here is fired. You have two hours to return them.'

Two hours later no CDs. I opened the door and told everyone to get their belongings and go. With a bitter taste in his mouth, Ronnie stared at me 'You know. You really are an asshole. I can't work with you. I'm out and I do not want anything to do with this any more.' He shook his head, picked up his helmet and walked out.

In disbelief and hands on her hips, Laura silently protested my latest actions 'Bobby, how are we going to open now?'

'We will do it ourselves. Fuck the second floor! We will only open downstairs and, once we get money, we will invest in the second floor.'

We needed business cards, but we did not have any idea of the logo. I liked the card of Gravellier in Bordeaux, a great restaurant where I was able to do a stag and named after the chef, Eave Gravellier. So we simply copied it, adjusting shapes and colour, and adding a spoon to the original fork and knife logo. Without a computer we were forced to spend much of our time at the Internet Café to design the logo. Its owner observed our total lack of computer competency, and out of sheer guilt started to design it for us, as he felt sorry for our struggles and us, as our story had circulated around town.

'What are we going to call it?'

'Saigon Joe's'

'You can't name it Saigon Joe's.'

'Why not?'

'You can only name a business after a Vietnamese city or province if it's a joint venture.'

'You're kidding me!'

'No.'

'Okay, then I will still call it Saigon Joe's. There is no city in Vietnam called Saigon; it's called Ho Chi Minh City.'

'You know what I mean!'

'Yeah, but come on, that is not a big deal.'

'Yes it is! It is part of the Social Evil Decree. You're serving liquor, you have female staff, and you have music. That means you could be potentially in the entertainment business. If you have a sign in English, then you have to make another sign three times the size in Vietnamese. Just look around! My government does not want foreigners in this business. You are not really welcomed in this business.'

I did not really need it explained to me. I had already seen the way business was being conducted. There were too many risks. Firstly, you needed a Vietnamese national to front for you, which meant everything was in their name. Once you put the money in and if it made money, you would not have a leg to stand on. Changing laws, new cops, staff boycotts, the market ripping you off, the list could go on and on, but somehow I was determined, and we were in too deep not to go through with it. I was prepared to lose it all as I really had nothing left to lose.

On completion of the logo, the Internet café was closed down. The owner said he was accused of spying, his business closed and his computers confiscated. It was another painful day for entrepreneurs in the early days of an economy opening up. It wasn't just the foreigners that were having a bad time; the Vietnamese were having a tough ride as well, if not tougher. We were all pioneers in the changing face of Vietnam, but didn't know it. As the market shifted from being centrally controlled to a free-market economy, there would be teething problems and a lot of victims.

Across the street from the restaurant was a man who sat with a bicycle pump and a little plastic bottle of gasoline. He sat there morning, noon and night. During that entire period of time, he never fixed one tyre, nor did he do anything but stare through our windows. He was what was regarded as a cell.

I convinced Laura that we would be better off sandblasting the window, so we could see out but no one could really see in. It was not as if the view of a bunch of stores selling alcohol was that pleasing to the eye. The only part of the window that would not be sandblasted would be our logo. It gave the place a very cool look, both inside and out.

Tet was quickly approaching, and the city was rapidly coming to a standstill. People just stopped working, prices were going up day by the day and the streets were becoming incredibly colourful and crowded.

Our natural fear was that, after Tet, the staff we'd hired would have a change of heart and would not show up for work. We were advised by all our friends to leave and take a break, since no one would be in town, plus we both really needed one. Down to our last $500, we decided to take a cheap vacation at the beach in Phan Tiet. Laura was worried, but Laura was always worried about money. She was begging me to get assistance from my father, not understanding that my Chinese father was not like other fathers.

In order for me to have any credibility in his eyes I needed to do everything by myself. I needed to suffer. Because suffering builds character, and if it was not enough that I was born in New Zealand, lived on four continents, was half Egyptian, and half Chinese, and been sent through the English boarding school system, the last thing on earth I would do is ask him for help.

Phase 1 was to build a kitchen on the top floor, build a bar and paint the downstairs, so we could open immediately. Once we were open and had enough money, we could open the second floor. I designed the layout of the kitchen, while Ronnie supervised the construction. The construction took forever with no end in sight.

The firepower was limited. I had a 5-top Electrolux that did not provide enough BTU to sear anything in volume. We simply put a hotel pan on top, filled it with water and in smaller pots, kept all out sauces and some of our mise en place in containers to keep warm.

We used a wok burner sat on a wooden stool to fire up two frying pans for searing.

Because of the very high cost of decent frying pans, we decided to go with a griddle – a large iron plate with a Chinese wok burner below it. I had observed the most efficient use of griddles at La Taqueria on 24th and Mission, and at Fleur de Lys.

It would take time to learn and understand the timing of cooking items like fish and chicken, but once you could gauge the heat, it would be pretty much easy cooking, with very little washing up. We would learn to cook on equipment that was totally different from any cooking apparatus I had ever encountered before. We also quickly saw that the reason why all the people use electric fans for their grills on the street was not for the same reason I had originally thought. The humidity is so high, that charcoal is rather damp and does not last very long lit by itself. It needs to be fuelled by a strong air supply to keep it roaring, which actually helps the whole smoky flavour. In time we would learn and implement Vietnamese techniques to our cooking. It became a management issue of understanding how to grill Western meats in Vietnamese style.

Suppliers were also eager to sell us new food products, both imported and locally produced. The locally produced smoked meats allowed us to make sandwiches that would be relatively cheap and provide us with great margins, although we needed to have enough money in profits to cover our monthly operational costs.

The first dollar we ever made came from my closest friends at the time, Eric Freed and David and Nicky Morgan. They all wanted to lend us their support. We sold three or four sandwiches, closed the restaurant and jumped on our bikes to head for the beach.

After several days of hanging on the beach we returned. Some of our staff also returned and some of the ones that didn't never got paid. We were understaffed and needed to open. When we went to the market, Laura was incredibly relaxed, but never stress-free.

'What are you going to buy? All we have left is $100 and I need to know what you're going to buy.'

'I don't know, the market will tell me.'

As we walked through, there were beautiful pencil-tip asparagus, cherry tomatoes and pumpkin flowers. I would just walk through pointing and calling out the amount.

1 kilo, 2 kilo, 1 kilo-...'

'What are you going to do with that?'

'I'm not sure yet.'

'What do you mean you are not sure? All we have is $100!'

'Great! You said that already!'

'We have staff; we have our rent, our laundry, living expenses. You have to tell me! This is all we have left!'

'I don't know! If I knew I would tell you! What difference does it make now. Either we blow it or we succeed, it is too late to worry about $100 now!'

At the back of my head I started to visualize all the money wasted. I was scared, but the last thing she needed was to have me lead her with no confidence. Our only option was to succeed. How could I fail in front of all my friends and more importantly in front of my enemies?

We returned to the restaurant with some of the staff waiting to enter. The roll-up gates were locked and it was turning out to be a scorcher of a day. The ingredients were quickly rushed upstairs to the kitchen, which was 10 degrees hotter then the rest of the place. The tin roof did not help, but the extraction fan did. The problem with the fan was that it sounded like a jet plane to most of the neighbours.

The first day we opened it was only for friends. They came, ate, and offered us their much-needed moral support. Who would boycott us? Who would say good things or bad things? None of this made any difference once we collected our first day at the till. The next day was busier. After that, we were pretty much full every day. Lunch was busy and all the tables were taken.

Laura took to running up stairs to forewarn me about various tables that she thought might say bad things about us. They were either close to Alexander and Thi, the husband and wife team who owned Camargue, or they were just regular difficult customers. Most of the time they would be French. The French like to express their opinion about food and Laura was out to ensure that I was aware of every table.

'Bobby, you will never guess who is here?'

'Who?'

'Table two is Xavier, who is sitting opposite Jean Pierre and Laurent!'

'Fuck! What are they ordering?'

'They said you could decide, but they want to talk to you.'

'Fire a sea bass and a burger!' I ordered, quickly adjusting the flame of the wok burner, shooting out the outer ring with deep blue flames while adjusting the inner flame.

As the iron griddle plate started to get hot, Mr. Hung sprayed the griddle with a little oil. While that oil got hot he turned to his work surface where one of the prep cooks delivered him his mise en place. A piece of sea bass appeared and he sprayed that with oil, rubbing his fingers over the flesh to ensure that it was well coated. Then he sprinkled salt twelve inches from the fish, followed by some freshly ground pepper. He stopped and stared for approval.

He had learned well, but the tricky part is to make sure that the fish sears on the griddle plate, so it does not stick. I waved my hand to stop him and get him to learn the next step. As I walked into his space, I placed my hand over the griddle to gauge its heat. The oil was just about at smoking point. I placed the sea bass right over the middle section of the griddle and reduced the heat of the burner below. We did not have a name for a griddle. But everyone knew what a pan was. The griddle was a large pan to all of us. I turned to Mr. Hung.

'Okay, I go downstairs. I come back quickly.'

He nods his head to acknowledge that he understood what I was saying.

'Okay? Do me a favour. Do not touch the pan, watch the pan okay?'

He looked at me a little confused.

'Watch the pan, do not touch the fish and just watch the pan.'

The hardest part of cooking for me was gauging temperatures on this homemade griddle. It was either luck or confidence. I had really no idea of how busy kitchens could fire an array of different dishes at the same time to get perfectly executed food. Cooking on a slab of iron with a round wok below was a real challenge.

To make it easier, I would simply sear a fish to develop a nice crispy skin, and then reduce the heat so it would cook slowly. I would only cook it on one side until the outer circumference of the fish became opaque. Once it reached this stage, I could simply flip it over for a minute or two and it would be cooked perfectly.

I removed my apron, ran downstairs, repeating myself one final time to Mr. Hung 'Watch the pan, do not touch the fish, just watch the pan'. I greeted the guests. I received compliments for the food, for the setting and for the ability to change the menu daily. I was finally feeling appreciated. The French had come to supply us with wines and the rest were there for the food. The thought of food quickly shot me back upstairs to check on my slow-cooking fish. When I arrived, the fish was turned over.

'WHAT THE FUCK DID I SAY? WHAT THE FUCK DID I TELL YOU TO DO!!!'

The kitchen fell into a deep silence. No one was talking. No one was looking at me, with heads down and ashamed of my insensitive ways I was now being ignored

'Can someone tell me!'?

Nothing. It was like talking to the deaf. I stood there screaming to myself. Laura quickly ran up the stairs and asked me to keep it quiet because she could hear me!

'Then turn the music up louder!'

I cooked another piece of fish because the last thing I wanted was overcooked fish to be sent out – especially to people who would be more then happy to bad-mouth me and my cooking.

At the end of the service, Mr. Hung grabbed my hand and led me to the other end of the kitchen, where the floor was not stable. His eyes were glazed. As he tilted his head down, a teardrop fell to the dry wooden planks. Teardrop after teardrop fell as we squatted side by side. With his head bowed to the floor he finally spoke.

'Chef, I do you a favour, because I like you, chef. Tomorrow I come to work; I come to work to help you. You no need pay me, but I help you until you find someone else to work.'

'How the fuck do you think this is helping me? If you want to quit, just quit, don't do me any favours.'

His face quickly rose up, teary-eyed and perplexed.

'But chef, I want to help you!'

'Yeah, great, now tell me how the hell are you helping me?'

'Because, after you pay salary today, everyone here is going to quit.'

I hadn't learned my lesson. I couldn't control my temper. We were only open for a month and I was facing a revolution. Am I that evil? Shit, I cannot do it on my own. I needed serious help. There was no time to waste. I needed to address the problem quickly.

I immediately went downstairs to Laura.

'We have a very serious problem.'

'I know.'

'The kitchen staff are all quitting.'

'NO! So are the front of the house staff. Some of them are really good.'

'Well we're seriously screwed then aren't we?'

'What are we going to do?'

'I've no idea. I'm going to run and see if Alex could help.'

I ran off to Alex to find him sitting over the gas burner, sipping on ice tea with a cigarette in his mouth. I proceed to tell him the latest.

'You are a crazy fucker! You know that?'

'Tell me something that I don't know.'

'I tell you, the Vietnamese will follow you, but you can't yell and scream!'

'You yell and scream!'

'Yes, but they know me! You yell and scream like a crazy man!'

'Okay, tell me what I'm suppose to do now.'

'I give you my guys and they all want to come back!'

I hadn't learned my lesson. I couldn't control my temper. We were only open for a month and I was facing a revolution.

'Then you join me!'

'Are you fucking crazy?'

'That has already been established. You are just as crazy as me!'

A big smile ripped through his face.

'I know.'

'I will teach you Western food and you can teach me Asian.'

'I always wanted to learn Western.'

'Well I learned from the best. On top of that I will make you a partner. No one will be able to do what we are going to do. I have people interested in me setting up in Hanoi, so we will be able to leave you with this place to run for yourself. We will have a sister restaurant in Hanoi.'

'How many people do you need?'

'We have nobody!'

'Okay, I get my maid to help you now.'

Alex's maid, Miss Cuc arrived hours later with a couple of relatives. She was to be our steward. Alex arrived ten minutes later.

'I tell you, my maid is tough. You fuck with her, I tell you. She will kick your ass.'

Laura arrived upstairs to get an update on if we would be open tomorrow. Miss Cuc took one look at Laura and smiled.

'I tell you another thing, my maid, she likes women!' He laughed hysterically to himself.

'Yeah!'

He quickly stopped laughing, then put on a stern face.

'Yeah, she also has a side business; she has a karaoke bar and a massage parlour in her house.' Once again he returns to hysterical laughing, driving his blood pressure up, while his face rose brighter shades of red.

'Dude, how long do you think a pimp will want to work as a steward for? She can make more money on her side business in an hour than what we pay her in a day!'

'Because I tell her to help you!'

'Okay what do we do?'

'You choose dishes that you want to do and that your guys know how to do.'

'What do you want?'

'I really would love to have a curry.'

I make the greatest fish head curry. Easy, profitable.

'Okay, how about we do this? I show you all my food and then once it is set up, you do your food. I have a very limited menu, and we start to collaborate on Eastern and Western dishes.'

That day, we opened. Laura was running the floor. She was taking the orders and those that did not speak English were running up and down the stairs dropping off the orders and picking up food. It was like clockwork.

Once again we were packed. At the end of our busiest day Kathy, Ronnie's girlfriend came in to talk to me.

'I need to talk to you.'

'What can I do?'

'I need a thousand dollars.'

'Um, so do I. What do you need it for?'

'Because you are making a lot of money, and I want a thousand dollars.'

'Well, that is a little difficult. I do not have a thousand dollars.'

'I know how much money you have. The cashier is my cousin.'

This was very common in the classic joint venture deals. Family members were brought in to watch and protect the investment, so usually the accountant, the human resource manager and security were related one way or another.

'Well, Kathy, the money we make goes into buying more food, paying our staff, electricity, etc.

That doesn't include paying David his percentage and Laura and me are working for free!'

'I do not care, I want a thousand dollars.'

'That is not our agreement. Our agreement is that you get paid once we have recouped our investment.'

'But I do not know how long that will take or if you ever get the money back, so I want the money now.'

'I honestly do not have that kind of money.'

'You get it, because if you do not get it, then I will close you down.'

'Have you talked to Ronnie about this?'

'I do not have to talk to anyone. I am the general director and this is my company'

It was not looking good. She stormed out and when I called Ronnie he suggested that I learn how to deal with people and hung up the phone. Once again Laura requested that I see if my father would help, but his response was that I was a big boy and to take care of myself.

The next day we arrived at work to find the keys to the locks did not work. I turned behind me to see what the cell had to say about it. Instead of sitting on his stool, he was standing up. Staring at me animated. His head shook like he had something to say. He walked over making noise.

'What is he saying?'

'He says that the white man came here 30 minutes ago and changed the locks.

I hadn't taken back the keys from Ronnie when he walked out.

I got the locksmith on the corner to rip the locks off and opened for lunch. Thirty minutes later Kathy drove by. It was all over. We were informed that we were illegal and that we had 30 minutes to remove ourselves from her restaurant as the police were on their way.

We left pretty quickly, never to return. All the staff were now unemployed as we were run out of town, losing everything, except our reputations and passion for what we did.

Sweet Things

Vietnamese desserts are, admittedly, somewhat limited. There are ceremonial cakes made for weddings, lunar holidays and other special occasions, but desserts following a regular meal are not very common. You only have to give the Vietnamese people some sliced fresh fruit and they're as happy as clams. You can even give them sour, unripe fruit and they'll cheerfully dip it in chilli and salt and eat it, just like the Thais. There are more elaborate options, such as coconut flan and crème caramel, a relic of French colonial times, but che is distinctively Asian: you mix and match whatever you want – black beans, lima beans, sweetcorn – with glutinous rice flour. It's kinda gooey, but some people like it. My main contribution to this chapter is the mangosteen sorbet, which is so easy. People often ask me what inspires me to create new dishes and in this case it was a new kitchen tool, an ice cream machine.

Lychee sorbet

MAKES ABOUT 575ML
enough canned lychees to produce 575ml liquid and 230g lychees
about 1 tbsp lime juice

In a food processor or blender, pulse the lychees to a purée.

Pass this through a fine-mesh strainer, pressing to extract as much juice a possible.

Mix this juice and the reserved syrup together and add lime juice to taste.

In a medium pot, heat the sugar in 240ml water until all the granules are dissolved. Place in the fridge.

Place in an ice cream machine and follow the manufacturer's instructions.

Sweet Lotus Seed Soup CHÉ SEN

All of the following dishes are called che. Right across the street from my favourite Bun Bo restaurant, by the Hang Xa market, used to be a slew of che restaurants. One by one they folded up and ventured into the newly popular retail, cosmetic and other businesses. Out of four, today only one remains and still packs them in.

The table is covered with matching glass bowls filled with a rainbow of colours from the rows of bowls. Red beans, green beans, black beans, lotus seeds, a corn porridge, multicoloured jellies made from Agar, thicken coconut cream, toasted shreds of dried coconut, freshly grated coconut, peanuts, and the list goes on and on.

There I would stand, wondering what mixtures to add into a glass of shaved ice. It was almost self-serve, and I would fill the glass up with whatever flavours, colours or textures my heart desired. There are many variations of che, and I have listed some of my favourites. They are all generally refreshing and light but quite filling.

In the recipe below, the lotus seeds can be a single dish, or it can be added to any combination on the following pages.

SERVES 5
200g dry lotus seeds
175 g sugar
½ tbsp tapioca flour
crushed ice, to serve (optional)
shredded coconut, to serve (optional)

Soak the lotus seeds in water to cover for about 2 hours, then rinse well and drain.

Put in a pot with 1.5 litres water and place over medium-high heat. Bring to the boil, reduce the heat and cook for 40 minutes uncovered. The liquid should reduce by about a third.

Add the sugar and cook for 20 minutes more. Check to make sure the lotus seeds are cooked

through and that they are also a little sweet.

Add the tapioca flour in stir well to ensure that it is well dissolved. Remove from heat and let cool to room temperature.

This dish can be served hot or cold. If cold, add some crushed ice and shredded coconut.

Sweet Black Bean Soup CHÉ ĐẬU ĐEN

This simple soup can either be added as an additional ingredient to the Sweet Mung Bean Soup (page 201), or served separately on its own. Either way, if you like these sweetened bean desserts, it is pretty easy to make a bunch at the same time. Obviously beans differ in flavour and size, and need different cooking times and amounts of sugar to get it to your personal taste and preference. In this black bean soup we use brown sugar and you can also use palm sugar for a more complex flavour. If you want to get a little more creative you also add spices like cinnamon, vanilla, cardamom, etc., to generate even more levels of flavour.

SERVES 4

200g black beans
350g brown sugar

Soak the black beans in cold water to cover generously overnight.

Next day, drain, rinse them well and drain again.

Put them in a pot with 3 litres of water, place over medium-high heat and bring to the boil. Reduce the heat to a simmer and continue simmering for about 1 hour, uncovered. The liquid will reduce and the water will become black. Make sure that you stir the beans on occasion to prevent them sticking to the bottom corners of the pot.

Once the beans get a little tender but are still al dente, add the sugar and cook for another 15–30 minutes, so the liquid and the beans are sweet and tender. Remove from the pot from the heat.

This can be served hot in winter months as well as chilled in summer months.

Sweet Mung Bean Soup CHÉ ĐẬU XANH

Like the black bean soup, this can either be added as an additional ingredient to the Che dish, or served separately on its own. Either way, if you like these sweetened bean desserts, it is pretty easy to make a bunch at the same time. This one is very popular in Singapore, where they purée it into a thick creamy soup. I prefer them in their natural form, where the texture and individual tastes of the beans come through.

SERVES 2

100g mung beans
180g sugar
½ tbsp tapioca flour
crushed ice, to serve (optional)
4 tbsp shredded coconut, to serve

Soak the beans in cold water overnight. Make sure to cover the beans with enough water so in the morning the beans are still submerged in water. I usually use a 1:4 ratio of beans to water.

Next day, drain, rinse them well and drain again. Put the beans in a pot, cover with water and place over medium-to-high heat. Bring to the boil, then reduce to a simmer and cook for another 30 minutes or until the beans are still a little undercooked, or just al dente.

Add the sugar and mix well. Cook for another 10–15 minutes, or until the beans have absorbed some of the sugar water and are tender and sweet.

Add the tapioca flour and stir well. Remove from the heat.

This soup can be served hot or cold. If serving cold, add crushed ice and garnish with shredded coconut.

Bananas in Coconut Milk CHÉ CHUỐI

This is a really simple dessert that is quite commonly found in neighbouring Asian countries. I love coconut milk in desserts and there is a wonderful affinity between coconut, bananas and the wonderful texture of tapioca. The bananas can be replaced with taro and/or pumpkin. Serve at room temperature or hot.

8 tbsp very small tapioca pearls

240ml coconut milk

225 g sugar

4 large bananas

crushed ice to serve (optional)

4 tbsp toasted sesame seeds

4 tbsp toasted chopped peanuts

4 tbsp shredded coconut

Place the tapioca pearls in a bowl and cover with warm water. Soak for about 20 minutes until they slightly translucent. Drain under cold running water and reserve.

In a pot over medium heat, combine the coconut milk, sugar and 240ml water. Bring to a simmer, but do not allow it to boil. Simmer for another 10 minutes.

Peel the bananas and cut them into 5 cm chunks. Add to the coconut mixture with the tapioca pearls. Simmer the mixture for another 10 minutes or until the tapioca pearls are perfectly cooked. Remove from the heat.

Serve hot in individual serving bowls, or in a glass with crushed ice. Garnish with toasted sesame seeds and chopped peanuts with shredded coconut.

Rice Pudding

One of my favourite desserts of all time is Thai coconut sticky rice with mangoes and a dollop of thick coconut cream. I fell in love with it the first day I tried it.

I was staying at the Oriental Hotel, and it was my first trip to Thailand since supposedly being conceived there. I love Thailand so much that I make it a point to use it as my travel hub to and from Vietnam. I always find an excuse to stop over there. The people are so friendly and the street vendors are always glad to teach me their food. I learned so many dishes from street vendors, from curry and laksa to stir-fries using what I refer to as condiment food: dishes that are created by mixing a variety of mass-produced pre-made bottled sauces and mass-produced jars of chillies and spices.

The only dish I could never really duplicate with the same authenticity was the coconut sticky rice. It is suppose to be easy, but I never got the opportunity to learn the dish by observation from start to finish. I did try, however, but if a Thai person ever tried mine, they would tell me something like, 'It is not the same as the Thai people'. One of my policies is, if I cannot duplicate a dish so it's as good as the original, then I disguise it to the point that it becomes my original! My lack of skills in duplication sometimes yields dishes that are unique - and good in their own right. This is a pretty good example of a dish that is derived through my culinary experience and upbringing.

In Egypt as a kid, I learned the love of making rice pudding. It was pretty simply – get leftover rice, cook it with milk and sugar, as if making a congee, and then throw in some raisins and nuts, and top with cinnamon. I would make six to eight bowls of the dish and leave them in the fridge to see how long they would last. I would then proceed to eat one after the other until nothing was left. I was a rice pudding addict. I loved rice and I was simply crazy about nuts…. all nuts.

Still when I walk through my kitchen, my staff hide all their pre-cooked, peeled nuts, as I would take handfuls of the stuff. I found out that when my mother was pregnant with me she also had a similar addiction. But that is another story!

Because I could never really get the Thai's execution of their rice, I decided to make it a cross between an Egyptian rice pudding and a Thai 'coconut sticky rice' the process would be very different, though as cooking sticky rice is tricky. I needed to simplify the dish to make it very easy to make for the kitchen staff, so it would be consistent. But I also needed a dish that would have some Vietnamese style and flavour.

The rice we would soak and later steam with a pandan leaf, a technique I learned from my travels to Bali. Once the rice was cooked, I would throw in sweetened coconut milk, raisins that had been plumped up in water, and nuts, giving a pudding with a similar texture to risotto, where the grains were individuals, but bound somewhat by the creamy coconut milk.

I recognized all the staff liked the dessert, but in some way there was nothing Vietnamese about it. I needed to make it more Vietnamese, so one of my staff suggested that we add young green rice, for a wonderful texture and colour. Yet somehow it wasn't enough. I started thinking of encircling the dish with a sauce, but needed something that was a dessert in its own right.

Here I got the idea from a dessert drink where they toast rice and add sugar, giving a wonderful nutty drink. The drawback was that visually this was a brown sweet water, lacking the consistency as well as the visual appeal necessary to round off a meal. Walking through a supermarket, I discovered that the Vietnamese have a grounded black sesame powder drink similar to the toasted rice drink. I purchased the powder and mixed it with the pre-sweetened coconut milk and the dish was complete.

The flavours, when combined, were simple and bold. We garnished the dish with additional black sesame seeds to punctuate the dish even further. The nutty sesame sauce smoothed out by the coconut was enough to make it the most requested dessert recipe from my customers.

SERVES 5

Sticky rice mixture

2 cups sticky rice, presoaked

1 pandan leaf (optional)

4 tbsp chopped hazelnuts

4 tbsp presoaked raisins (you can soak it in Frangelico liqueur for real decadence)

2 tbsp young green rice (optional)

Coconut sauce

175 g sugar or to taste

350ml coconut cream

Toasted Sesame Sauce

½ cup sesame powder

To serve

toasted sesame seeds or peanuts

Steam the drained presoaked rice with the pandan leaf until tender, about 35 minutes.

Once it is cooked, place in a baking sheet and spread it out evenly. Let it cool with a wet towel over the top.

Make the coconut sauce: in a mixing bowl, mix the sugar with the coconut cream and place in cool place. You may wish to use caster sugar to ensure the sugar dissolves quicker if in a hurry.

Reserving three-quarters of the coconut mixture for the rice, mix the remainder with the sesame powder for the sesame powder sauce.

Fold the sweetened coconut cream into the warm rice. Should there be any lumps, break them down with a fork. Taste to ensure that the sweetness is to your liking. Once you have a homogenous mixture that resembles a perfectly cooked risotto, throw in the nuts, raisins and young rice, if using.

Spoon the rice pudding on to a plate and garnish with sesame seeds. Spoon the coconut sesame sauce on the rim of the plate.

Tropical Fruit Soup with Mangosteen Sorbet

Sometimes I am inspired by what others do. Other times it is something that someone says. With this dish, it was all about buying a new kitchen toy. I wanted an ice cream machine, but they are generally very expensive. I couldn't really afford a $10,000 machine to make ice cream or sorbet, but at William Sonoma they had a new machine that could make a litre of ice cream for $500.00. I stood admiring the machine, trying to justify its purchase. It was difficult to do, especially when I was broke and the machine was wired for the US 110v, 50 cycles supply. It clearly stated that it could not be used for commercial use. I bought it against the protests of Laura.

'What are you going to do with that?'

'I'm going to make a sorbet that people would only dream about!'

'Like what?'

'Mangosteen sorbet with a tropical fruit soup! No one can afford to make it with the price of mangosteens being what they are.'

'She smiled and loved the idea.

You can choose any of your favourite fruit for this dish, but choose things that are in season. If you would like other flavours for the soup, you can also add spices, like star anise, cinnamon or even black pepper, to give it a little bit of a kick.

SERVES 4

200g lemon grass

20g ginger

500ml simple syrup (475g sugar dissolved in 150ml water over a low heat)

2 apples, peeled, cored and diced

1 orange, segmented and deseeded

1 Asian pear, peeled, cored and diced

¼ pineapple, peeled, cored and diced

2 bananas

2 star fruit, cut into 5mm slices

Mint leaves, cut into thin slices, for garnish

Mangosteen Sorbet

50 g sugar

2.5kg fresh mangosteens

2 tbsp lemon juice

lime juice, to taste

First make the mangosteen sorbet: in a pot, mix the sugar with 240ml water over a low heat until the sugar dissolves. Let it cool.

Juice all the fruit by passing them through a food mill. Keep the fruit from browning by storing in water acidulated with the lemon juice. Pass the juice through a fine-mesh strainer until you have 500ml. Mix together with the cooled syrup and add lime juice to taste.

Place in an ice cream machine and follow the operating instructions.

Chop the lemon grass and ginger, then add these to the simple syrup and bring to the boil. Once the mixture reaches boiling, remove from the heat and let the ingredients infuse and cool down to room temperature

Once the mixture has cooled to room temperature, strain it through a chinois, squeezing the lemon grass and ginger to extract as much flavour as possible. Chill the mixture and place 4 soup bowls in the refrigerator to chill for a few hours.

Once the mixture is chilled, cut the fruits into bite-sized pieces. Add the chopped fruit to a chilled soup bowl and pour the chilled soup over the fruit to cover (if the soup is too sweet you can add a little more iced water). Garnish with the shredded mint.

Sweet Pumpkin Soup with Yellow Mung Bean CHÈ BÍ NGÔ ĐẬU XANH

This is a recipe I've never seen before. I have seen pumpkin in coconut milk, but never have I seen pumpkin almost as a drink.

When writing this book we needed to research many dishes, and some of the recipes were hard to come by. I asked for a simple che recipe and this one came up. Most of the office staff were delighted with this recipe, myself included. Far too frequently, the wonderful taste of pumpkin is lost or the palate is overwhelmed with spices and sweetness, as in the traditional pumpkin pie with which we are all so familiar.

This dish is light and simple, with a wonderful flavour of pumpkin sweetened ever so slightly with sugar. This is a dish to whip up when you have too much pumpkin lying around!

SERVES 7

100g yellow mung beans

500g pumpkin

175g sugar

4 tbsp cassava flour

1 tbsp vanilla essence

crushed ice, to serve

70g grated coconut, to garnish

Soak the mung beans in warm water for about 1 hour. Rinse well, drain and reserve.

While the beans are soaking, peel the pumpkin and remove the seeds. Cut the pumpkin flesh into 2.5cm cubes.

Place a pot with 1.2 litres of water over medium-to-high heat, add the pumpkin and the beans, bring to the boil, then reduce to a simmer and cook for about 1 hour. Add the sugar and continue cooking for 5 minutes.

In a mixing bowl, mix the cassava flour and 2 tablespoons of water until it is nice and smooth. Pour the mixture into the soup, stir well and simmer it for 15 more minutes. Remove the mixture from the heat and allow to cool.

Serve this mixture in a glass with crushed ice and some drops of vanilla essence. Sprinkle some grated coconut on the top.

Sticky Rice with Mung Bean Paste

XÔI VÒ

This is another one of those dishes that you just can't find in restaurants. This wonderful dessert is sold from large bamboo baskets on the backs of bicycles by villagers who sell it all wrapped up in little lotus leaf parcels. It is food on the go and I have yet to meet a person that did not enjoy it. Banana essence might have a huge role to play, as it is a unfamiliar flavour to many of us.

The dish is generally eaten with your hands, especially when it is served from a back of a bicycle. Despite its informal nature, it always makes the banquet menus at many of the weddings I have attended over the years.

SERVES 5

400g raw glutinous rice
200g dried yellow mung beans
60g grated coconut
60g sugar
1/2 tsp salt
4 tbsp lotus seeds
1 tbsp vegetable oil
1/4 tsp banana essence or vanilla essence
1 tbsp icing sugar

Soak the rice, mung beans and lotus seeds separately in water overnight. Drain and set aside

Put 750ml water in a saucepan over medium-to-high heat, add the lotus seeds, and bring to the boil. Reduce the heat and simmer for 1 hour.

Drain, and leave about half a cup of the water in the pot. Add the coconut and sugar, and cook until the water has almost completely gone and is reduced to a glaze. Do this over a lower heat to prevent the sugar from burning. Reserve.

In a steamer, steam the mung beans for 20 minutes, or until they are tender.

In a food processor, pulse the mung beans until they form a fine paste. Form the paste into 2 firm balls and let stand for 20 minutes.

Place the rice in a mixing bowl and rub the mung bean balls between your hands, breaking them down into little crumbs over the rice. Season with a little salt and fold together so they are well combined and homogenous.

In a steamer, spread the rice so it is about the same thickness all over and steam for 45 minute or until the grains are nice and tender. You may wish to rework the rice by mixing it around on occasion to insure that it all gets cooked equally.

Once the rice is tender, transfer the steamed rice mixture to a baking sheet and spread it out to allow it to cool quickly and evenly. Once cool enough to handle, drizzle the oil over the mixture and work your hands through it, doing your best to coat all the grains with the oil to separate the grains from one another. Sprinkle with the lotus seeds and grated coconut mixture and continue to mix.

To finish the dish, add the banana essence and icing sugar, and serve.

Doughnuts with Sticks

QUẨY XIÊN

MAKES 6

125g flour
1 egg
1 tbsp baking powder
3 tbsp honey
1/4 tsp yeast
pinch of salt
1 tbsp vegetable oil, plus more for deep-frying
2 tbsp sugar, for decoration

In a mixing bowl, place the flour, egg, baking powder and honey, and stir well. Add 4 tablespoons of water and work the dough into a ball. Set aside and let it rest for 10 minutes.

Divide the dough into 6 pieces, each about 20g. Roll each into the form of a log about 7cm long, then twist them a couple of times. Using a presoaked bamboo skewer, pierce it through the dough so it will act as a handle .

In a deep pan, heat oil for deep-frying to 130°C or close to smoking. Place the doughnuts in the oil (you may want to do this in batches of 2 or 3 at a time to avoid lowering the oil's heat too much) and fry for about 8 minutes, or until the doughnuts are golden brown.

Remove from the pan and sprinkle with the sugar all over their surface while still hot.

Coconut with Taro CHÈ KHOAI MÔN

I am not really sure if this is a Vietnamese dessert or whether it is a dish that was borrowed from Thailand. The desserts in South Vietnam are generally much sweeter then their counterparts in the North. A good friend of mine turned me on to eating desserts in the Benton Market. One of the reasons is that you can find dozens of different desserts all over one roof. I am a sucker for any dessert with coconut milk. To me, it is the wonderful nutty alternative to cream.

SERVES 4

500g taro, peeled ad cut into 5cm cubes
1 tsp salt
100g sugar, or to taste
1 tbsp pandanus juice or a pandan leaf
1 can (400ml) coconut milk (unsweetened)
5 tbsp tapioca flour
2 tsp cornflour
crushed ice to serve (optional)
60g freshly grated coconut, for garnish

Put the taro and enough water to cover it in a medium-sized pot over medium-to-high heat, add salt and bring to the boil. Once it reaches the boil, reduce to a simmer and cook until the taro is tender. To test, remove a taro, and run a knife through it; there should be no resistance. Once tender, drain and reserve.

Place 1 litre of water in a large pot over medium-to-high heat and add the sugar, pandanus juice or leaf and coconut milk. Bring to the boil and reduce to a simmer. Add the cooked taro and continue cooking for about 5 minutes.

While the mixture is simmering, in a mixing bowl, mix the tapioca flour and cornflour and gently pour in 120 ml water in a steady stream to get a nice uniform mixture. Once the mixture is nice and smooth, pour it into the coconut mixture, stirring to make sure that it is evenly distributed. Cook for another 4–5 minutes, until the mixture has a nice creamy consistency.

This can be served at room temperature, or hot during the winter months. I generally prefer it served cold with crushed ice and garnished with freshly grated coconut.

Coconut Sticky Rice Pudding with Taro CHÈ KHOAI MÔN

Once again, I am not really sure if this is a Vietnamese dessert or whether it is a dish that was borrowed from Thailand. I used always to order this at the food court in Thailand's old international airport. I would bring bags of the stuff to my staff to see if they liked the Thai version of the dish. They would eat it all of it and then complain it was too sweet! You can replace the taro with bananas, pumpkin, sweet potatoes, you name it. Many tropical desserts are perfumed with pandan leaves which is now sold as a chemical concentrate all over Asia. If you are not into chemicals, try a vanilla bean, or use vanilla essence or pandanus juice.

SERVES 2

1 (400g) can unsweetened coconut milk, not shaken
1 tsp cornflour
small pinch of salt
5 tbsp glutinous rice, rinsed and soaked
1 tbsp pandanus juice
225g taro, peeled, cut into 5-cm inch cubes and rinsed
75g sugar, or to taste
pinch of salt

To make the thick creamy coconut sauce garnish, open the can of coconut milk, ensuring sure that it is not shaken, and scoop off as much of the thick coconut cream from the top of the coconut milk and place in saucepan (there should be about 120ml). Stir in the coconut, then add the cornflour and a pinch of salt, and bring the sauce up to a simmer. Cook for a couple of minutes, remove from the heat and set aside.

Put the rice and 850ml water in a pot over medium-high heat and bring to the boil. Reduce the heat, add the pandanus juice and simmer until the rice is almost soft, about 15 minutes.

Add the taro, sugar and salt. Cook until the taro is soft, about 15 minutes.

Add the remaining coconut milk and gently stir to incorporate. The pudding should be slightly thick, and the grains soft but still maintaining their shape, like overcooked risotto.

Ladle the rice and taro into individual soup bowls and then give each a nice healthy dollop of the coconut cream on top. This can be served hot or at room temperature

Deep-fried Banana with Rice Flour Batter CHUỐI CHIÊN

As a sweeping generalization, the Vietnamese are not really big on rich desserts or chocolate desserts to die for. More often then not, a fruit plate will suffice. As in Japanese cuisine, they are light and simple and there to clean the palate. I think the same applies to Thailand and many Asian countries. Fruit is the cornerstone of desserts in one shape or form.

This recipe is comforting. Banana is one of those fruits that can taste better fried. In Thailand you can often find grilled bananas, sometimes grilled in banana leaves. In Vietnam, they have some of the tastiest bananas I have ever eaten and in the cold months you can walk the back streets of the Old Quarters and find these gems being fried to order. There are many varieties of bananas, but traditionally they use a short thick banana for this dish.

To accelerate the cooking time as well as ensure that it is soft and moist after frying, it is rolled out with a rolling pin between two sheets of paper or plastic to make it thinner and wider. This dish is a real treat as the batter is light and fluffy. If you want to get creative, throw in some chocolate sauce and serve it with coconut ice cream, or you can flame it with rum. Call it a banana split if you will.

I have more complicated versions where I roll the banana in warm chocolate, then nuts, then roll them in rice paper, then douse it with the batter. Either way, when you have dishes this simple, you really should keep it simple, and then once you have mastered it, play with it… again just a little!

SERVES 4
4 bananas
vegetable oil, for deep-frying
icing sugar, for dusting

Batter
4 tbsp rice flour
7 tbsp cornflour
4 tbsp sugar
¼ tsp salt
1 tbsp baking powder
1 tbsp vegetable oil

First make the batter: in a mixing bowl, combine the rice flour, cornflour, sugar, salt and baking powder. Slowly whisk in 240ml water until you have a smooth batter. Add the vegetable oil and stir until it is well incorporated. Allow this batter to rest in the refrigerator for about 1 hour.

Peel the bananas and cut them in half lengthwise.

Heat oil for deep-frying in a wok or a deep pan to about 190°C.

While the oil gets hot, prepare the bananas by dusting them in cornflour, making sure they are evenly coated but also tapping off any excess.

Dip the bananas into the batter and carefully slide them into the hot oil. Fry them one at a time to ensure that the oil is the right temperature. Perhaps once you get the knack of it you can add a couple at a time, ensuring that you do not overcrowd the pan. Fry for about 4–5 minutes on each side, or until they develop a golden brown colour on both sides and are crisp. Remove with a slotted spoon and drain on a draining board covered with a kitchen towel and pat lightly with the towel to absorb as much oil as possible. You can also makes these in advance and hold them in a warm oven.

Serve on a platter, dusted with icing sugar. Consider serving with coconut ice cream or flaming it with rum. Either way, a crispy hot banana melts in the mouth and is a serious treat to any banana connoisseur. If you flame it, please read the Baked Alaska story on page 214!

Sweet Young Rice with Pearl Strands
CHÈ CỐM TRÂN CHÂU
Young rice is rather aromatic compared to its fully grown counterpart. It is a light green in colour and in its raw form, rather tender. It used to be hard to come by when I first arrived in

Vietnam, where it would be sold wrapped in banana leaves on the back of a bicycle from people from the villages. It was eaten as a little snack. I later saw it introduced in the ice cream at Fanny's, a very popular ice cream parlour, but had simply not noticed it in many of the che concoctions. If you can't get young rice, make a point of trying it when you are in Vietnam.

SERVES 4

100g young rice

60g pearl tapioca

125g sugar

35g cassava flour

crushed ice, to serve

1 tbsp vanilla extract

60g grated coconut, to serve

Place the young rice and tapioca in a saucepan with 1 litre of water and bring to the boil, then reduce the heat to a simmer. Let it simmer for 20 minutes. Add the sugar and cook for a further 5 minutes.

In a mixing bowl, combine the cassava flour with 4 tablespoons of water and mix well until nice and smooth.

Slowly pour this mixture into the young rice soup and stir well until the flour goes clear. Remove from the heat and allow to cool.

Serve in glasses with crushed ice, a few drops of vanilla extract and grated coconut on the top.

Sweet Rice Dumplings with Ginger Syrup BÁNH TRÔI NƯỚC

SERVES 10

Mung Bean Filling

100g dried yellow mung beans

2 tbsp sugar

1 tbsp roasted white sesame seeds, for decoration

Ginger Syrup

5cm (50g) fresh ginger, finely chopped

225g sugar

600ml hot water

2 tbsp cassava flour (optional)

Dough

250g glutinous rice flour

120ml boiling water

Presoak the mung beans in warm water until al dente, about 30–40 minutes.

Drain the beans and steam for 15 minutes or until tender.

Pour the beans and sugar in a blender and pulse a couple of times, pushing the mixture down the sides of the blender to make sure that the beans are puréed evenly. The mixture should still retain a little texture, so do not worry about getting a perfect purée. A paste with a little texture is fine.

Remove the mung bean paste from the blender and, using a measuring spoon, scoop the purée out and roll into about 30 small balls. Place in the fridge for later use.

To make the ginger syrup, place the sugar in a saucepan and cook over medium heat until the sugar melts. Turn the heat up and swirl the pan, making sure the sugar cooks evenly. Once the sugar develops a nice caramel colour, reduce the heat and add the ginger (the ginger will release water as steam, so be careful). After a couple of minutes, add the hot water and stir. You can stir in the cassava flour at the end if you prefer a thicker syrup.

To make the dough, place the flour in a mixing bowl, make a well in the middle and pour the boiling water into that. Using a fork, quickly fold the flour into the water, mixing it well and constantly incorporating more flour until all the water is absorbed and you are left with a sticky ball of dough. Cover with a damp towel and let the dough rest for 5–10 minutes, or until it is cool enough to handle, but still warm.

Knead the dough until it is smooth and a little moist, but does not stick to your hands.

Pinch the dough and roll out into small balls the size of 50p piece. Cover again with a damp cloth.

To assemble, roll out each piece of dough into a 2.5cm disk, place a mung bean ball in the centre and fold the edges of the dough around the bean. Press the dough around the mung bean until the bean is totally covered. Once they are all rolled out, cover and set aside.

Bring a large pot of water to a boil, and add the dumplings. Like gnocchi, they are ready once they float to the top. This should take about

3 minutes. Remove the doughnuts with a perforated spoon and drain on absorbent paper.

To serve, place the dumplings in a bowl, ladle some of the ginger syrup over them and then sprinkle with the toasted sesame seeds.

Coconut Crème Brûlée

This is a really simple recipe and I went through a repertoire of crème brûlées, from regular classic to lemon, chocolate etc. I then started to venture into Asian flavours like ginger, lemon grass, and eventually stumbled on coconut.

I sometimes like to add nuts, like pistachios, but swirled into the mixture in a powdered form, or add bananas on top, as the combination of those two ingredients works very well.

SERVES 6

240ml double cream
240ml milk
240ml coconut milk
5 egg yolks
225g sugar, plus more for sprinkling on the tops

Preheat the oven to 180°C/Gas 4.

Bring the milk, cream and coconut milk to the boil. While it heats, whisk the egg and sugar together in a bowl until pale yellow in colour.

When the liquid mixture comes to the boil, gradually pour the hot liquid into the egg mixture, while whisking continuously to prevent the egg from scrambling.

Pour the mixture into 6 ramekins and place in a deep container with hot water reaching halfway up the sides of the ramekins. Place in the preheated oven for 30 minutes or until done – when you wiggle a ramekin the middle of the custard wobbles a bit.

Remove from the oven and allow to cool, then place in the fridge.

When ready to serve, simply sprinkle enough sugar on top of each to cover the top completely. Using a blow-torch (or under a very hot grill, if your ramekins are heatproof), melt the sugar, or place under a hot grill until the sugar caramelizes.

Grapes Rolled in Goats' Cheese With Pistachio Crust

This is a dish I learned when cooking in France with Yaffa Edry. It is so simple and I have yet to meet anyone who did not enjoy it. The juicy sweet grapes are offset by the saltiness of the creamy goats' cheese with the chopped pistachio nuts.

These little mouthfuls are fun to serve at cocktail parties and work very well with both red and white wine.

At the restaurant we usually serve them as an amuse bouche, but for those who like serving fruit and cheese after a meal this is a good and unusual option.

MAKES ABOUT 50

250g chilled soft goats' cheese
300g red grapes, preferably seedless
180g pistachio nuts, roughly chopped

Take the grapes from their stalks, twisting them off. You do not want to pull them off, as the skin will tear and it will absorb too much of the cheese. I like to chill the grapes in the refrigerator.

Using a melon baller, or your fingers, scoop or roll the chilled goat cheese into 10g balls.

Press each cheese ball down in the palm of your hand. Place the grape in the middle of the cheese, and with both hands, quickly roll the grape back and forth until the grape is fully coated with the goat cheese. You can do up to this stage a day in advance.

Fill a large bowl with chopped pistachio nuts, throw in the cheese-coated grapes and roll them in the chopped nuts until totally coated. It is easier if the cheese is a little soft. So you do not want to take these out from the fridge just before starting the rolling process.

With a sharp knife, cut each in half and serve.

And for dessert, Baked Alaska

Mr Z was a handsome gentleman who worked for the ministry of foreign affairs and seemed very well connected in government. His dark tan gave him the ultimate Colgate smile and he was very well spoken. A couple of friends who had brought him in as a partner in a restaurant-bar introduced him to me. These friends – one a reporter, one a graphic designer – were part of the local media but decided to open their own place where they could drink and eat. The restaurant was in the heart of the Old French Quarter but was failing miserably. It was a time of over-expansion in the restaurant industry with no tourism and the expatriate market was fickle and thinning out. Mr Z called to request some advice on how to turn his restaurant around. He was a little hard-pressed, having partnered with the right people at the wrong time. They could muster up a lot of local press, but there was noone involved who actually knew how to run a restaurant.

Replicating one of the hotspots in Saigon, the idea was to sell tapas and drinks to the thinning expat community. They plugged it in their magazine as having the best margaritas, the best bar, and the only tapas in Hanoi. Month after month pictures of the restaurant appeared in the magazine, but unfortunately it wasn't paying off.

I met Mr Z in the downstairs bar of the restaurant. As he escorted me up the stairs, we walked past two floors of empty tables and chairs. On the third floor we walked through some swinging doors into a kitchen that smelt of rancid oil. I had been hoping a job would come of the meeting but one look at the kitchen put me off doing anything but giving free advice. I couldn't produce any of my food in a kitchen like this. There was really no refrigeration to speak of, except a couple of very old domestic refrigerators that were rusting all over the place, with cracked plastic seals and warped doors. There were a couple of wok burners sitting on small plastic tables next to propane gas canisters. A large circular chopping board sat next to the lone sink in the corner. Spatulas, strainers, tongs… non-existent.

As I stood there looking at the rat shit spread all over the usual areas, Z opened up the window that overlooked the roofs of the neighbouring buildings. 'What do you think? It has a lot of space and natural light.'

'There is no shortage of space,' I replied. 'There is a shortage of equipment, and work surfaces. If you want to be successful you will need to get more equipment. You have no work surfaces. You can't cook on that wok for long as it will melt through the table.'

I took a closer look and sure enough the table was scarred with melted holes. A two-hundred seat restaurant with one refrigerator that was not plugged in, as electricity was too expensive, one wok, and a thirty-page menu. No inventory, no risk control. It was all pretty simple. Restaurants did not work because of this, and everyone thought they could do it better simply because someone said, 'Boy you cook really well, you should open a restaurant,' or 'You throw great parties, you should open a restaurant.' There was no hope of saving this place in my mind. It would need a lot of money, and there was none to be found.

Off the top of my head, I suggested that I help them with a very limited menu that the kitchen could produce and execute consistently for the bar, and then for the restaurant they could hire a Hue chef to produce Imperial Hue food, since there were no really good Hue restaurants in Hanoi at the time. Hue dishes are intricate and bite-sized – rather like tapas like in style – so they could in theory keep their tapas concept and do Vietnamese food for the Vietnamese market rather than the depleted expat community.

Three weeks later my phone rang and it was Mr Z asking if I could come by with some friends, Laura and Thao, and test out his new menu.

On arrival Mr Z greeted us warmly. I looked around to see if I could spot any changes – there

were none. He was relying fully on his newly-hired chef from Hue. We made light-hearted small talk as we ascended the stairs to an empty dining room with thirty-odd tables that were fully set.

'I have followed your advice, and I would like to get your idea about the food here,' said Mr Z.

In the corner of my eye I could see a chef peering from behind a pillar next to the kitchen. 'My chef is from Hue and I think he is pretty good, but I would like to get your opinion as you have the understanding of what the foreigners taste.'

Within seconds of sitting at the table the first course arrived: duck à la orange served in an orange shell, a warm soupy dish filled with sautéed slivers of duck with onions and lotus seeds. The sauce was a mixture of duck stock and orange juice. The execution was poor at best, but you had to like the effort he made. The stock had boiled, so the flavours were muddled and cloudy. The orange juice was simply sour, and there was no balance between it and the stock. The dish had no culinary integrity or merit.

'What do you think?'

'Well, I really like the orange cup, it is a nice touch, and the use of the lotus seeds gives it some added texture and Asian finesse. The sauce is light, and delicate… I did not have the heart to tell him what I really thought. Here we were being invited to lunch at the expense of a restaurant that is loosing money. Should I lecture him on well-balanced stocks, sauce reductions, and the use of orange in Asian and Western cuisine? No, I did not say a word, and a light kick under the table from Laura silenced any attempts to tell the truth.

Next was a classic stir-fry of water spinach, garlic and fermented tofu, watered down with an MSG mixture that made it overly salty. Another stir-fry arrived, crowding the table: rouge pieces of beef with lemongrass, but it tasted more like water buffalo. Then came slivers of semi-transparent pigs' ears lost in opaque oil laced with onions.

The table was now so overcrowded with food that none of us were eating. Thoa pretty much parked her chopsticks over her bread and butter plate. It was clear Mr Z had hired a cook who could not cook. More importantly, this guy was not cooking Hue dishes, but food that could be found on any street corner in Hanoi – except that Hanoi's street food was perfectly executed and cheaper. It was impossible for them to compete with. They couldn't compete with the foreign restaurants given the kitchen they had, so they had to cook Vietnamese food for Vietnamese customers, and Hue food was the only gap in the market. How else could anyone turn this place around? There wasn't a kitchen to attract anyone good. They could not pay a competitive salary. They needed to cut their losses, yet needed to spend more money.

As I sat marvelling at the problem, a flashback of Hubert Keller's voice came ringing in my ears, as it always did during times like these. It was my last day at work at Fleur de Lys, and we sat drinking beers in the downstairs prep kitchen with some of the kitchen staff. I was so blown away by all his technique, his eye for making food visually stunning, the ingredients he used. He was a chef's chef.

'You are the chef's chef!'

'Bobby, it's a business.'

'Yeah, but the combination of flavours and techniques…'

'It's a business.'

'…the colours and the ideas, man you are great!'

'Bobby, it's a business. Whether you are selling sandwiches or haute cuisine, it's a business.'

And there I finally was, sitting in this failing business in Vietnam and understanding why it was failing. But it would not be that easy to explain it to Mr Z and his chef. No-one wants their work criticised that way.

We sat in silence, my mind wandering off in all directions, then the chef appeared. The waiter stood over his shoulder as the chef proceeded to clear some of the untouched food. It was a little strange to clear the table while Mr Z was still eating from the bowl of rice nestled in his hand, but this did not stop them.

Then I looked over my shoulder to see a Baked Alaska coming to the table. I started to think again: boy, this guy's got balls! I would never dare to do a Baked Alaska in Vietnam. This classic dessert consists of ice cream layered with sponge cake, which is then covered with a blanket of meringue. With the meringue acting as insulation, the cake is placed in an oven and baked until the meringue browns. Simply put, the list of potential ways to screw up this dish would put me off in a heartbeat – it would never even be a consideration. We used to serve Baked Alaska at a restaurant I worked at called The Coconut Grove, and it was so difficult that the chefs resorted to using blowtorches to brown the meringue.

Where would the problem lie? Would the ice cream melt? What would melt it – the warm plates, the timing, or the dilapidated freezer? No, no, no, no! A Baked Alaska – what balls! I was beginning to like this guy.

The waiter placed the Baked Alaska in the middle of the table, then the chef, with an open bottle of Vietnamese vodka, proceeded to douse the meringue. Instead of baking the dessert, he was going to flambé it at the table. Once he doused it, he put the bottle of vodka back on the table and started fumbling unsuccessfully for some matches in his pocket. Laura's face was shocked as she counted up all the tableside service mistakes.

Suddenly the waiter came up with a lit match, but he did not know what to do with it. So with his arm stretched out, he leaned over Mr Z's shoulder towards the Baked Alaska and proceeded to burn holes in the tablecloth, aiming the burning matchstick as close to the base of the Baked Alaska as he could. Laura and I stared at each other in shock.

I turned back to watch the waiter try it again while the chef busily focused on striking his own match. He then realised that he had been beaten by the waiter, who was now on his way to adding a third hole to the tablecloth. The chef, angry at the waiter's lack of tableside knowledge, decided to administer immediate justice by smacking him on his shoulder with a rather loud and serious thump, then grabbed the matches from him, took him by the shirt and shoved him away from the table. It was like Fellini meets the Three Stooges.

Then the chef turned to the waiter, to show him how it was supposed to be done. The waiter watched attentively. The chef struck the box and moved the match quickly towards the surface of the Baked Alaska and panned across the surface

in the hope of igniting it. He failed. He tried again, to no avail.

So he picked up the bottle of vodka and shook it all over the Baked Alaska, with his thumb half-covering the top of the bottle. He quickly put the bottle back on the table, picked up the matches, struck one and waved it over the Baked Alaska. Once again it failed to ignite.

He then doused the meringue with even more vodka, lit two matches and with their flames blowing bright blue and yellow, inserted them in the meringue with no results. The matches burnt out. He lit them again and, holding the bottle with the open flame burning close to the bottle top, began pouring the vodka over the flame.

I quickly shouted 'NO!' It had been one of my first lessons when training; I was using whisky to deglaze a pan of lobster over a hot flame, when wushhhhhhh, the fire came up into my face and seared off most of my facial hair. I was a little shy of facial hair for a while but learned: never deglaze over an open flame, always remove the pan from the fire, just in case!

But it was too late. Just as I screamed, a ball of fire roared across the table in my direction. My head instinctively tilted and my eyes closed. The heat filled my nostrils with the smell of scorched hair. But the fire was quickly gone.

Mr Z was ooohing and aaahing in a rather excited tone. I peaked one of my eyes open in the hope that everything was okay. Mr Z was batting his arm with a napkin that was on fire. Both his arm and his napkin were on fire!

I wiped my forehead to relieve myself of the heat and as my hand ran over my eyebrows shriveled hair fell from my face. I'd lost my limited quantity of eyelashes as well.

Mr Z extinguished the fire on his arm, the burnt white napkin reduced to a quarter of the size it was just seconds ago. He quickly and calmly told the chef he should concentrate on his cooking and let the waiter be a waiter.

I could not help but smile at Laura, who found none of it amusing. 'This is something that I did not like,' she said. 'Why do chefs want to come outside and act like waiters?' But given the events, that was the last thing that to cross my mind.

Index

From Bobby

The amount of work it takes to write a book is so tremendous that I find myself just as stressed trying to make sure that I can thank all the people that made this possible. I would like to thank each and every one of them that touched my life to give me the courage to do all that I have done. I cannot mention all of you so spare me if you are not on the page and consider it your contribution to not adding any more petroleum based products and paper.

I have always been very lucky and to work with editors Jenni Muir and Lewis Esson was a privilege. If I was the queen I would give them both an OBE.

None of this would have been possible without Borra Garson, my agent. Although she is responsible for my TV career, I would have never pursued any of the projects without her incredible support and belief in me to the point that she did not knock on doors, she pretty much kicked them down.

Lorraine Dickey, for fuelling belief in me when I was in doubt of such a project during a tremendously crazy schedule of filming and the restaurant. Even when I lost most of the manuscript, she remained poised, and supportive.

A special thanks to Sybella Marlow, Jonathan Christie and all the wonderful people at Conran Octopus who made this book possible.

Anthony Bourdain for writing the foreword. Even with a crazy travel and filming schedule, coupled with a new addition to the family of a baby girl, I appreciate all your efforts to find the time for your contribution. Your support to the projects that I have pursued are deeply appreciated.

I would like to pay tribute to my two loving grandmothers, for teaching me two different styles of food, table manners and bringing me up as best they could. Their guidance and love was a comfort that surpassed the food and knowledge that I have been able to replicate. It was their philosophy and love that makes good food great. When you care it shows and I could even taste it. While I am at it, forgive me for any heartache I may have ever caused.

Jason Lowe, the photographer that was quite extraordinary and a true artist at heart. He seemed to have captured the beauty and essence that I love about being out here. It was a privilege to work with a photographer of such high talent.

To my parents, like many of us, who I took for granted all that they gave me. My parents might have found it difficult to understand how I could ever walk away from years of education, and a promising career in finance, but they somehow encouraged me with hope that I could find passion in whatever I pursued. For the years of silence or tears, I thank you from the bottom of my heart for allowing me to pursue my dreams no matter how stupid they may have appeared to you.

None of this would have been possible without the countless people that encouraged me when I was soul searching. I would like to thank Laura Flourens. Without her help and support from the very start, I would not have made many good professional decisions in my pursuit to the culinary arts. From my job choices and her critical palate, I learned and was encouraged when not many people believed in me. Never forgotten and deeply appreciated.

Roland Flourens, who encouraged supported and shared all of his thoughts with respect to food, wine, service and the business. Although he recently passed away, his impact on me will never be forgotten.

Duyen Kauffman who walked me through the back streets and alleys of Hanoi to discover flavours and tastes that I had never experienced before. It was her knowledge that guided me to the finest establishments the street had to offer, which in accelerated my learning curve to understand what was really achievable.

Christine Vu, who organized my life, gave me love when there was none, and did all that she could in the darkness of the night to schedule this book. Thank you for your relentless support.

Arthur Ting, my friend who helped and supported me in my struggles of opening up the restaurant. Without such a platform I doubt whether anyone would have ever taken me seriously.

My childhood friend John Larson, with Elizabeth Larson Grossman and Kevin Cottrell for helping me throughout my life.

David and Lydia Bransten who have both helped me in their own right. David shared with me his culinary secrets, fed me great food at some of the finest restaurants and inspired me in my early years. Lydia Bransten who helped me with logo's, stories and memories that were lost. Thank you for your memory and being a good friend through the years.

To the all the chefs and cooks that ever taught me, encouraged me and supported me with my dreams and my struggles. Not to mention the recipes that I had obtained, and shared in this book. I'd like to pay a serious tribute to Gary Danko, Hubert Keller, all the kitchen staff at Elka, who gave me their time and attention during my free time to teach me, Jeff Inahara, Scott Newman, David Duke, Traci des Jardin, Elka Gilmore, Drea, Tim Hilt and John Nelson and Michelle (Mitch) Drea.

I'd like to thank all the staff at San Francisco Bay Medical Center who helped me to deal with an injury that changed my life.

Special thanks to Yaffa Edry and Eave Gravilier, for allowing me to cook in their kitchens when I was crippled.

To my sister Nina Grivakes who let me prep in her kitchen when I wanted to learn.

To Joana Gregorous for her creative ways with seasonal ingredients.

To Lena, Maggie, Itch, Tarek, Dac, Long and Ho.

To all my staff who worked so hard to help me with the laborious task of testing each and every recipe until the book was completed. Many of the recipes have been tested several times to insure that we got it right. Jeff Richardson, Huong, Peanut, Ditz, Bich, Chi, Ha, Cuchi, Hai, Duyen, Skinny, Tuan (Donkey), Tuan (not donkey) Hoa, Hiep, Hien, Nga, Den, Duyen, Van Huong, Giang and anyone else I've forgotten.

Special thanks to Cham who I kept up all night typing out recipes when my memory stick lost all the updated files.

Michael DiGregorrio who introduced me to people that I did not know existed.

Warm thanks for the support of all my friends including Mark McDonald, Phil Karber, Donald Berger, Quyen Van Minh, Deborra Aronson, Richard Moore, Tina Sparkle & Bob Shiffer, Adam Sitcoff, Jinny Foote, Dana Doan and Steve Adams.

And finely, believe it or not, I would like to thank all the people that have fired me over the years. Without your rejection, snobbery, insubordination, lack of respect, insecurity and dysfunctional attributes, broken promises, I would have probably stuck it out and enslaved myself to working a life without ever trying to fulfil any of my dreams. To all of you from the bottom of my heart, thank you so much I salute you!